CURRENT ISSUES *in* POLICING

CURRENT ISSUES *IN* POLICING

CHRISTOPHER JAMES UTECHT
College of Lake County

cognella
SAN DIEGO

Bassim Hamadeh, CEO and Publisher
Mary Jane Peluso, Senior Specialist Acquisitions Editor
Alisa Munoz, Project Editor
Abbey Hastings, Associate Production Editor
Emely Villavicencio, Senior Graphic Designer
Danielle Gradisher, Licensing Associate
Natalie Piccotti, Senior Marketing Manager
Kassie Graves, Vice President of Editorial
Jamie Giganti, Director of Academic Publishing

Printed in the United States of America.

ISBN: 978-1-5165-9597-6 (pbk) / 978-1-5165-9598-3 (br)

cognella® ACADEMIC PUBLISHING
3970 Sorrento Valley Blvd., Ste. 500, San Diego, CA 92121

In Memoriam

Lt. Dr. Brian D. Fitch, PhD. (Ret.)

1961-2019

Education is the most powerful weapon which you can use to change the world.

-Nelson Mandela

CONTENTS

PREFACE

One of the major goals of criminal justice education is to help many students obtain the tools to become successful criminal justice practitioners or, at the least, to understand the diverse issues facing the field today. There are certain skills that need to be integrated across all courses in a curriculum, such as oral communication, written communication, and critical and creative thinking. The last one is arguably the most important. Criminal justice practitioners of all stripes are called on to critically and creatively interpret the situations into which they are injected.

This can be a tough job for any instructor. The criminal justice professions are known for being hands on, learn as you go in the field. Any time someone can get a "view-from-the-field perspective," he or she is able to integrate his or her existing knowledge with practical application. Integrating primary literature into a criminal justice course presents one of these opportunities to prepare students to function as practitioners. Many undergraduate criminal justice classes follow a textbook and use the textbook to guide the content of the class, but using a textbook to support the content of a course does not necessarily help students learn these important concepts they need to know to become successful practitioners. The perspective of practitioners can present rich dimensions because they offer a direct reflection of what practitioners do.

The book is unique because it combines theory with practice from the perspective of practitioners turned academics. The experience base for the authors covers a wide range of policing-related activities, including assignments in field operations, private security, investigations, prosecution and defense, training, crime analysis, and supervision. It provides the practical view of policing necessary to better understand the function of police in society and as well as functioning of the police organization. These original essays are written by authors possessing credibility as both academic and criminal justice practitioners. This is not simply a book of "war stories." Rather, it is envisioned as a collection of the most important topics viewed from those who have a knowledge of what it is to be a criminal justice practitioner working as or with the police.

The book is conceived to generally follow any mainstream, popular policing textbook. It can easily supplement any of those texts or be used as a stand-alone book in any course focused on the issues facing law enforcement agencies and personnel today. The individual chapters are written to highlight one of the most important issues in that chapter's topical area. For instance, for chapter 9, the corresponding mass market policing textbook topic is "Career Issues: Hazards of the Job." The essay for chapter 9 is about police suicide, a great hazard to law enforcement officers that is often overlooked or given scant attention in mass market policing textbooks.

This book opens with the history of policing as an evolution of a profession; moves into the place of the police in the criminal justice system through an examination of a partner that usually gets limited coverage, private security; then moves to legal factors affecting the police, including the reasonable expectation of privacy in the digital age and the ultimate current issue, racially differential views on police use of force; then moves to the importance of quality front-line supervisory leadership and to a review of police career issues, including police training and education, use of discretion through the lens of interactions with the mentally ill, police subculture and race relations, and the unspoken hazard of the police profession, suicide; then moves to specific areas of the profession, including patrol and investigations (domestic violence investigations), community policing (the need to move to *humanistic policing*), ethics (a call for *values-based policing*), accountability (body camera program implementation), homeland security (the effect of the fourth industrial revolution on policing); and finally moves to a final chapter by Dr. Ken Peak looking toward the future of policing.

It is my hope that the breadth of topics, as well as the currency of the topics addressed, will serve to make this a useful book for undergraduate and graduate criminal justice scholars and academics, as well as criminal justice practitioners and anyone in the general public who hopes to better understand the sometimes opaque, often controversial, and always interesting world of the police.

Christopher Utecht

ACKNOWLEDGMENTS

To all the scholars who have contributed their work to this volume, without your dedication, hard work, and timeliness, this book would not have been possible. Thank you.

To Dr. Cullen Clark, thank you for the inspiration.

To Jerry Westby, I offer you special thanks for your faith, support, and guidance throughout this process.

To Mary Jane Peluso and the staff at Cognella Academic Publishing, thank you so very much for your hard work and dedication in bringing this book to publication.

To the reviewers of this book, thank you all for your feedback and insight regarding this work.

Reviewers:

Daisy Ball, Roanoke College
Naomii Brack, City Colleges of Chicago, Richard J. Daley College
Joseph R. Carlson, University of Nebraska at Kearney
Dr. Lee H. DeBoer, Collin College
Richard C. Helfers, University of Texas at Tyler
Steven Hundersmarck, Ferris State University
Charles Klahm, Wayne State University

To Harvey and Arlene, Randy and Sandy, Adeline, Otto, Helen, and Hazel, thank you for being a constant source of motivation, strength, and encouragement.

Finally, to my wife Erica, you have my thanks and praise for your support, patience, understanding, forbearance, insight, and proofreading skills.

History of Policing

The Evolution of a Profession

By Charles J. Kocher and Darren K. Stocker

CHAPTER 1

Opening Questions

Answer the following question before reading this chapter:

> What do you know about the history of policing prior to reading this chapter?

Answer the following question while reading the chapter:

> What are some concepts from the chapter that stand out to you? Why do you think they are important?

Introduction

This chapter examines the history of policing within the United States and how law enforcement has transformed itself throughout the years. The concepts of uniform policing and patrol methods have evolved and adapted to technological advances as well as the needs of the community. The basis of policing is crime control and public service. The term "police" originates from the Greek word *Politeia* meaning civic government (Harding, 1960). Policing in the United States is rooted deeply within the English tradition where modern law enforcement is believed to have originated. The history of policing has experienced a paradigm shift toward the philosophy of community policing, which is based in proactive policing methods rather than the initial concept of responding to calls for service. These approaches include such models as predictive policing, intelligence policing, and smart policing. Policing within the United States has morphed into what it is today based on needs in various sections of the country adapting to a fragmented, federal system of justice, unlike its counterpart in England. Contemporary law enforcement may first appear as an industry that is stable and congruent, but it was initiated through a somewhat disjointed development of legal and implementation ideologies on all levels of government. Political differences throughout history created an inability for agencies to coordinate at an optimum level or prevented the consolidation of agencies for fear of the danger to democracy that a powerful consolidated agency would present (Schedler, 2001).

Contemporary society debates the true sense of policing. What exactly is the job or responsibility of a police officer? Are they crime fighters, problem solvers, peace makers, or social workers? Where do the responsibilities of enforcing criminal laws, patrolling neighborhoods, enforcing traffic laws, investigating crime, arresting violators, and keeping the peace fall? The answers to these questions are philosophical, ideological, political, and, through time, generational. The responsibility for these and many other public tasks has consistently fallen on the shoulders of those who are provided with the most discretion of any government official within the criminal justice system: the police.

England's Experiment

Enforcement that led to the development of policing is often traced to the early "hue and cry" under the reign of Alfred the Great around 870 A.D. If the community did not catch the individual or participate with the capture, that person could not be prosecuted for the crime. By the 15th century, most historians point to the **Frankpledge system**, as the earlier systems established were no longer appropriate and working very well. Groups of 10 individuals were sworn in to protect the shire and placed under the direction of the count of the stable, which later became the **constable** (Crowleye, 1975). Shires were small villages scattered throughout the countryside of England and consisted of several families that cared for the land. As the population increased, the noblemen of the land appointed a reeve who ruled over the shire (county). The land owners were becoming preoccupied with the king and other issues pertaining to the residents and, as such, appointed a reeve, who was responsible for the safety of the shire. Hence, we see over time the term shire-reeve become what we refer to presently as the **sheriff**. The reeve needed assistance and later the count of the stable was placed in charge of the supplies needed should someone commit a violation within the shire. This person and term became the basis for the constable (Harding, 1960).

History illustrates that most attempts at policing were viewed by the populace at large with a degree of contempt. By the 19th century in England, farming was very difficult, and many of those from the rural areas migrated to London. Sir Robert Peel, often regarded as the father of modern policing, was largely responsible for the Irish Peace Preservation Force Act of 1814 and proposed to the English Parliament an act to create a similar force in London called the Metropolitan Police Department. The English Parliament approved the Metropolitan Police Act in 1829. The design of this department developed into policing as we know it and ushered in the modern era of policing (Lyman, 1964).

Often referred to as the new police, Peel incorporated a military organizational plan that provided constables, sergeants, and other ranks for motivating the members for future positions within the agency. However, he did not want his **bobbies** to have a military representation. Therefore, they wore navy blue uniforms, were fitted with a wooden rattle used as an alarm, a pair of handcuffs, and a wooden baton. For England, this was the next phase for the former night watch guard who took care of lighting street lights and watching for fires, among other services (Corfield, 2000).

Peel's idea was to have the very best representation of the public to serve the community. The power of the English policing style promotes minimal force and draws on the support of the community or what is referred to as **policing by consent** with a foundation of trust. The police force in England was designed to be a servant of the community rather than of the government. Peel's saying that "the police are the community and the community are the police" has remained a constant and is often referred to throughout the United Kingdom and the United States (Goldstein, 1987). It is also the foundation for modern community policing efforts.

Reith (1956) explains the philosophy of policing or paradigm shift for policing would, from this point forward, center on trust among the community and policing in a cooperative spirit, as enumerated by the so called *Peelian principles*:

1. To prevent crime and disorder, as an alternative to their repression by military force and severity of legal punishment
2. To recognize always that the power of the police to fulfill their functions and duties is dependent on public approval of their existence, actions and behavior, and on their ability to secure and maintain public respect
3. To recognize always that to secure and maintain the respect and approval of the public means also the securing of the willing cooperation of the public in the task of securing observance of laws
4. To recognize always that the extent to which the cooperation of the public can be secured diminishes proportionately the necessity of the use of physical force and compulsion for achieving police objectives
5. To seek and preserve public favor, not by pandering to public opinion, but by constantly demonstrating absolutely impartial service to law, in complete independence of policy, and without regard to the justice or injustice of the substance of individual laws, by ready offering of individual service and friendship to all members of the public without regard to their wealth or social standing, by ready exercise of courtesy and friendly good humor, and by ready offering of individual sacrifice in protecting and preserving life
6. To use physical force only when the exercise of persuasion, advice, and warning is found to be insufficient to obtain public cooperation to an extent necessary to secure observance of law or to restore order, and to use only the minimum degree of physical force that is necessary on any particular occasion for achieving a police objective
7. To maintain at all times a relationship with the public that gives reality to the historic tradition that the police are the public and that the public are the police, the police being only members of the public who are paid to give full-time attention to duties that are incumbent on every citizen in the interests of community welfare and existence
8. To recognize always the need for strict adherence to police-executive functions and to refrain from even seeming to usurp the powers of the judiciary of avenging individuals or the state, and of authoritatively judging guilt and punishing the guilty
9. To recognize always that the test of police efficiency is the absence of crime disorder and not the visible evidence of police action in dealing with them

Since their inception, the principles established by Peel have come under significant scrutiny and discussion and perhaps should be recast to fit more civic police practices that include trust-producing and democracy-enhancing performances (Adegbile, 2017). While these foundational standards have provided value to law enforcement agencies past and present, having a "one-size-fits-all" set of ideals is not only fundamentally unreasonable, it is also impractical in a world so diverse.

Policing in America

"And to make an end is to make a beginning, and the end is where we start from."

—Eliot, 1971

The history of policing within the United States follows a different path than that generated through the English parliament. The terms are worth noting as early history developments for what would be the basis for policing in America. Policing in America was at a relatively young stage as the needs were not the same as in Europe. By the early 1800s the cities were forming primarily along the eastern seaboard in places such as New York, Boston, Philadelphia, and Baltimore. Evening watch operations in municipalities were being established about the same time London was creating the Metropolitan Police Department. Unlike London, the need for an organized policing effort for America in the early formation of towns throughout the United States was not required. Additionally, because of the political differences, there was no central control for the existing police agencies. Each city, town, or municipality would have to form their own law enforcement agencies, as they did the early states and territories (Kelling & Moore, 1999).

The oldest federal policing organization, the U.S. Marshal's Office, was created by the first Congress in 1789. The individuals serving as marshals carried out orders issued by judges and the United States Congress (Pope, 1998). In the Western territories, self-appointed enforcement groups were prevalent during the 1800s. These areas were part of the westward expansion and were considered dangerously overrun by bandits and wanted felons. One individual, Bass Reeves, was the first African American Deputy U.S. Marshal (Nelson, 2009) and served in the areas now known as Oklahoma and Arkansas. He is credited with the apprehension of more than 3,000 criminals. Paradoxically, in parts of the deep South, **slave patrols** continued to keep slaves from running away or rebelling against the racist values of the antebellum South.

It is not until after the Civil War (1861–1865) that the true emergence of police departments for most cities were realized. If one attributes the declining conditions and overall deterioration for both minor and major crimes within the city of London for the creation of the Metropolitan Police Act, then the rapid expansion of the railroads may be attributed to the development of policing throughout the United States. As the rail lines began to link both the East and West together, there were many robberies of the railroad trains that were carrying the payroll for the employees. The answer became the hiring of private investigators that pursued those destined to rob the trains. Many attribute private security to the early development stages of law enforcement throughout the United States (Stenning, 2000).

Modern Eras in Policing

Political Era 1840s–1930s

The police profession in the United States has gone through several transformations. George Kelling and Mark Moore found a division of eras designated by the **political era**, **reform era**, and the **community era** (Stewart & Morris, 2009). The first notable era of policing, the political era, lasted from the 1840s through the 1930s. This era includes the formation of cities, the creation of unions, and later the prohibition period, all influencing policing. The police officer was usually from the community and the primary function for the police was crime control.

Early policing has been characterized largely with both corruption and discrimination. Police departments took their instructions from the political authorities. Perhaps, as Greene (2000) suggests, police were the visible form of the existing government. As governments evolved and changed, so did the local law enforcement. Corruption during this era in government was rampant and, in many respects, so were the police who mirrored the government. Those who controlled the local political offices also controlled the police. Police officers were harsh to those who were not part of the established political power and were credited with widespread exploitation and organized crime.

Reform Era 1930s–1970s

The reform era favored a reactive policing approach more than a proactive approach. The United States was to some extent preoccupied with the two world wars, and crime was not center stage in the minds of the public. There has been a gradual shift away from the community approach that was observed through the Peelian principles to a more reactive-type response to issues within the community. Post-World War II observed more quantifiable methods designed to measure the effectiveness of the police agencies rather than concentrating on arrests and how quickly the police responded to emergencies. The primary focus was on the professionalism of police officers and less political interference. Scrivener (1995) proposes this was a different way of thinking and a different strategy for managing the police function. This was realized with the implementation of the civil service system. This was a different direction from the community-based approach of the earlier period or era. It was considered a means of separating personnel from existing political influence (Tolbert & Zucker, 1983).

August Vollmer, who may be one of the most important figures to influence policing in the United States, experientially stated that the police officer was required to have

> the wisdom of Solomon, the courage of David, the strength of Samson, the patience of Job, the leadership of Moses, the kindness of the Good Samaritan, the strategic training of Alexander, the faith of Daniel, the diplomacy of Lincoln, the tolerance of a Carpenter of Nazareth, and finally the intimate knowledge of every branch of the natural, the biological and the social sciences. If he had all of these, he might be a good police officer. (Johnson, 1968)

Vollmer, often referred to as the father of criminal justice, was responsible for bringing technology into the police environment during the early 20th century and for reshaping the methods and tools for more effective law enforcement. His writings are credited as early as the 1930s when he was addressing the issues of *the* scientific policeman and police progress. Vollmer, the police chief of Berkeley, California, was also preeminently responsible for bringing professionalism to modern policing and implementing initiatives such as bicycle patrols, and, later, automobiles equipped with flashing lights and a radio system. He also believed that police should be educated, and his officers were referred to as "college cops" (Wilson, 1953).

One of the key differences of the reform era was the emergence of the patrol vehicle, which permitted the police to escape the public by remaining inaccessible. The idea was for an immediate response to calls for service. The incorporation of portable radios would change the method of contacting police officers for emergencies. One-way broadcasts could be made to patrol cars, and the invention of two-way communications permitted the officers to converse with their dispatchers. Reiss (1992) contends that the changes in technology favored the methodology of policing, which was becoming the norm for the era where the public was demanding greater services and quick responses. These technological changes were quickly adopted and remain utilized in contemporary law enforcement nationwide.

A Golden Age of Policing

Despite the relative distance from the community created by technology, especially the squad car, police officers during the 1950s and early 1960s were considered the ones to turn to if someone was in need of assistance. The common theme was the policeman was your friend (Frank, Smith, & Novak, 2005). The term "policeman" was still a very common term as women were not as prevalent in the workforce as police officers. The rise of women actually on patrol would finally increase during the early 1980s. During the golden age of policing, the police officer was your proverbial friend. The police officer was known as someone who could be trusted to help and assist in any way. The officer was familiar with the neighborhood and often from the community in which he served.

Training for police officers was still limited until the early 1960s. On-the-job training was the basis for most police officers until formal police academies became most prevalent during the early 1960s. There was a move toward better training, specifically in the area of police recruitment and standardization. Those with degrees in higher education were encouraged to serve as police officers as economic compensation was beginning to increase (Reiner, 1992).

The United States Supreme Court during the 1960s began to shape police departments into a more professional organization because of several decisions of the court led by Chief Justice Earl Warren. Police training became more formal in all parts of the country. Issues for arrest, search and seizure, stop-and-frisk procedures, and formal investigations began to change. This was motivated by constitutional challenges by citizens and civil rights groups that perceived tactics used by the police were punitive and unjust (Simmons, 2008). By the mid-1960s, civil disobedience exposed another shortcoming for law enforcement. The handling of large crowds and public perception of how police handled unruly individuals came to the forefront and continues to the present day.

Many police agencies dedicated police officers to specific forms of training. Areas such as accident investigation, tactical patrol, and crime scene specialists evolved. However, the basic educational credential was the high school diploma, which has remained somewhat constant. Therefore, specialization made sense for the police agencies as a way for officers to improve their skills and knowledge base. Even today, officers specialize in crime scene investigations and fatal accident investigations. Investigators concentrate on fraud investigations, personal crimes, and property crimes. One specific specialization that emerged was community relations (Greene, 2000).

Random patrols remained the hallmark of patrol strategy during the golden age, with highly marked vehicles patrolling a designated area. Technology influenced radio frequencies and the ability to communicate more effectively with officers on patrol. It was not until 1972 that the Kansas City patrol experiment begin to ask questions as to whether policing through evidence-based researching was effective with the citizens they served (Larson, 1975).

This landmark study provided different degrees of visibility of police officers to various areas for 12 months and measured the findings. The results suggested that citizens did not find a difference among the styles of patrol presented, and there was no notable reduction for the fear of crime (Kelling, Pate, Dieckman, & Brown, 1974). The study would lead to new types of patrol and a reduction in the use of random patrols. Directed patrol and other programs would develop as new technologies for tracking became available. The earlier terms of computer-aided dispatch (CAD) would later morph into crime analysis. By the early 1990s, **COMPSTAT** became a current theme within the city of New York, and there was a paradigm shift toward proactive policing (Willis, Mastrofski, & Weisburd, 2007). Today, **intelligence-led policing** and other such programs are major parts of all police agencies. Ratcliffe (2010) believes this recently accepted method of policing leads to constructive trends in crime prevention and reduction.

Community Policing Era: 1970s–Present

Both visible patrol techniques and community relations remained major themes throughout the late 1970s and into the 1980s. By the mid 1980s, the earlier programs of community relations experienced a makeover. A new philosophy known as community-oriented policing took a new approach to policing, which appeared to revert back to Sir Robert Peel and the Peelian principles. Goldstein (1987) argues that these changes in policing are not simply designed to proactively respond to crime, but to address the fear of crime that is present in many communities. There has been much debate as to whether community policing is a philosophy or a set of various programs implemented to address the needs of a community. Palmiotto, Birzer, and Unnithan (2009) imply that as a philosophy there is a need for a cultural change in a police agency focused on problem solving and partnerships, while others argue about the true definition of the concept and what it means (Maguire & Mastrofski, 2000).

Whatever scholars and practitioners conclude, community policing has made a noted impact on how police do their business and respond to the needs of the public. Nothing clarified this more than what took place before and after the horrific event of September 11, 2001. Prior to 9/11, the federal government continued to pour funds into community-oriented policing. In 1992, President Bill Clinton proposed the hiring of 100,000 new police officers for community policing programs. Police agencies were required to have a written procedure of a community-oriented policing program to qualify for funds to permit the appointment of more police officers and to fund equipment for implementation (Marion, 1997). Although the number of police officers never reached 100,000, program changes allowed departments to purchase equipment that would free officers from clerical positions and return to a more visible patrol presence.

The overall organizational structure of policing was being challenged by many sides. Empowerment in policing allowed officers at the lowest level to enhance the quality of life for their residents within the community (Lurigio & Skogan, 1994). The officers *knew* their neighborhoods and were representative of fulfilling the desires of the populace. Police managers were reluctant to relinquish specific leadership strategies and oversight for street cops to implement problem-solving methods outside the norm of the agencies. The overall idea was to work *with* the community and not *separately* from it. Critics suggest that lack of police oversight can lead to the corruption that was prominent in the earlier eras of policing.

Broken Widows

One study that gained prominence during this era was **broken windows theory**. Introduced by Wilson and Kelling in 1982, the concept was that if broken windows and other quality-of-life issues were left unchecked, it would potentially lead to criminal behavior (Maskaly & Boggess, 2014). The theory has a basis on social disorganization, one of the most recognized criminological theories of the 20th century. Because of its popularity and underlying pragmatic approach to crime, it was adopted by many urban police departments. Detractors of the theory suggest that those who live in minority neighborhoods and the economically disadvantaged are most affected (Fagan & Davies, 2000).

Recent Changes in Policing

Horne (2006) and others have noted that throughout its history, policing has been a predominantly male profession. During the beginning of policing, the term **matron** was utilized to describe women whose job it was to assist male police officers with various functions following arrest procedures if the arrestee was a female or a juvenile. The increased numbers of females applying for positions within police agencies has transformed recruitment methods and entry requirements, especially for physical agility examinations, which were traditionally set up to test male applicants. Schuck (2006) evaluated 4,000 police agencies and has found that females are mostly associated with organizations that have community policing models. Leadership is another area that is changing for female police officers. In 2008, there were approximately 212 female police chiefs representing less than 2% of the total number of police chiefs nationwide (Mallicoat & Ireland, 2013). Although initially seen as a predominantly a male occupation, the increase in women in policing has grown far beyond the use of matrons.

Hiring practices for police officers are changing as well (Sklansky, 2005). All agencies generally desire a candidate of good moral character, which usually requires a written examination followed by a medical, physical agility, and psychological examination to judge the fitness of a potential police recruit. Once met, the applicant enters a rigorous training program through a police training academy to prepare for the job ahead. However, the skill sets for those in law enforcement have changed, and a better educated and trained candidate in nontraditional areas has become the norm for many of the larger and more contemporary police agencies. While the fundamentals of policing remain consistent, practice and philosophy are ever changing, and the scope of law enforcement will change as well to endure effectiveness and success (McLeod, 2003).

Conclusion

The history of policing is rich in culture and tradition. Tracing the history through uniforms, patrol tactics, and the use of technology demonstrates that law enforcement is constantly transforming itself to provide the finest service possible to the residents and businesses they serve in any community. Today, knowledge and expertise dominate law enforcement, and changes continue to take place throughout the United States. However, there is an emphasis on relationship building in today's community era that hearkens back to the Peelian principles that governed the political era. In general, policing is a profession that has evolved over time by keeping good aspects and reforming or casting off aspects that have been detrimental to its success. The future will find that the face of policing will continue to change into a new exciting chapter.

Key Terms

bobbies: A colloquial term for the officers of the London Metropolitan Police Department. Derived from Sir Robert (Bob) Peel.

broken windows theory: A concept stating that if broken windows and other quality-of-life issues were left unchecked, it would potentially lead to criminal behavior.

community era: The present era of policing, lasting from the 1970s through today. This era is defined by an emphasis on police-community relations and partnering with the community to keep the community safe.

COMPSTAT: Short for compare statistics. A computer program used by police organizations to track crime trends and inform patrol strategies.

constable: A local law enforcement officer in the United Kingdom. Analogous to a local police officer in the United States.

Frankpledge system: An early English system of criminal justice, wherein members of a village were responsible for bringing to justice any members of their village who had committed an offense (Crowleye, 1975).

intelligence-led policing: A policing strategy that utilizes an integrated intelligence structure, key performance indicators, and collaboration with outside agencies to inform police decision making and leverage limited assets (Ratcliffe, 2010).

matron: A woman whose job it was to assist male police officers with various functions following arrest procedures if the arrestee was a female or a juvenile.

policing by consent: A philosophy of policing that argues the legitimacy of policing in the eyes of the public is based on a general consensus of support that follows from transparency about their powers, demonstrating integrity in exercising those powers and their accountability for doing so (Police Transparency Unit, 2013).

political era: The first era of policing in the United States, lasting from the 1840s through the 1930s. This era was characterized by decentralization of policing services, little to no training for officers, a lack of supervision of officers, and a great reliance on officer discretion. These characteristics served to facilitate much corruption and graft.

reform era: The second era of policing in the United States, lasting from the 1930s through the 1970s. This era was characterized by a centralization of policing services, increased training, greater supervision of officers, and a more controlled use of officer discretion. There was also an emphasis placed on efficiency, facilitated by technology. By the end of the reform era, this emphasis on efficiency led to an estrangement of the police from the communities they served.

sheriff: A county-level law enforcement officer.

slave patrols: A form of law enforcement in the pre-Civil War southern United States that was concerned with the apprehension and return of runaway slaves.

Discussion Questions

- What do you think about the history of policing after reading the chapter?
- What was the significance of the Peelian principles or what is referred to as a paradigm shift?

- Discuss the major difference between policing in England and policing throughout the United States.
- What was the significance of the Civil Service Reform Act?
- Define and discuss the three eras of policing.
- What are the differences between reactive and proactive policing?
- Describe the significance of the Kansas City patrol study.
- Describe the reasoning of the broken window theory.
- What was the golden age of policing, and why is it referred to as a golden age?

References

Adegbile, D. P. (2017). Policing through an American prism. *Yale Law Journal, 126*(7), 2224–2258.

Corfield, P. J. (1990). Walking the city streets: The urban odyssey of 18th-century England. *Journal of Urban History, 16*(2), 132–174.

Crowleye, D. A. (1975). The later history of frankpledge. *Bulletin of the Institute of Historical Research, 48*(17), 1–9.

Eliot, T. S. (1971). *Complete poems and plays 1909–1950*. New York, NY: Hartcourt Brace and World.

Fagan, J., & Davies, G. (2000). Street stops and broken windows: Terry, race, and disorder in New York City. *Fordham Urban Law Journal, 28*(2), 457–504.

Frank, J., Smith, B. W., & Novak, K. J. (2005). Exploring the basis for citizens' attitudes toward the police. *Police Quarterly, 8*(2), 206–228.

Goldstein, H. (1987). Toward community-oriented policing: Potential, basic requirements, and threshold questions. *Crime and Delinquency, 33*(1), 6–30.

Greene, J. R. (2000). Community policing in America: Changing the nature, structure, and function of the police. *Criminal Justice, 3*(3), 299–370.

Harding, A. (1960). The origins and early history of the keepers of peace. *Transactions of the Royal Historical Society, 10*(1960), 85–109.

Horne, P. (2006). Policewomen: Their first century and the new era. *The Police Chief, 73*(9), 56–61.

Johnson, E. H. (1968). Sociological interpretation of police reaction and responsibility to civil disobedience. *Journal of Criminal Law and Criminology, 58*(3), 405–409.

Kelling, G., & Coles, C. (1982) *Fixing broken windows: Restoring order and reducing crime in our communities.* New York, NY: Touchstone.

Kelling, G., & Moore, M. (1999). The evolving strategy of policing. In Victor Kappeler (Ed.), *The police and society* (2nd ed.). Long Grove, IL, Waveland.

Kelling, G. L., Pate, T., Dieckman, D., & Brown, C. E. (1994). *The Kansas City preventive patrol experiment: A summary report.* Washington, DC: Police Foundation.

Larson, R. C. (1975). What happened to patrol operations in Kansas city?: A review of the Kansas city preventive patrol experiment. *Journal of Criminal Justice, 3*(4), 267–297.

Lurigio, A. J., & Skogan, W. G. (1994). Winning the hearts and minds of police officers: An assessment of staff perceptions of community policing in Chicago. *Crime and Delinquency, 40*(3), 313–330.

Lyman, J. L. (1964). The metropolitan police act of 1829. *Journal of Criminal Law and Criminology, 55*(1), 141–154.

Maguire, E. R., & Mastrofski, S. D. (2000). Patterns of community policing in the United States. *Police Quarterly, 3*(1), 4–45.

Mallicoat, S. L., & Ireland, C. E. (2013). *Women and crime*. Thousand Oaks, CA: Sage.

Marion, N. E. (1997). Symbolic policies in Clinton's crime control agenda. *Buffalo Criminal Law Review, 1*(1), 67–108.
Maskaly, J., & Boggess, L. N. (2014). Broken windows theory. In Miller, J.M. (Ed), *Encyclopedia of Theoretical Criminology* (pp.76–78). Hoboken, NJ: Wiley.
McLeod, C. (2003). Toward a restorative organization: transforming police bureaucracies. *Police Practice and Research, 4*(4), 361–377.
Nelson, V. M. (2009). *Bad news for the outlaws: The remarkable life of Bass Reeves, deputy US Marshal.* Minneapolis, MN: Carolrhoda.
Palmiotto, M. J., Bizer, N., & Unnithan, P. (2000). Training in community policing. *Policing: An International Journal of Police Strategies and Management, 23*(1), 8–21.
Police Transparency Unit. (2013). *Surveillance camera code of practice.* London, UK: Stationery Office.
Pope, J. (1998). *Bounty hunters, marshals, and sheriffs: Forward to the past.* Westport, CT: Praeger.
Ratcliffe, J. (2010). Intelligence-led policing and the problems of turning rhetoric into practice. *Policing and Society, 12*(1), 53–66.
Reiner, R. (1992). Policing a postmodern society. *Modern Law Review, 55*(6), 761–781.
Reiss, A. J. (1992). Police organization in the twentieth century. *Crime and Justice, 15*(1992), 51–97.
Reith, C. (1956). A new study of policing. Edinburgh, UK: Oliver & Boyd.
Schedler, A. (2001). Measuring democratic consolidation. *Studies in Comparative International Development, 36*(1), 66–92.
Schuck, A. (2006). Female representation in law enforcement: The influence of screening, union, incentives, and community policing. *Police Quarterly,17*(1), 54–78.
Scrivener, E, M. (1995). Community policing: New roles for police psychology. In Kurke, M.I. & Scrivener, E.M. (Eds.), *Police Psychology into the 21st Century* (pp. 419–434). New York: Taylor and Francis.
Simmons, K. C. (2008). The politics of policing: Ensuring stakeholder collaboration in the federal reform of local law enforcement agencies. *Journal of Criminal Law and Criminology, 98*(2), 489–546.
Sklansky, D. A. (2005). Not your father's police department: Making sense of the new demographics of law enforcement. *Journal of Law and Criminology, 96*(1), 1209–1223.
Stenning, P. C. (2000). Powers and accountability of private police. *European Journal on Criminal Policy and Research, 8*(3), 325–352.
Stewart, D. M., & Morris, R. G. (2009). A new era of policing?: An examination of Texas police chief's perception of homeland security. *Criminal Justice Policy Review, 20*(3), 290–309.
Tolbert, P. S., & Zucker, L. G. (1983). Institutional sources of change in the formal structure of organizations: The diffusion of civil service reform, 1880–1935. *Administrative Science Quarterly 28*, 22–39.
Willis, J. J., Mastrofski, S. D., & Weisburd. D. (2007). Making sense of COMPSTAT: A theory-based analysis of organizational change in three police departments. *Law and Society Review, 41*(1), 147–188.
Wilson, O.W. (1953). August Vollmer. *Journal of Criminal Law and Criminology, 44*(1), 91–103.

CHAPTER 2

The Intersection of Private Security with Public Law Enforcement

Working Together Instead of Working Against Each Other

By Holly Dershem-Bruce

Opening Questions

Answer the following question before reading this chapter:

> What do you know about the intersection of private security with public law enforcement prior to reading this chapter?

Answer the following question while reading the chapter:

> What are some concepts from the chapter that stand out to you? Why do you think they are important?

Introduction

The profession of **private security** has a long and storied history in the field of criminal justice, and private security officers often do not receive the professional recognition they deserve when positioned against other members of the criminal justice system. This chapter will provide a history of the private security industry and address security's contemporary role in protecting the public. Legal complexities surrounding the private security industry will be examined, along with a general summary of the training and licensing requirements for individuals working in the field of private security. Finally, the chapter will conclude with a discussion regarding the need for a strong working relationship between the private security industry and **public law enforcement**.

The History of Private Security

The notion that private individuals are responsible for protecting their own property and lives hearkens back multiple centuries to a time when public law enforcement agencies did not exist. Various efforts were taken by the people to protect themselves. Early examples can be found in the natural and man-made barriers that groups often utilized to protect themselves. Natural barriers included the use of caves, large boulders, or high cliffs located well out of the easy reach of human or animal threats that limited or prohibited access. Man-made barriers included the Great Wall of China, which served as a defense against invasion; the cliff dwellings of the ancient Pueblo Indians; as well as the use of walled cities or moats and drawbridges to protect one's castle and the people within. Other protections included the use of animals, such as geese or dogs, that would create an incredible racket when disturbed, thereby alerting people to the presence of some threat (Dempsey, 2011; Hess & Wrobleski, 1996; Johnson & Ortmeier, 2018; Smith, Schmalleger, & Siegel, 2017).

As the world evolved and became more civilized, so too did the means to protect life and property. It is generally accepted that the first organized police force was established in London by Sir Robert Peel in 1829. However, prior to the establishment of the London Metropolitan Police Force, communities shared a collective responsibility for their own safety and security. Hess and Wrobleski (1996) summarized this collective responsibility, or the need to protect oneself and one's property, in four stages: First, people came together for mutual protection and a sense of security in groups; second, people soon determined that large groups of people needed rules or laws to coexist; third, people discovered that not all members of the group would obey said laws or rules; and fourth, a mechanism was needed to compel individuals to obey the laws or rules (Hess & Wrobleski, 1996). Hence, the need for enforcement became essential. During the middle ages and throughout feudal times, these early communities relied on the monarchy and their armies to enforce established rules and laws. However, as these systems fell by the wayside, a more formal means of protecting the people and their property became necessary.

English Roots

Some of the earliest significant and organized means to protect property developed in England and other parts of Europe during the 13th, 18th, and 19th centuries. Issued by King Edward in 1285, the Statute of Westminster established three measures by which the people participated in the protection of themselves and their property. The *watch and ward* required that eligible men take their turn at watching over the village at night; threats to the well-being of the community resulted in the raising of the *hue and cry,* which required that all men immediately join in the pursuit of a criminal or deal with other threats such as fires or floods; and finally, the *assize of arms* required that all males between the ages of 15 and 60 keep a weapon in their home so as to help maintain the peace (Dempsey, 2011; Hess & Wrobleski, 1996; Johnson & Ortmeier, 2018). The Statute of Westminster would remain an obligation of the people for the next several centuries but did not afford the people elevated levels of security or result in the prevention of crimes.

As the English feudal system slowly came to an end, the people found themselves without many formal protections beyond their own personal efforts coupled with the existence of a magistrate that meted out punishments to law breakers brought before them. Merchants who experienced a theft would often have to track down the thief themselves or pay someone to locate and return their property to them for a fee. It was considered everyone's obligation and responsibility to obey the laws, protect the village, and aid in the capture of criminals (Dempsey, 2011). This collective responsibility helped pave the way for the establishment of several practices that attempted to provide more formal protection to the people. One of the first efforts was the use of "thief-takers" who served as a quasi-private police force during the 16th, 17th, and 18th centuries. These individuals would capture thieves and other criminals and/or recover stolen property for a fee or commission normally paid by the victim of the crime, or, later, by the government. Too often, the thief-taker was a criminal in his or her own right and was being paid to essentially remove his or her competition (Dempsey, 2011; Johnson & Ortmeier, 2018; Smith et al., 2017).

The use of thief-takers evolved into a more formal effort during the 18th century when Henry Fielding became the chief magistrate of Westminster. Living in a small house on Bow Street in London, he established the Bow Street Runners, a group of private citizens who formed an investigative unit that searched out criminals and brought them to justice. Privately funded at first, the group was so successful that eventually they were rewarded by the government and paid with public funds (Dempsey, 2011; Hess & Wrobleski, 1996; Johnson & Ortmeier, 2018). Over the next several decades, the Bow Street Runners became highly effective at preventing crimes through patrolling the streets, often on horseback; responding to and investigating crimes; and capturing wanted criminals (Johnson & Ortmeier, 2018). Later taken over by half-brother John Fielding after the death of Henry, the Bow Street Runners would become the precursor to the formal establishment of the London Metropolitan Police Force in the 19th century (Dempsey, 2011; Hess & Wrobleski, 1996; Johnson & Ortmeier, 2018).

The industrial revolution of the 18th and 19th centuries brought many changes and challenges to England. During this time, London and its surrounding areas experienced increased industrialization and urbanization as people moved to the cities in search of work. Along with the people came increased crime and incivilities, thus driving business and industry to increase their private protection efforts. Wealthy landowners often hired private "gamekeepers" to keep people from poaching on their property while middle-class merchants and business owners in the villages and towns formed volunteer groups to protect each other and assist in crime control and prevention. The use of night watches increased and were often supplemented with day watches. Some neighborhoods even went so far as to hire their own private police forces for added protection (Dempsey, 2011). It was during this time that discussions began in earnest about the establishment of a formal, government-backed police agency.

The establishment of a formal police agency was initially resisted by the public due to a belief that the establishment of such a formal government agency would diminish people's rights and freedoms (Dempsey, 2011). However, as the industrial revolution changed the appearance of London's urban areas and brought with it rising crime and disorder, the foundations were laid for passage of the Act for Improving the Police in and near the Metropolis (Dempsey, 2011). Referred to as the Metropolitan Police Act, Home Secretary Sir Robert Peel wrote and introduced the act to the English Parliament and worked toward its eventual passage in 1829. The act replaced the watch system that had been in use and established a 1,000-man civilian police force that was paid by the government (Johnson & Ortmeier, 2018). Considered the first public and organized police force in Europe, the London Metropolitan Police would eventually become a model for law enforcement agencies around the world (Dempsey, 2011; Hess & Wrobleski, 1996; Johnson & Ortmeier, 2018). Nevertheless, while these new, publicly funded police agencies were created all over Europe and eventually in the United States, people would continue to pay private guards and private police to protect their persons and property or to recover stolen goods (Dempsey, 2011; Heitert, 1993; Hess & Wrobleski, 1996). The private security industry was born.

Early Colonial Experiences

Life for the colonists in what would eventually become the United States was extremely difficult in the early years. The colonists had to rely on themselves and each other for protection from the constant threats created by wild animals, brutal winters, lack of food, hostile Native Americans, foreign nations, and the other colonies (Dempsey, 2011). Having limited or no military protection, and since many of the original colonies were settled by the English, the colonists soon established a system of protection very similar to the familiar English system they had left behind (Heitert, 1993; Johnson & Ortmeier, 2018). As in England, colonists assumed a collective responsibility for the security and safety of their villages and towns, and watches were often relied on to provide a measure of security and protection for the inhabitants (Johnson & Ortmeier, 2018; Smith et al., 2017). Eventually, these night watches would be replaced by more formally organized entities, including several law enforcement agencies modeled after London's first police force. Throughout the founding and expansion of the United States, police agencies were established in many of the largest urban areas in the East, slave patrols were common in the South to keep slaves in line, and the wild west frontier was often protected by U.S. marshals, a local sheriff, or railroad police hired to keep the peace along the routes of the intercontinental railroads (Heitert, 1993; Hess & Wrobleski, 1996; Johnson & Ortmeier, 2018; Walker, 1992). Nevertheless, even with the creation of these formal police agencies, the challenges of a growing country overwhelmed what limited law enforcement resources existed, and the eventual result was the establishment of the private security industry in America.

The American Experience

The rapid pace of expansion in the United States created ongoing challenges for the people and the young nation. The industrial revolution brought masses of people into urban areas and resulted in overcrowded ghettos with inadequate housing, no services, and an overabundance of incivilities. Crime and discord were common and newly minted police agencies could not keep up. Labor strife was common in many factories, as was the theft of goods and property. Public law enforcement was often unable to provide protection to these industries; hence, corporations and merchants hired private guards to protect life, limb, and property (Dempsey, 2011; Heitert, 1993; Johnson & Ortmeier, 2018; Smith et al., 2017).

The establishment of the modern American private security industry is largely attributed to Allan Pinkerton, a Scottish-born immigrant who served briefly as a deputy sheriff in Cook County, Illinois and later as the first detective for the Chicago Police Department (Dempsey, 2011). Pinkerton would eventually open his own detective agency, the Pinkerton National Detective Agency, in the 1850s. Trademarking an open eye with the slogan "The Eye That Never Sleeps" (Dempsey, 2011, p. 8), the Pinkerton detectives soon became known as *private eyes*, and the business became a resounding success. Pinkerton helped develop many investigative techniques including handwriting analysis, mug shots, undercover operations, and suspect surveillance. The company was also the first to hire a female detective, establish a code of conduct for its employees, and prohibit the acceptance of gratuities and rewards. In 1857 Pinkerton would establish the Pinkerton Protective Patrol to provide watchman-like services to private individuals and industry (Dempsey, 2011; Pinkerton Our History, n.d.)

The Civil War resulted in a new arena for the Pinkerton Detective Agency as the Pinkertons served as a precursor to the Secret Service (Pinkerton Our History, n.d.) and took on the dual roles of protecting President Abraham Lincoln and providing military intelligence to the Union Army (Johnson & Ortmeier, 2018; Dempsey, 2011; Hess & Wrobleski, 1996). After the war, the Pinkerton Agency went back to its original services and provided railroad and stagecoach security, bank security, and tracked down several notorious criminals such as the Younger-James Gang (e.g., Jesse James and Frank James), the Dalton Brothers, and Butch Cassidy's Wild Bunch (Pinkerton Consulting & Investigations, n.d.a.).

Allan Pinkerton died in 1884, and his sons, William and Robert, took over the agency. They would lead the Pinkertons into a tenuous period when Pinkerton officers were often hired by mining and manufacturing companies to quell labor unrest and work as strike breakers to suppress the labor union movements of the late 19th and early 20th centuries (Dempsey, 2011; Heitert, 1993; Hess & Wrobleski, 1996). These activities lead to a poor image of the Pinkertons, and while they were not the only company involved in strike breaking, they were one of the more notable. After a congressional inquiry into strained labor-management relations in 1937, the Pinkertons adopted a policy whereby its agents would never again become involved in covert strike-breaking activities (Dempsey, 2011; Heitert, 1993; Hess & Wrobleski, 1996).

The Pinkerton Agency was able to repair its image over the next several decades with such important activities as safely escorting Leonardo da Vinci's priceless Mona Lisa painting across the Atlantic Ocean in 1968, assisting over 430 expatriates in leaving Indonesia due to the Asian Currency Crisis in 1998, and mobilizing agents to assist clients in the aftermath of Hurricanes Katrina, Rita, and Wilma in 2005 and after Hurricane Sandy in 2012 (Pinkerton Our History, n.d.a.) In 1999 the Pinkerton Agency was acquired by Securitas AB, one of the largest security firms in the world (Pinkerton Our History, n.d.b.; Securitas, n.d.) and is now considered a leader in **applied risk science**.

Other forms of security were developing during the late 19th and early 20th centuries. According to Johnson and Ortmeier (2018), "[T]he American [e]xperience reveals that the growth of security paralleled the growth of industries, society, technologies, and various social movements. One of the underlying themes ... is that the private security industry was (and still is) entrepreneurial, finding new opportunities based on market and societal needs, 'filling the voids' that the public sector could not provide" (p. 7). Other early companies involved in private security included the Rocky Mountain Detective Association, Wells, Fargo & Company, the Baldwin-Felts Detective Agency, the Wackenhut Corporation, and the William Burns International Detective Agency (Dempsey, 2011; Hess and Wrobleski, 1992; Johnson & Ortmeier, 2018). The discovery of electricity and the invention of the telegraph led to the development of the alarm industry and central alarm-monitoring stations. Companies utilizing the technology included AFA Protection, Holmes Protection, and the American District Telegraph Company (ADT). Likewise, J.W. Woolworth's changes in the retail industry led to the problem of shoplifting and the need for store detectives and retail security officers. In 1859, Washington Perry Brink provided the first secure package and freight delivery service, and eventually the company began transporting company payrolls and other valuable goods in the first armored cars (Dempsey, 2011; Hess & Wrobleski, 1996; Johnson & Ortmeier, 2018). It was clear that the private security industry was becoming a vital component for businesses, banks, and other trades.

20th-Century Private Security

The World Wars led to tremendous growth in the private security industry. The federal government often relied on private defense contractors to secure federal facilities, and the protection of the United States' infrastructure was (and still is) often relegated to private protection employees. Munitions factories and companies that built military equipment were required to implement stringent security procedures to protect their plants from espionage or sabotage before being awarded lucrative contracts from the government. Many of these factories were protected by the FBI or came under the control of the War and Navy departments as their protection employees were often inducted into the military as civilian auxiliaries to the military police. Over 200,000 such employees were granted the status of auxiliary military police with the responsibility of securing and protecting countless war goods and products, equipment, and supplies (Hess & Wrobleski, 1996; Johnson & Ortmeier, 2018).

The post-World War era led to further enhancement and **professionalization** of the private security industry. The American Society for Industrial Security (now known as ASIS International) was founded in 1955 and was the first professional organization dedicated to the professionalization of the security industry. Today, ASIS International has over 35,000 members worldwide and includes representatives from all aspects of the security industry (ASIS International, n.d.). The Korean War and the Cold War led the creation of the federal government's Industrial Defense Program in 1952, as new concerns about espionage and sabotage surfaced. Now referred to as the National Industrial Security Program and administered through the Defense Security Services (DSS), the program is responsible for providing oversight, advice, and assistance to nearly 11,000 defense-related facilities (Dempsey, 2011; Johnson & Ortmeier, 2018).

The 1960s would bring new challenges and opportunities for the private security industry. The civil rights movement would bring social unrest and violence to the South and to major cities around the United States and further increased the need to protect private property and possessions (Smith et al., 2017). In 1968, Congress passed the Omnibus Crime Control and Safe Streets Act in response to the 1967 President's Crime Commission report (Johnson & Ortmeier, 2018). The act was responsible for establishing the Law Enforcement Assistance Administration (LEAA). A year later the LEAA helped establish the Research and Development (RAND) corporation. Among its many publications, the RAND corporation would conduct an in-depth analysis of the private security industry in its report "The Private Police Industry: Its Nature and Extent." The report would examine the increasing use of private security in the United States and examine other trends in the industry. Among other concerns, the report concluded that the private security industry was in dire need of increased training, professionalism, and licensing and regulatory oversight (Johnson & Ortmeier, 2018; National Advisory Committee on Criminal Justice Standards & Goals, 1976).

Further advances in the professionalization of the private security industry included the creation of the Private Security Advisory Council (PSAC) in the early 1970s. The PSAC was responsible for monitoring the private security industry and issued many different reports and publications in the early 1970s, including one report that identified problems between law enforcement and the private security industry, including a "lack of mutual respect, communication, law enforcement's [limited] knowledge about the industry, low employment standards, and perceived competition and corruption that needed to be addressed to ensure strong working relationships between the two" (Johnson & Ortmeier, 2018, pp. 13–14). Subsequent reports on the private security industry also acknowledged the importance of the private security industry while identifying the need for additional training and regulation. These included the Task Force on Private Security in 1976, the Hallcrest

Report I in 1985, and the Hallcrest Report II in 1990 (Dempsey, 2011; Hess & Wrobleski, 1996; Johnson & Ortmeier, 2018). The formal professionalization of the private security industry was launched, and the growth of the industry was about to explode.

In response to the various reports, articles, and documents surrounding the private security industry, many states began passing statutes, establishing rules, and defining training requirements to govern the private security industry. Many of those states grappled with just how much supervision and regulation was necessary over an industry designed to protect private property while concurrently dealing with the public. "Historically, the private security industry, primarily at the entry and nonmanagerial levels, ... suffered from a lack of professional standards" (Dempsey, 2011, p. 45). As the security industry continued to evolve, the amount of training and professionalization evolved as well. According to information from the U.S. Department of Labor Bureau of Labor Statistics (2018c), today most states require that private security officers must be registered or licensed with the state, and many require pre-licensing training of 8 hours or more, coupled with an additional 8–16 hours of on-the-job training after hire. Security officers who are armed normally complete additional training and often must meet stricter background checks along with annual firearms qualifications.

Johnson and Ortmeier (2018) write that "[d]uring the last quarter of the twentieth century, the security industry continued to grow rapidly due to increasing concern over crime and the limited availability of law enforcement resources" (p. 14). As law enforcement numbers grew steadily but slowly, the number of private security personnel consistently out-numbered public law enforcement personnel during the mid-to-late 1900s, with the number of security personnel eventually numbering more than twice that of public law enforcement personnel (Dempsey, 2011; Hess & Wrobleski, 1996; Johnson & Ortmeier, 2018). Likewise, several major events, including the 1993 bombing of the World Trade Center and the 1995 Oklahoma City Bombing, would lead to the recognition that private security was crucial to a safe and secure infrastructure within the United States (Greenspan, 2013; Johnson & Ortmeier, 2018; National September 11th Memorial & Museum, n.d.). In the wake of the terror attacks of September 11, 2001, the U.S. Department of Homeland Security (DHS) was established to respond to the security challenges facing the United States. Often working alongside private security, the DHS works to coordinate the country's response to the increased threats caused by terrorism, natural disasters, crime, and violence at the federal, state and local levels (Johnson & Ortmeier, 2018). An upsurge in recent years in the numbers of violent attacks at schools, workplaces, concerts, churches, theaters, stadiums, and other venues where large numbers of people gather serves to solidify the relevance of private security as a necessary component to the safety and protection of the people in the 21st century.

The Private Security Industry Today

The private security industry has evolved into a massive and complex entity responsible for the protection of people, possessions, and property all over the world. Over 40 countries have more private security officers than they do police officers, and an estimated 20 million private security workers encompass the globe in an estimated $180 billion market. In the United States alone the private security industry is worth an estimated $44 billion (Finkel, 2017).

Categorizing Security Services

Private security can function either as proprietary security (e.g., the company's own in-house security) or as contract security (e.g., an external security company hired to provide protection). Private security can be found in both the private and public sectors as officers routinely protect and guard both government and private buildings. According to Johnson and Ortmeier (2018), the dual categories of public and private security can be "further subdivided into defense-related, public security, homeland security, corporate security, private security, and individual or personal security sectors" (p. 15). Other categories of private security may include physical security, information security, information systems security, and personnel security. Another area of the security industry includes operational security, which can include but not be limited to educational institution security, financial services security, gaming/wagering security, healthcare security, lodging security, manufacturing security, utility security, or retail security (Dempsey, 2011; Hess & Wrobleski, 1996; Johnson & Ortmeier, 2018; Smith et al., 2017). Each category has its respective mission, but all share the mutual task of keeping their respective industry and the people within safe and secure.

In addition to the categories and subfields of private security previously mentioned, multiple types of private security personnel exist within the profession. The most common occupations include armed and unarmed private security guards, private patrol officers, private investigators, armed couriers, alarm response runners, alarm installers, executive protection specialists, loss-control agents, security managers, fugitive recovery agents (bounty hunters), and security consultants, to name a few. According to the U.S. Department of Labor's Bureau of Statistics, there are currently over 1.1 million private security officers employed in multiple capacities within the United States. This compares to roughly 807,000 law enforcement officers and detectives at all levels (Occupational Employment Statistics [OES], 2018). The top industries that employ private security personnel include investigation and security services (73%), followed by real estate (1.7%), traveler accommodations (1.6%), medical facilities (.7%), and elementary and secondary schools (.4%) (OES, 2018). According to the *Occupational Outlook Handbook*, growth in the private security industry, particularly in the category of private detectives and investigators, was expected to increase *much faster than the average* for 2016–2026 when compared with other occupations (Bureau of Labor Statistics, 2018b). These facts are testament to the ongoing need for increased and enhanced security services throughout the United States.

Legal Issues and Private Security

As noted previously, each state is responsible for establishing its own requirements for the regulation and control over the private security industry. Because most private security-related activities fall under the private sector, the environment within which the private security industry must function includes a combination of criminal, civil, and administrative laws. The result is a complex mixture of laws, regulations, and requirements that must be met for private security companies to function successfully within each state.

To fully comprehend the complexity of the legal issues impacting private security, it is helpful to consider the similarities and differences between private security and public law enforcement. Both types of officers share a similar mission to prevent crime and protect the public. They often engage in similar activities including investigations, patrols, and monitoring and directing people. The private security officer and the law enforcement officer may both be in uniform with badges or insignia, and both may be armed. Each possesses authority over the public he or she controls, and both may face hostilities, aggression, or other mistreatment at the hands of the public. Likewise, both private security and public police officers face liability in their interactions with the public and may be subject to civil lawsuits (Heitert, 1993; Hess & Wrobleski, 1996; Johnson & Ortmeier, 2018; Meadows, 1995; Smith et al., 2017).

Private security differs from public law enforcement in that private security is normally a for-profit entity that serves specific, private clients. Its primary role is to regulate the noncriminal behavior of its clients' employees and customers and to prevent crime, control access, protect assets, and reduce losses. In contrast, the public police officer is a nonprofit, government entity that serves the general public and is charged with combatting crime, enforcing laws, and apprehending criminal offenders (Hess & Wrobleski, 1996). The police are responsible for enforcing society's laws; private security is responsible for enforcing its employer's rules or regulations. For the private security officer, any allegiance belongs to its employer and not necessarily to the public it is hired to manage or protect.

In addition to a difference in their focus and loyalty, private security and public law enforcement also differ in their jurisdictions. Law enforcement is limited to a specific legal jurisdiction, either at the local (city, municipality, county), state, or federal government level. By contrast, private security can cross over these traditional legal jurisdictions, and personnel can be employed by companies that may operate in several cities, counties, states, or internationally (Strom et al., 2010). Consequently, the security professional has to be aware of any differences in the legal responsibilities and obligations when crossing jurisdictions in the course of his or her employment.

While the private security officer may appear to possess law enforcement-like authority, the reality is that, unlike public law enforcement, security officers often have no more authority than the average private citizen (Dempsey, 2011; Heitert, 1993; Hess & Wrobleski, 1996; Johnson & Ortmeier, 2018; Meadows, 1995; Smith et al., 2017). According to Dempsey (2011), the "[c]ourts have generally held that private security personnel obtain their legal authority from the same basic authority that an employer would have in protecting his or her own property. This authority is extended to security guards and other employees hired by an employer" (p. 94).

This chapter turns now to a brief overview of some of the more common powers and authority of private security. The reader is reminded to check with each state regarding specific laws and grants of authority for private security personnel.

Arrest Powers

As with most private citizens, private security officers have a general power to effect an **arrest** of an individual. They are subject to the same laws and obligations as the private individual, such as the requirement to turn the arrestee over to police authorities as soon as practicable. Unlike the police, however, a private security officer must usually *observe* the criminal activity and must be sure that the behavior observed is actual criminal activity. A police officer that can demonstrate probable cause for an arrest is normally shielded from accusations of false arrest. On the other hand, no matter how well intentioned a security officer may be or how justified he or she believes his or her arrest happens to be, should the behavior of the accused turn out not to be a crime, the security officer could face liability for a false arrest or worse (Dempsey, 2011; Hess & Wrobleski, 1996; Johnson & Ortmeier, 2018; Meadows, 1995; Montana Code Annotated [MCA], 2018; Smith et al., 2017).

Detention

Detention differs from arrest in that a detention usually is shorter in duration and normally has a specific purpose. The detention does not require restraints, nor does it require moving the accused to a different location. The actions of the security officer, however, must be reasonable and appropriate to the situation. Many states have merchant detention laws that protect retailers from liability and afford them and their employees the right to investigate shoplifting within their businesses, to detain suspects for a specific period of time (usually no more than 30 minutes), to verify the suspect's identity and place of residence, to determine whether a theft has occurred, and to recover any stolen merchandise. Upon completion of an investigation by the private security officer, the detainee is usually allowed to leave or is turned over to law enforcement for further processing (Dempsey, 2011; MCA, 2018; Meadows, 1995; Smith et al., 2017).

Search and Seizure

As with private citizens, private security officers have more latitude than the police when it comes to searching others they have detained or arrested. Public law enforcement officers must establish probable cause to conduct a legal search of most persons or their immediate surroundings. Should an officer fail to establish probable cause, the exclusionary rule could result in the evidence being excluded from a criminal court. The same rule doesn't apply to the actions of a private security officer. As mentioned previously, "merchant detention laws" afford a retailer or its agents the ability to reasonably search a suspected shoplifter and to seize stolen merchandise. Further, that seized property could be turned over to law enforcement as evidence of a crime having been committed, even if the security officer didn't formally establish probable cause. The differences in how the private security officer and the police officer may behave stem from the U.S. Supreme Court's rulings that the exclusionary rule only applies to government actions (Dempsey, 2011; Meadows, 1995, Smith et al., 2017). It should be cautioned, however, that should a private security officer conduct a search or seizure while assisting a law enforcement officer, his or her behaviors must meet the same legal requirements as those for the public officer. Likewise, a security officer who conducts an illegal search may be subject to civil liability for violating the privacy rights of the individual, regardless of whether a crime was committed or if the individual was convicted of a crime (Dempsey, 2011; Hess & Wrobleski, 1996; Johnson & Ortmeier, 2018; Meadows, 1995; Smith et al., 2017).

Interrogations

Just as the exclusionary rule doesn't apply to private security officer actions, the same is true with the requirement for the Miranda warnings. It is long-standing legal precedent that public law enforcement officers must put suspects on notice of their Fifth and Sixth Amendment rights prior to any interrogation. In contrast, private security officers are not obligated to Mirandize suspects prior to questioning as they are not considered agents of the law. "The *Miranda ruling* and the *Miranda warnings* apply only to government agencies and not to private employers; thus, in a private investigation, suspects do not have to be warned that what they say may be used against them" (Dempsey, 2011, p. 98; emphasis in the original). Nevertheless, some states do require that private security officers give a modified version of the Miranda warnings prior to any questioning, and many states require that the rights of the suspect be protected. In essence, the rights of an individual should be safeguarded by all officers, whether they are functioning in the private- or public-sector security realm (Dempsey, 2011; Meadows, 1995; Smith et al., 2017).

Use of Force

It is commonly understood and accepted that private citizens have the right to protect themselves, others, and their property from physical force or attack. Such a right depends on individual statutes and is subject to various restrictions and limitations, depending on where the person is located. Consequently, private security officers possess the right to reasonably defend their employer's property and the people within; however, they typically have no more power than the average citizen when it comes to the amount of force they may use. Further, the policies and procedures of their employer will dictate what, if any, force can be used in the course of carrying out their duties. In comparison, police officers have more discretion in the use of force and have a wider latitude in the types actions they may take against individuals. The right to use force notwithstanding, both private security and public police officers must be cognizant of the amount of force that they do use and be aware of the liability associated with this right (Dempsey, 2011; Heitert, 1993; Hess & Wrobleski, 1996; Smith et al., 2017).

In sum, while there are several distinct differences between the legal actions that private security officers and public police officers can take, the basic principle remains the same for both: Everyone's rights should be safeguarded, regardless of the circumstances. Further, both the private security officer and the law enforcement officer have a mutually shared obligation to protect and defend the public they are hired to serve.

The Intersection of Private Security and Public Law Enforcement

As noted previously, private security officers and law enforcement have a similar mission and share many common goals. Similarly, public law enforcement can engage in activities that private security cannot and vice-versa. Thus, working together can benefit both entities in the long term. The interaction of private security and public law enforcement can (and should) produce a symbiotic relationship, provided that challenges and differences can be worked out between the two entities. Working together can make both entities stronger and provide an even greater level of safety to the public they are both ultimately charged to protect (Hess & Wrobleski, 1996).

One of the challenges that exists between private security and public law enforcement can be traced to the differences in entry-level requirements, licensure, and training standards between the two entities. "Forty-one states, plus the District of Columbia, license security officers, but requirements vary greatly from state to state. ... [N]ine states do not license security officers at the state level. ... And 22 states have no training requirements for unarmed security guards; 15 of those have none for armed guards, either" (Bergal, 2015, para. 8–9). On average, the entry-level private security officer is required to be 18 years of age, possess a high school diploma or equivalent, complete a few hours of pre-employment or on-the-job training, pass a background check, and become licensed by the state in which he or she intends to work. In contrast, the average entry-level police officer must be a U.S. citizen, 21 years of age, possess a high school diploma or equivalent, pass an extensive background investigation, and complete several hundred hours of training from an approved law enforcement training academy (BLS, 2018a). It is no wonder that these differences in standards have led many police officers to consider private security officers deficient in professional training) and to discount the role of private security as a first line of defense in protecting the public (Dempsey, 2011).

Efforts to improve the professionalization of the private security profession have not been limited to state legislative or regulatory efforts. ASIS International has been instrumental over the past several decades in developing professional training and standards that led to the certification of private security professionals in several different areas of the profession (American Society of Industrial Security International, n.d.; Dempsey, 2011; Fisher & Green, 2004; Hess & Wrobleski, 1996; Johnson & Ortmeier, 2018). Education standards have increased as well with several hundred associate, bachelors and graduate degree programs in private security or specialized options now in existence nationwide (criminaljusticeprograms.com, n.d.).

Nevertheless, while many states and the private security industry have diligently worked to improve training standards, employment requirements, and educational opportunities, the standards for private security have remained stagnant in many instances. "Many states—never the federal government—first set and then increased, and sometimes decreased, standards over the years. With the shock from the events of 11 September 2001 (9/11) and the subsequent war on terrorism, the pace of regulatory growth increased. Even so, regulations for security personnel—especially security guards—remain at an indefensibly low level with 12 states having no requirements at all for unarmed security personnel and 14 having none for armed" (McCrie, 2017, p. 287). While great strides have been made to enhance the reputation of the private security industry, the differences between private security and public law enforcement cannot be ignored, and a concerted effort should be made to identify those areas in which private security and public police can work together seamlessly, regardless of the differences in training, education, licensing, or regulatory standards.

The need to improve the working relationship between private security and public law enforcement was identified early on as various law enforcement or criminal justice related commissions studied the field in the late 20th and early 21st centuries. Reports such as the Task Force on Private Security in 1976; the Hallcrest Reports I & II in 1985 and 1990, respectively; and the Private Security Industry Review in 2010 all identified the importance of cooperation between public law enforcement and the private security industry (Cunningham, Strauchs, & Van Meter, 1990; Cunningham & Taylor, 1985; National Advisory Committee, 1976). Two of the more notable efforts to facilitate that understanding and cooperation between private security and public law enforcement predates the 9/11 attacks and includes the International Association of Chiefs of Police's (IACP) Private Sector Liaison Committee and the Law Enforcement Liaison Council of the American Society for Industrial Security International (Morabito & Greenberg, 2005). These types of cooperative arrangements helped launch Operation Cooperation, a national effort to increase collaboration between the private sector, particularly private security, and state and local law enforcement agencies (Morabito & Greenberg, 2005). In 2005, the Law Enforcement Private Security Consortium was formed to "provide research, training, and technical assistance services that support development of effective law enforcement-private security collaborations nationwide" (Law Enforcement Private Security Consortium, 2009, p. 5). The result was Operation Partnership, which identified successful partnerships, practices, and trends between private security and law enforcement.

Both Operation Cooperation and Operation Partnership assisted police agencies and private security companies to improve their relationships, and success could be measured by the sizeable number of positive working relationships between private security and law enforcement. "The best evidence from both of these projects suggests there were many more LE-PS partnerships in the United States in 2007 than there were 7 years earlier. Operation Partnership identified more than 450 LE-PS partnerships, compared to about 60 identified through Operation Cooperation" (Law Enforcement Private Security Consortium, 2009, p. 7).

Many benefits to both private security and public law enforcement were realized from Operation Partnership and included advantages such as the following (Law Enforcement Private Security Consortium, 2009):

- The development of professional contacts between private security and law enforcement, which led to better relationships between individual officers on both sides
- The force multiplier effect, which allowed the private sector to aid the public sector in addressing various crimes within the community on both the private and public levels
- Cost savings associated with protecting the public by enabling private security to provide additional "eyes and ears" to law enforcement
- The ability of private security to assist the police in the investigation of computer and high-tech crimes
- Additional cost savings to law enforcement when private security would address minor workplace incidences such as financial crimes or intellectual property crimes internally
- Law enforcement's access to and increased use of advanced technology developed by private security
- Critical incident planning and responses through coordination between law enforcement and private security
- Increased sharing of information and intelligence between both entities
- Increased training opportunities and shared resources;
- More effective community policing
- Enhanced career opportunities and recognition as a profession for private security

And, while the benefits and advantages of a cooperative partnership were numerous for both private security and public policing, barriers and challenges to those successful arrangements were also identified by the Law Enforcement Private Security Consortium (2009):

- A lack of awareness and knowledge on the part of private security in not realizing the full capabilities and resources of law enforcement and on the part of law enforcement in not fully understanding the specialized nature within the private security field
- A lack of trust between the two entities
- Concerns regarding the sharing of privileged information with each other
- The high expense of some technologies
- Personnel issues, particularly the low pay, poor benefits, and high turnover rates for some parts of the private security industry
- Slow and cumbersome decision making on the part of public law enforcement when private security could make decisions much quicker and capitalize on immediate opportunities
- Taxpayer support for public police and private security services

Operation Partnership concluded that while the partnerships between private security and public law enforcement included unique challenges, the overall result was a positive outcome for both, and the ultimate winner was the public (Law Enforcement Private Security Consortium, 2009).

Conclusion

In summary, cooperation between private security and public law enforcement has taken a long and arduous journey, and connections between the two entities continue to be built. However, more needs to be done. Recent events in the United States continue to demonstrate the importance of law enforcement and private security working together toward mutual goals and outcomes. When Stephen Paddock opened fired in Las Vegas in October 2017, it was a private security officer who was the first responder on scene (McKirdy, Hanna, & Almasy, 2018). The epidemic of school shootings in recent years has resulted in school security becoming a growth industry as school districts scramble to find ways to keep their students, teachers, and staff safe (Hsu, 2018), even though no guarantees can be made that the billions spent on increasing security will keep anyone safer (Schuppe, 2018). It should be obvious that one entity alone, be it law enforcement or private security, is unlikely to have the impact that the two can have when working together. It is time for the intersection of private security and public law enforcement to become fully realized.

Key Terms

applied risk science: An analytical tool that utilizes the newest technology to identify, manage, and mitigate total risk for clients.

arrest: Taking someone into custody for violation of a law.

detention: Taking someone into temporary custody for purposes of investigation.

private security: Agents employed in the private sector who are used to patrol and protect property against theft, vandalism, and other illegal activity (BLS, 2018a).

professionalization: A process where members of an occupation develop standards. This process changes the occupation from unskilled labor into a profession.

public law enforcement: Sworn law enforcement officers working for a governmental entity.

Discussion Questions

- What do you think about the intersection of private security with public law enforcement after reading the chapter?
- Describe the history and evolution of private security.
- Explain the concept of "collective responsibility" for safety and security and discuss its relevance to private security.
- Describe the significant events that have impacted the evolution of the private security industry in the United States.
- Compare private security with public law enforcement. How are they similar and how are they different?
- Discuss the common legal powers of private security officers. How do these powers compare to the same powers of public police officers?
- Describe some of the challenges that exist between private security and public law enforcement and offer your own assessment of these challenges. How can these challenges be addressed by both entities?

- What steps have been taken in recent years to improve the relationship between private security and public law enforcement. Discuss whether you believe these efforts have been successful. What more needs to be done?

References

American Society of Industrial Security International. (n.d). *Membership*. Retrieved from https://www.asisonline.org/membership/asis-membership/

Bergal, J. (2015). In many states, security guards get scant training, oversight. *PEW*. Retrieved from http://www.pewtrusts.org/en/research-and-analysis/blogs/stateline/2015/11/10/in-many-states-security-guards-get-scant-training-oversight

Bureau of Labor Statistics (BLS). (2018a). Security guards and gaming surveillance officers. *Occupational outlook handbook*. Retrieved from https://www.bls.gov/ooh/protective-service/security-guards.htm

Bureau of Labor Statistics (BLS). (2018b). Private detectives and investigators. *Occupational outlook handbook*. Retrieved from https://www.bls.gov/ooh/protective-service/private-detectives-and-investigators.htm

Bureau of Labor Statistics (BLS). (2018c). Occupational employment and wages, May 2017. *Occupational employment statistics*. Retrieved from https://www.bls.gov/oes/current/oes339032.htm

Cunningham, W. C., Strauchs, J. J., & Van Meter, O. W. (1990). *The Hallcrest report II: Private security trends 1970–2000*. Retrieved from https://www.ncjrs.gov/pdffiles1/Digitization/126681NCJRS.pdf

Cunningham, W. C., & Taylor, T. H. (1985). *The Hallcrest report: Private security and police in America*. Portland, OR: Chancellor Press.

Dempsey, J. S. (2011). *Introduction to private security* (2nd ed.). Belmont, CA: Wadsworth.

Finkel, E. (2017, December 1). Top security guarding companies report 2017. *Security Magazine*. Retrieved from https://www.securitymagazine.com/articles/88535-top-security-guarding-companies-report-2017

Fisher, R. J., & Green, G. (2004). Introduction to security (7th ed.) Burlington, MA: Butterwroth-Heinemann.

Greenspan, J. (2013). Remembering the 1993 World Trade Center bombing Feb 26, 2013. *History*. Retrieved from https://www.history.com/news/remembering-the-1993-world-trade-center-bombing

Heitert, R. D. (1993). *Security officer's training manual*. Englewood, NJ: Regents/Prentice Hall.

Hess, K. M., & Wrobleski, H. M. (1996). *Introduction to private security* (4th ed.) Minneapolis/St. Paul, MN: West Publishing.

Hsu, T. (2018, March 4). Threat of shootings turns school security into a growth industry. *New York Times*. Retrieved from https://www.nytimes.com/2018/03/04/business/school-security-industry-surges-after-shootings.html

Johnson, B. R., & Ortmeier, P. J. (2018). *Introduction to security: Operations and management* (5th ed.). New York, NY: Pearson.

Law Enforcement Private Security Consortium. (2009). Operation law enforcement: Trends and practices in law enforcement and private security collaborations. *U.S. Department of Justice, Office of Community Oriented Policing Services*. Retrieved from https://www.nationalpublicsafetypartnership.org/clearinghouse/Content/ResourceDocuments/OperationPartnership-TrendsandPracticesinLawEnforcementandPrivateSecurityCollaborations.pdf

McCrie, R. (2017). Private security services regulations in the United States today. *International Journal of Comparative and Applied Criminal Justice, 41*(4), 287–304. doi:10.1080/01924036.2017.1364281
McKirdy, E., Hanna, J., & Almasy, S. (2017, October 20). Las Vegas police: Security responded to door alarm, drew fire from killer. *CNN*. Retrieved from https://www.cnn.com/2017/10/06/us/las-vegas-shooting-investigation/index.html
Meadows, R. J. (1995). *Fundamentals of protection and safety for the private protection officer*. Englewood Cliffs, NJ: Prentice Hall.
Montana Code Annotated. (2018). *46-6-506 temporary detention by merchant—liability*. Retrieved from https://leg.mt.gov/bills/mca/title_0460/chapter_0060/part_0050/section_0060/0460-0060-0050-0060.html
Morabito, A., & Greenberg, S. (2005). Engaging the private sector to promote homeland security: Law enforcement-private security partnerships. *U.S. Department of Justice, Office of Justice Programs*. Retrieved from https://www.ncjrs.gov/pdffiles1/bja/210678.pdf
National Advisory Committee on Criminal Justice Standards and Goals. (1976). *Private security – Report of the task force on private security*. Retrieved from https://www.ncjrs.gov/App/Publications/abstract.aspx?ID=40543
National September 11th Memorial & Museum. (n.d.). *FAQ*. Retrieved from https://www.911memorial.org/faq-about-911
Occupational Employment Statistics. (2018). *Security guards*. Retrieved from https://www.bls.gov/oes/2017/may/oes339032.htm
Pinkerton Consulting & Investigations. (n.d.a.). *Our history*. Retrieved from https://www.pinkerton.com/our-difference/history
Pinkerton Consulting & Investigations. (n.d.b.). *Risk science*. Retrieved from https://www.pinkerton.com/our-difference/risk-science
Securitas. (n.d.). Retrieved from https://www.securitas.com/
Schuppe, J. (2018). Schools are spending billions on high-tech security. *NBC*. Retrieved from https://www.nbcnews.com/news/us-news/schools-are-spending-billions-high-tech-security-are-students-any-n875611
Smith, C. F., Schmalleger, F., & Siegel, L. J. (2017). *Private security today*. Boston, MA: Pearson.
Strom, K., Berzofsky, M., Shook-Sa, B., Barrick, K., Daye, C., Horstmann, N., & Kinsey, S. (2010). *The private security industry: A review of the definitions, available data sources, and paths moving forward*. Retrieved from https://www.ncjrs.gov/pdffiles1/bjs/grants/232781.pdf
Walker, S. (1992). *The police in America: An introduction* (2nd ed.). New York: McGraw-Hill.

CHAPTER 3

Technology Versus the Reasonable Expectation of Privacy

A 21st-Century Perspective

By Tiffany Wasserburger

> *"Technology is changing people's expectation of privacy ... maybe 10 years from now 90 percent of the population will be using social networking sites and they will have on average 500 friends and they will have allowed their friends to monitor their location 24 hours a day, 365 days a year, through the use of their cell phones. Then—what would the expectation of privacy be?"*
>
> —Oral arguments, *US v. Jones* (2012)

Opening Questions

Answer the following question before reading this chapter:

> What do you know about the effect technology has on an individual's reasonable expectation of privacy prior to reading this chapter?

Answer the following question while reading the chapter:

> What are some concepts from the chapter that stand out to you? Why do you think they are important?

Introduction

Police today operate in a world never envisioned by the founding fathers. Our instantaneous public consumption of information has raised myriad issues in the quest to protect public safety while respecting personal privacy.

Law enforcement in the United States struggles to keep abreast of technological changes, oftentimes before the courts have outlined proper procedure, leaving critical evidence at risk of exclusion and our system at risk of failing to hold offenders' accountable. This dilemma is occurring on a world stage where criminals move freely and temporarily unite to victimize hundreds, thousands, and even millions of people at a time.

The question has now become, "Who is winning the technology race: police or the criminals?" This chapter will help you decide by exploring the history of technology in police work, issues at the forefront of today's crime fighting, and landmark Supreme Court decisions that dictate the proper use of technology within today's police organizations.

History of Technology in Policing

As society has developed, so too has our use of technology. Police departments around the country work to implement new methods of locating and identifying suspects and evidence, transmit information, and prevent new criminal activity. Some of the most important technological advances relevant to policing have been identified as follows (SEASKATES, 1998):

1854–1859	San Francisco becomes the site of systematic photography for criminal identification
1877	Police begin using the telegraph in Albany, New York
1878	Washington D.C. precinct houses begin to use the telephone
1923	Los Angeles Police Department establishes the first police crime lab in the United States
1928	Detroit police begin using the one-way radio
1934	Boston Police use the two-way radio
1930	Prototype of polygraph machine is developed
1932	FBI opens its crime lab
1948	Law enforcement begins using radar
1948	American Academy of Forensic Sciences meets for the first time
1955	New Orleans Police Department begins using an electronic data-processing machine
1960s	First computer-assisted dispatching system is installed in the St. Louis Police Department
1967	The National Crime Information Center begins. It is a computerized national filing system on crimes
1968	911 established
1970s	Large-scale computerization of police departments begins
1975	First fingerprint reader installed at FBI
1986	First use of DNA evidence in a criminal investigation (England)
1990s	Internet becomes part of mainstream society
1990s–Today	Advancing technology now includes smart phones, tablets, artificial intelligence, and enhanced DNA

As rapidly as law enforcement works to incorporate the latest technology, criminals are doing the same thing, often with more success. Those whose goal is victimization are not bound by the same constitutional constraints as law enforcement. Privacy concerns of citizens are of no importance to those intent on using technology to make money. These diametrically opposed principles have raised legal issues with which the court system and law enforcement continue to grapple.

General Context

Most issues raised by law enforcement's use of technology center on the Fourth Amendment: Does the method constitute a search? Do citizens have an expectation of privacy that is being violated by the use of the technology? Is a warrant required to use the technology? The Court has provided general guidance to law enforcement through its decisions in *Weeks v. U.S.* and *Mapp v. Ohio.*

Weeks v. US **(2014)**

Summary: The defendant was arrested at work on charges including use of mail for transporting shares in a lottery or gift enterprise. Police officers went to defendant's house, found the key, and entered. They searched the defendant's room and took possession of various papers and articles, which were turned over to the U.S. marshal. Police returned later the same day to search again. They were allowed into the home but not by the owner; additional paperwork was removed by the officers. Documents removed during the searches were offered and received at trial against the defendant, who was convicted. No search warrant was issued for either search.

Issue: Was the warrantless search of the defendant's home lawful?

Holding: No. For the first time, the Court held that the Fourth Amendment prohibited the use of evidence secured through illegal searches and seizures in federal prosecutions.

This decision in effect created the Exclusionary Rule, which bans the use of any evidence unlawfully discovered by law enforcement at trial. The rule was established to deter police misconduct, but this decision applied it only to federal officers.

Reasoning: The Court reasoned that the "letters in question were taken from the house of the accused by an official of the United States, acting under color of his office, in direct violation of the constitutional rights of the defendant." The Court further reasoned that "[t]he effect of the Fourth Amendment is to put the courts of the United States and Federal officials, in the exercise of their power and authority, under limitations and restraints as to the exercise of such power and authority, and to forever secure the people, their persons, houses, papers and effects again all unreasonable searches and seizures under the guise of law."

***Mapp v. Ohio* (1961)**

Summary: In May 1957, three Cleveland police officers arrived at Mapp's home based on information that a wanted person was hiding there. After officers demanded entrance, Mapp consulted her attorney and refused to admit them without a search warrant. Officers then began surveillance of the home and several hours later attempted to gain entrance again. When Mapp did not immediately respond to the door, officers forcibly entered the home. Mapp demanded to see the warrant, and a paper, claiming to be such, was held up by one of the officers. A physical altercation then ensued between Mapp and the officers. Mapp was forcibly taken upstairs to her bedroom where officers searched several items and then expanded the search to the entire second floor and basement of the building. It was during this expanded search that obscene materials were found, leading to Mapp's criminal charges. At trial, the obscene materials were offered and received and Mapp was convicted. Appeals led to review by the United States Supreme Court.

Issue: Does the Exclusionary Rule apply to state actions?

Holding: Yes. The Court found that the Exclusionary Rule is an essential part of both the Fourth and 14th Amendments and "makes very good sense." The Court further stated that "[t]he criminal goes free if he must, but it is the law that set him free. Nothing can destroy a government more quickly than its failure to observe its own laws."

The Fruit of the Poisonous Tree doctrine came about as a natural extension of the Exclusionary Rule. This doctrine holds that any evidence discovered from an initial unlawful process must be excluded at trial, including even later-discovered evidence.

Trending Topics

DNA

DNA provides a useful study of how novel evidence can become routine and readily admissible in the court system. Common usage, consistent guidelines, scrutiny of the technology, known rates of error, and acceptance in the technological community can all help establish the reliability and admissibility of evidence obtained through modern technological techniques.

DNA has been called "the single greatest advance ... and the gold standard of forensic science" (Hodge, 2017). First developed to help establish child paternity, its use started in criminal cases in England during a 1986 rape investigation (Geberth, 2017). The first use of DNA profiling in America was in Orange County, Florida, during a rape case (Geberth, 2017). The first DNA-based conviction in the United States was in 1987, when Tommy Lee Andrews was convicted of rape (Geberth, 2017).

As the use of DNA increased, courts struggled with determining what must be proven for the evidence to be admissible. First came the "**Frye standard**." In this case, the court ruled that scientific evidence must be sufficiently established to have gained general acceptance in the scientific field (*Frye v. United States of America*, 1923).

More recently, the Court established the **Daubert Standard**, which imposes additional requirements for the admissibility of scientific evidence. Here, the court required that the admissibility of scientific evidence be determined by (a) whether the theory or technique employed by the expert is generally accepted in the scientific community, (b) whether the technique has been subjected to peer review and publication, (c) whether the technique can be and has been tested, (d) whether the known or potential rate of error is acceptable, and (e) whether the research was conducted independent of the litigation (*Daubert v. Merrell Dow Pharmaceuticals*, 1993).

During the early days of DNA evidence, defense counsel issued many challenges to its use in the courtroom. However, most court decisions found the evidence to be reliable and admissible. Problems were found when issues of improper collection, cross-contamination, improper lab procedures, or unqualified technicians were raised. These problems sometimes played out on the national field, damaging law enforcement credibility but also encouraging new and stricter guidelines to ensure the validity of test results.

The judicial acceptance of DNA has provided additional tools for law enforcement. The **Combined DNA Index System (CODIS)** stores samples from offenders in every state. States vary on who is required to provide a sample, but the collection has resulted in "cold hits," providing matches to cases in which offenders could not previously be identified (Geberth, 2017). According to Vernon Geberth "as of January 2017, CODIS contained 12,647, 876 offender profiles, over 2 million arrestee profiles and more than 700,000 casework profiles. As of November 2016, CODIS produced approximately 355,535 DNA database 'hits' and aided nearly 340,552 investigations" (Geberth, 2017).

DNA collection has also provided for the creation of **"John Doe" warrants**. These warrants are used when the offender is unknown but an identifiable DNA sample has been collected. These warrants are used as a technical approach to toll the statute of limitations on certain crimes (Geberth, 2017).

DNA has also allowed law enforcement to expand their sources for DNA comparisons. Familial DNA allows police to test known samples from family members to samples from unknown offenders and can help provide leads to direct the investigation (Geberth, 2017). Utilizing collections of DNA samples, such as those collected in commercial DNA testing sites, can provide law enforcement potential links that may have otherwise gone unknown.

Captivating national attention in 2018, the use of a familial database led to the arrest of Joseph DeAngelo, believed to be the brutal Golden State Killer. The Golden State Killer is a suspect in the rapes of at least 50 victims, the murders of 12, and hundreds of burglaries in California from 1974–1986 and yet evaded detection for decades (Zhao, 2018). Paul Holes, a former Contra Costa County criminologist, submitted crime scene DNA to an open-source ancestry website that matched the offender's profile to a possible relative (Dillon, 2018).

DeAngelo, 72 years old, was identified through this method, and his DNA was collected from a car door handle and a tissue from his trash can. After analysis, the DNA was found to be a direct match to some of the Golden State Killer's crime scenes. An arrest warrant was issued and DeAngelo remains in custody on 12 murder charges (Dillon, 2018). Expected to be one of the main issues in the case is the how the Fourth Amendment may impact use of the familial database DNA.

Advances in DNA now also allow analysis of touch DNA, which analyzes skin cells left behind wherever offenders touch at the crime scene. The method used to analyze touch DNA means a much smaller sample is required to create a reliable analysis.

The use of DNA has also led to the exoneration of those wrongfully convicted. In 1989, Gary Dotson became the first person exonerated by DNA testing after serving over 10 years for a rape he did not commit (Hodge, 2017). In June 2018, Joseph DeAngelo, the suspected Golden State Killer, was cleared of involvement in the 1978 murder of a woman and her young son in Simi Valley, California (Dillon, 2018).

Social Media

Social media has proven to be an active arena as police and offenders struggle for dominance in the technological world. Today's ever-changing platforms, including Facebook, Twitter, Instagram, Snapchat, YouTube, etc., provide means for both to succeed.

Police now utilize social media to connect with the communities they serve. Countless agencies use these platforms to communicate with citizens in real time, request assistance in investigations, and promote their agencies. Social media has also allowed glimpses into the lives of offenders that were once inaccessible to law enforcement. Photos and videos posted, comments between users, and connected accounts allow police to conduct sweeping investigations from their desks.

Criminals have also perfected the use of social media to achieve their means. Crimes that once required time, thought, and contact can now be done behind the mask of anonymity. These crimes are difficult to investigate and prosecute, often leaving victims with a sense of violation, shame, and fear (McGovern & Milivojevic, 2016). Some believe the use of social media by offenders even exposes victims' families and friends to secondary trauma and victimization (McGovern & Milivojevic, 2016).

Cyberstalking, bullying, victim blaming, and revenge porn have ballooned with the advent of social media. The use of private Facebook pages and other online sites to spread nonconsensual pornography, commonly known as "revenge porn," has become a common occurrence. As legislatures struggle to develop consistent laws against revenge porn, victims have turned to the civil courts for relief. In early 2018, a federal district court in California entered a default judgement of $6.45 million in damages against a man who was accused of spreading an ex-girlfriend's nude pictures and videos online (O'Brien, 2018). The victim, identified only as Jane Doe was forced to copyright her breasts to have the images removed from the Internet (O'Brien, 2018).

In 2014, LexisNexis (2014) conducted a survey of law enforcement agencies to see how police are actually utilizing social media. The executive summary of the report stated,

> Law enforcement professionals throughout the US are increasingly turning to modern technology including social media, to aid in carrying out their public safety mission, with a primary goal of preventing and investigating crime. The frequency of social media use by law enforcement, while already high, is projected to rise even further in the coming years. Yet, few agencies have adopted formal training, policies or have dedicated staff in place, resulting in barriers to consistent and broad application throughout all of law enforcement. (LexisNexis, 2014)

The study further found that law enforcement utilized social media tools to prevent crimes by using real-time information to anticipate and prepare for public situations and request/convey information to the public (LexisNexis, 2014). Law enforcement also cited social media as a tool in closing investigations quickly through the real-time communications and the ability to connect people of interest through videos and postings (LexisNexis, 2014).

Cell Phones/Smart Phones

Cell phones have proven fertile grounds for the courts as police struggle to clearly delineate where personal privacy protection ends and investigative rights begin.

Katz v. United States of America **(1967)**

Summary: Katz was convicted in the district court for Southern District of California under an eight-count indictment charging him with transmitting wagering information by telephone, in violation of federal statute. At trial, the government was permitted, over objection, to introduce evidence of Katz's conversations held in a public telephone booth to which FBI agents had attached an electronic listening and recording device. No warrant was obtained authorizing the listening device. The Court of Appeals affirmed Katz's conviction and stated that no violation of the Fourth Amendment had occurred because "[t]here was no physical entrance in the area occupied by [the petitioner]."The U.S. Supreme Court granted certiorari to consider the constitutional questions presented.

Issue: Was the use of the listening device governed by the Fourth Amendment?

Holding: The listening device constituted a search and seizure. Use of the device without a warrant was a violation of Katz's Fourth Amendment rights.

Reasoning: Katz argued that the telephone booth was a "constitutionally protected area" and thus any evidence obtained by the electronic listening device was a violation of the right to privacy of the user of the booth. The state argued that the telephone booth was constructed partly of glass, making Katz as visible as if he were outside. Furthermore, the state argued that the listening device involved no physical penetration of the telephone booth.

The Court turned its decision on different grounds. Reasoning that the right to privacy protects people, not places, the court found that the listening device did constitute a search and seizure and violated Katz's "reasonable expectation of privacy."

***Riley v. California v. Brima Wurie* (2014)**

Summary: Riley was stopped by a police officer for driving with expired registration tags. During the stop, the officer determined that Riley's license had been suspended. Riley's car was impounded, and during an inventory search two loaded handguns were found under the car's hood. A search-conducted incident to the arrest found items associated with the Bloods street gang and a cell phone. The phone was a smart phone—a cell phone with a broad range of functions based on computing capability and Internet connectivity. The officer accessed information on the phone and found information believed to be associated with the Bloods gang. About 2 hours after the arrest, a detective specialist in gangs further examined the content of the phone, which included videos and a photo of Riley standing in front of a car suspected to be involved in a shooting a few weeks earlier.

Riley moved to suppress all evidence because the warrantless searches of his phone violated the Fourth Amendment. Riley was convicted of firing at an occupied vehicle, assault with a semiautomatic firearm, and attempted murder and was sentenced to 15 years to life in prison. After the appeals court upheld the convictions, the U.S. Supreme Court granted certiorari.

In a companion case, Brima Wurie was arrested for selling two packets of crack cocaine.

At the station, officers seized two cell phones from Wurie's person. One was a flip-phone that continuously received calls from a source identified as "my house" on the external screen. Accessing the call log on the phone, officers used this information to track Wurie's home address to an apartment building. Once at the building, they saw Wurie's name on a mailbox and observed through a window a woman who resembled the woman in the photograph on his phone. Officers obtained a search warrant and found 215 grams of crack cocaine, marijuana, drug paraphernalia, a firearm, ammunition, and cash. Wurie was charged with distributing crack cocaine, possessing crack cocaine with intent to distribute, and being a felon in possession of a firearm and ammunition. He moved to suppress the evidence from his apartment, arguing that it was fruit of the poisonous tree because no warrant had been obtained for his phone. The motion was denied and Wurie was convicted on all three counts and sentenced to 252 months in prison. Wurie's appeal was successful as to the convictions for possession with intent to distribute and possession of a firearm as a felon. The U.S. Supreme Court granted certiorari on this case as well.

Issue: Were the warrantless searches of the phones reasonable as searches incident to an arrest?

Held: No. "Our answer to the question of what police must do before searching a cell phone seized incident to an arrest is accordingly simple—get a warrant." The Court specified that a warrant is required for a phone, even when a search is conducted incident to an arrest. The Court did find that other exceptions to the search warrant requirement may be found applicable in future cases. Although the Court recognized the diminished privacy interests of those under arrest, the Fourth Amendment was still found to be a relevant consideration in determining the validity of the searches.

It is important to review and become familiar with the Court's reasoning in the *Riley v. California* decision as it will likely guide future decisions. The Court first explored the history of the search warrant exception granted at the time of an arrest in *Chimel v. California* (1969):

> When an arrest is made, it is reasonable for the arresting officer to search the person arrested in order to remove any weapons that the latter might seek to use in order to resist arrest or effect his escape. Otherwise, the officers' safety might well be endangered and the arrest itself frustrated. In addition, it is entirely reasonable for the arresting officer to search for and seize any evidence on the arrestee's person in order to prevent its concealment or destruction. There is ample justification therefore, for a search of the arrestee's person and the area "within his immediate control" construing that phrase to mean the area from within which he might gain possession of a weapon or destroy evidence.

The Court then moved on to the challenges of imposing precedent on modern technology. "These cases require us to decide how the search incident to arrest doctrine applies to modern cell phones, which are now such a pervasive and insistent part of daily life that the proverbial visitor from Mars might conclude they were an important feature of human anatomy" (*Riley v. California v. Brima Wurie*, 2014).

Without precise guidance, the Court stated that to determine whether a certain type of search should be exempted from the **warrant requirement** requires "an assessment of the degree to which it intrudes upon an individual's privacy and the degree to which it is needed for the promotion of legitimate governmental interests" (*Riley v. California v. Brima Wurie*, 2014, citing *Wyoming v. Houghton*, 1999).

The Court specifically discussed two ways in which the data on phone may be vulnerable to destruction after an arrest: remote wiping and data encryption. Remote wiping occurs when a phone, connected to a wireless network, receives a signal that erases stored data. This can happen when a third party sends a remote signal or when a phone is pre-programmed to delete data upon entering or leaving certain geographical areas (geofencing; see also recommendations for use of drones discussion in this chapter). Encryption protects data on a locked phone protected by a code that is almost unbreakable unless police know the password. Although both are very real concerns in today's law enforcement world (see San Bernardino discussion), the Court found that these issues were too far removed from Chimel's protection of a search of the person and the area under their immediate control.

The Court again returned to the argument that cell phones differ in "both a quantitative and qualitative sense from other objects that might be kept on an arrestee's person." The Court described cell phones as minicomputers with immense storage capacity.

> The storage capacity of cell phones has several interrelated consequences of privacy. First, a cellphone collects in one place many distinct types of information that reveal as much or more in combination than any isolated record. Second, a cell phone's capacity allows even just one type of information to convey far more than previously possible. The sum of an individual's private life can be reconstructed through a thousand photographs labeled with dates, locations, and descriptions; the same cannot be said of a photograph or two of loved ones tucked into a wallet. Third, the data on a phone can date back to the purchase of the phone or even earlier.

The Court concluded, "We cannot deny that our decision today will have an impact on the ability of law enforcement to combat crime. Cell phones have become important tools in facilitating coordination and communication among members of criminal enterprise, and can provide valuable incriminating information about dangerous criminals. Privacy comes at a cost."

In 2016, the federal government faced the exact situation explored by the Court in *Riley.* After a mass shooting in San Bernardino, California, the deceased shooter's work-issued iPhone was discovered in his car (Rubin, Quelly, & Paresh, 2016). The FBI attempted to review information on the phone for any evidence leading up to and including the commission of the crime, including anyone who may have helped the shooter (Rubin et al., 2016). Familiar with security features that make a phone inoperable after a certain number of failed login attempts, agents approached Apple and requested a bypass of the encrypted security system to access the phone (Rubin et al., 2016). Apple refused, asserting it was protecting the privacy interests of its customers (Rubin et al., 2016). The government then went to court to force Apple to cooperate. Before a final decision was issued, the government announced they were able to hack the shooter's phone with the assistance of an outside group that they refused to name (Rubin et al., 2016). Viewed as a test case pitting technology companies against law enforcement, the lack of a judicial resolution means this area remains ripe for future litigation.

***Carpenter v. United States of America* (2018)**

Summary: In April 2011, four men were arrested for involvement in a string of armed robberies. One of the men confessed to robbing nine different stores in Michigan and Ohio and identified 15 accomplices. This suspect provided the FBI with his cell phone number and the numbers of others he had named as accomplices. The FBI reviewed the information from the phone and obtained a court order under the Stored Communications Act to obtain cell phone records for several of the suspects. The burden for obtaining this order is reasonable grounds as opposed to probable cause for the issuance of a search warrant. When a cell/smart phone connects to a cell site, cell-site location information (CSLI) is generated. Because of increased cell usage, providers have built more sites, allowing the CSLI to become more specific. The CSLI showed Carpenter's movement for 127 days. Carpenter moved to suppress the cell-site evidence, claiming a warrant was needed to obtain the records. This motion was denied, the evidence was used at trial, and Carpenter was convicted. After several appeals, the U.S. Supreme Court granted certiorari.

Issue: Was the government's action of obtaining historical cell phone records, which revealed the location and movement of a cell phone user, a search under the Fourth Amendment? Was a search warrant required for the records?

Holding: Yes. The government's acquisition of the cell-site records was a search within the meaning of the Fourth Amendment. "Before compelling a wireless carrier to turn over a subscriber's CSLI, the government's obligation is a familiar one—get a warrant."

The Court made clear that this decision was a narrow one, applying to CSLI records:

> This is certainly not to say that all orders compelling the production of documents will require a showing of probable cause. The Government will be able to use subpoenas to acquire records in the overwhelming majority of investigations. We hold only that a warrant is required in the rare case where the suspect has a legitimate privacy interest in records held by a third party. Further, even though the Government will generally need a warrant to access CSLI, case-specific exceptions may support a warrantless search of an individual's cell-site records under certain circumstances. "One well recognized exception applies when '"the exigencies of the situation" make the needs of law enforcement so compelling that [a] warrantless search is objectively reasonable under the Fourth Amendment.'" *Kentucky v. King*, 563 U. S. 452, 460 (2011) (quoting *Mincey v. Arizona*, 437 U. S. 385, 394 (1978)). Such exigencies include the need to pursue a fleeing suspect, protect individuals who are threatened with imminent harm, or prevent the imminent destruction of evidence.

Reasoning: The Court found that tracking a person's movements through CSLI was very similar to information obtained by GPS monitoring. (See *U.S. v. Jones*, 2012) But, the Court found that historical cell site records present even greater privacy concerns than GPS monitoring. A court order requiring reasonable grounds for believing that the records were "relevant and material to an ongoing investigation" falls well short of probable cause required for a warrant. An order issued pursuant to this manner is not a permissible mechanism for accessing historical cell-site records. The Court found that any rule it adopted "must take account of more sophisticated systems that are already in use or in development" (*Kyllo v. U.S.*, 2001).

GPS

Cases involving global positioning systems (GPS) continue to be active in the courts as well. Again, most cases focus on whether the use of GPS is a violation of a person's expectation of privacy.

***U.S. v. Jones* (2012)**

Summary: Jones was suspected of drug trafficking. Police requested and received a warrant to attach a GPS tracking device on a vehicle registered to Jones's wife. The warrant authorized installation in the District of Columbia within 10 days. However, agents installed the device on the 11th day in Maryland and tracked the vehicle's movements for 28 days. The District Court suppressed the GPS data obtained while the vehicle was parked at Jones's residence but held the remaining data was admissible because Jones had no reasonable expectation of privacy when the vehicle was on public streets. The D.C. Circuit Court reversed, concluding that admission of the evidence obtained by warrantless use of the GPS device violated the Fourth Amendment.

Issue: Did the government violate Jones's Fourth Amendment rights by installing the GPS tracking device on his vehicle without a valid warrant and without his consent?

Holding: Yes. The Court found that installing a GPS tracking device to a vehicle and using the device to monitor the vehicle's movements constituted a search under the Fourth Amendment and thus the Circuit Court was correct in concluding that admission of the GPS evidence violated the Fourth Amendment.

In *US. v. Jones* (2012), although all justices agreed on the outcome, five held that police had committed a trespass against Jones's personal effects, which constituted a search per se. This was unexpected reasoning from the Court, as the decision in the *Katz* case seemed to move away from property rights and focus on expectations of privacy. However, the majority in the *Jones* case explained that the property rights approach had not been abandoned by the Court and was thus appropriate grounds on which to rest this decision. The remaining four justices rested their decision on the expectation of privacy argument, reasoning that the continuous monitoring of every single movement of an individual's car for 28 days constituted a search.

***U.S. v. Katzin* (2014)**

This case followed *Jones* and was decided in the U.S. Court of Appeals, Third Circuit.

Summary: In December 2010, law enforcement officers magnetically attached an independently battery-operated GPS device on the vehicle of Harry Katzin while the vehicle was parked on a public street. Although the officers had probable cause, they did not obtain a warrant. For two days, the GPS was used to track the vehicle's whereabouts on public roads. The vehicle never entered private garage, curtilage of home, or any other private area. The information from the GPS led to the seizure of evidence and the arrest of Harry Katzin and his brothers, alleging their involvement in an ongoing scheme to steal drugs from Rite Aid pharmacies.

Issue: Are police required to obtain a warrant prior to attaching a GPS device to an individual's vehicle for purposes of monitoring the vehicle's movements?

Holding: Yes. Police must obtain a warrant prior to a GPS search. Note that this is not a Supreme Court decision but may provide a groundwork for future decisions.

It is important to remember that law enforcement can also utilize GPS information for purposes of running a more efficient agency. According to Timothy Roufa (2018), GPS allows law enforcement to identify the location of a 911 call, determine the safest response route, and precisely document the locations of crimes and accidents, allowing agencies to study patterns and effectively provide coverage. GPS also allows agencies to increase accountability of officers, giving administrators the ability to track a range of risk management issues, from location to vehicle speeds (Roufa, 2018)

Child Pornography

Child pornography, as known today, began in earnest with the invention of the camera in the early 19th century (Wortley & Smallbone, 2006). Today's technology makes it ever easier for predators to identify and groom victims, share their work, and learn how to become more efficient offenders.

Users of child pornography reside everywhere. Investigations that once focused on individual offenders must now envelope hundreds or thousands of suspects located throughout the world. File sharing, encryption, social networking, and the **Dark Web** all provide extra security to those who seek to victimize children for their own sexual satisfaction. The Dark Web is a part of the Internet that requires special routers that allow users to remain anonymous and has become a central location for criminal activity.

The Internet has enabled offenders to provide numerous files of child pornography easily and efficiently to its users (Wortley & Smallbone, 2006). The distribution of child pornography may occur in many different ways. Primary methods used by offenders are web pages and websites, live web cams, e-mail, e-groups, newsgroups, bulletin board systems (BBS), chat rooms, and peer-to-peer (P2P) sharing (see Wortley & Smallbone, 2006, table 2: Distribution methods of child pornography on the Internet).

Law enforcement has had some success by utilizing the same technology used by offenders. Sources of evidence can become abundant in these types of cases: computers, flash drives, smart phones, tablets, cameras, servers, and even GPS may all contain evidence linking the offender to the crime.

Many law enforcement agencies have formed specialized groups to focus on child pornography. These task forces, known as **Internet Crimes Against Children (ICAC)**, allow officers to receive specialized technical training in identifying, tracking, investigating, and arresting perpetrators. Jurisdictional issues also require collaboration between multiple law enforcement agencies on the local, state, federal, and international levels.

Operation Safety Net, conducted in New Jersey, resulted in the arrest of 79 people suspected of exploiting children. Arrestees included a Trenton police officer and swimming coach (Parent, 2017). New Jersey Attorney General Christopher Porrino stated, "The men we arrested lurked in the shadows of the internet and social media, looking for opportunities to sexually assault young children or to view such unspeakable assaults by sharing child pornography. ... We set up a wide safety net in this operation to snare these alleged predators and to protect children, which remains our highest priority" (Parent, 2017). Although viewed as successful, the sting again raised the question, "Who is winning the war against online child abuse in New Jersey? Law enforcement or those who trade or engage in child exploitation?" (Park, 2018).

In 2017, the attorneys general of Virginia and South Dakota unveiled the Campaign for Child Rescue, a program launched in partnership Griffeye, Hubstream, and Project VIC (Miller, 2017). The purpose of the program is to provide cutting-edge technology to law enforcement to locate and rescue children from human trafficking and sexual exploitation (Miller, 2017). Crowdsourcing is utilized to enable investigators the world over to help identify victims and perpetrators (Miller, 2017). An additional goal is to reduce the amount of child pornography to which investigators are exposed, reducing stress and allowing them to work longer in the field (Miller, 2017).

Law enforcement is also struggling with the population of potential victims that now have their own access to technology. Ever-younger children have personal cell phones and computers in their bedrooms, evading oversight by adults. Social media platforms accessed by potential victims are also always changing, often promising communications and images that can be immediately erased. In a classroom presentation, New Jersey State Police Lieutenant Jon Pizzure conducted a poll of students who owned smart phones: Twenty-two had them and two did not. These responses came from a class of first-graders (Park, 2018).

Officers are also utilizing trained dogs to aid in the detection of hidden child pornography. Bear, a Labrador retriever, has been trained to sniff out electronic media devices (Kim, 2015). These may include thumb drives, iPads, and SD cards, often used by perpetrators to maintain their collection (Kim, 2015). Bear was dispatched during the Jared Fogle investigation and helped find a thumb drive initially missed during a search of Fogle's home during a child pornography investigation. In 2015, Fogle pled guilty to federal charges of child pornography possession and traveling to pay for sex with minors. Fogle is serving a maximum of 15 years, 8 months in a federal correctional institution.

As police work to stay abreast of technology changes, it is important to remember that child pornography is not a one-time victimizing event. Children once victimized are more likely to become future victims, and child pornography creates a permanent record of the victim's pain, shame, and powerlessness.

Human Trafficking

Like child pornography, peddlers in human trafficking have become very sophisticated in the use of media to push their "product": victims forced into the sex or labor trade. Social media, cell phones, and online sites allow predators to advertise their "wares" with disguised language and to receive electronic payments from their clients. Many identify technology use by predators as one of the most challenging factors in these cases. Rebecca Sadwick (2016) states, "Technology has historically been used to the detriment of victims; traffickers use social media, websites and anonymizing apps and networks to contact and recruit their victims (often through deceptive or coercive message), post online advertisements for the services that can be purchased from their victims, and communicate easily and anonymously with buyers and conspirators within their trafficking rings" (para. 2).

Law enforcement is using the same technology to identify, track, and locate both victims of human trafficking and their peddlers. Data analysis can provide trafficking patterns and trends as well as identify words commonly used in advertising victims of trafficking. For law enforcement to be successful, it is sometimes necessary to maintain sites on which known human trafficking is occurring. This allows police to maintain surveillance of known offenders who are quick to change methods when concerns about detection arise. Studies have also shown that even when law enforcement is able to shutdown sites, others become almost instantaneously available to offenders. Often, the known site can actually provide better investigative information and safety for victims.

A 2015 report on human trafficking found that certain patterns emerge in human trafficking cases (USC Annenberg Center on Communication Leadership and Policy, 2011):

1. Online classified sites are used to post advertisements of victims.
2. Social networking sites are used in the recruitment of victims.
3. Investigation may begin with a picture of what appears to be an underage girl in an online classified ad.
4. A number of victims have been identified as runaways.

Often, victims of sex trafficking are viewed as criminals themselves. Investigations are now attempting to prioritize victim support services. Malika Saada Saar, a panelist at Fast Company's 2016 Innovation Festival, stated that charging young women who have been forced into the sex trade with prostitution puts girls behind bars "for essentially being subject to commercial serial rape" (Titlow, 2016, para. 15).

Drones

Unmanned aerial vehicles, otherwise known as drones, have become an unexpectedly beneficial tool for law enforcement. Between 2006 and 2013, the FBI described using drones in eight criminal cases and two national security cases (Alderton, 2018). Drones have been utilized for location surveillance, drug interdiction, suspect tracking, and negotiations (Alderton, 2018). Drone sales are expected to top $11.2 billion by 2020 and an estimated 3 million were manufactured in 2017 (Alderton, 2018).

Police Chief Alejandro Lares in Tijuana told *USA Today* in 2014, "It's like having 20 officers on patrol or more. ... It may be a small step in community policing, but it's huge for our future" (Alderton, 2018, para. 9). In Ciudad Juarez, Mexico, aerial images collected in 2009 captured 34 murders as they occurred, including a cartel killing (Alderton, 2018). The San Jose Police Department obtained a drone to access a potential explosive device and avoid risk to Bomb Squad personnel in 2014, and Jon Noland, a lieutenant with the Santa Rosa Police Department in Santa Rosa, California, told the *North Bay Business Journal* in 2014 that the use of drones is "50 times quicker than you could put people on horseback, motorcycles, bikes or on foot. It gives you real-time intelligence" (Alderton, 2018, para. 18)

Once again, issues of privacy are raised by the use of drones, similar to the use of fly-overs. In 2012, the International Association of Chiefs of Police published a list of recommended guidelines for use of drones by law enforcement. These suggestions were endorsed by the American Civil Liberties Union and include the following (Alderton, 2018):

- Warrants should be obtained if the drone will be in an area where people have a reasonable expectation of privacy.
- Police should not retain images captured by drones unless relevant to crime.
- Police should give public meaningful notice of drone use.
- Police use of drones should be subject to tracking and audits with accountability for misuse.
- Police should not use weaponized drones.

Similarly, recommendations from Gregory McNeal, Pepperdine University School of Law, are as follows (McNeal, 2014):

- Legislators should follow property-rights approach to aerial surveillance, recognizing owner rights up to 350 feet above ground level.
- Legislators should craft simple duration-based surveillance legislation to place limits on how long law enforcement may surveil specific persons or places.
- Data retention procedures should require heightened levels of suspicion and increased procedural protections to access data as time passes.
- Transparency and accountability measures should be adopted, including publication by government agencies on a regular basis information about their use of drones.
- Legislators should recognize that technology advances may ultimately make aerial surveillance by drones more protective of citizen's privacy than human surveillance, as with the use of geofencing.

Additionally, McNeal (2014) recommends that if legislatures decide to require warrants for the use of drones, certain exceptions, including good faith and inevitable discovery, should be included.

As the use of drones explodes, expect to see numerous court cases based on privacy expectations and property rights. Because each state regulates the industry differently, most believe the ultimate issues will have to be decided in the courtroom rather than the legislature. A history of legal decisions regarding aerial surveillance is helpful in trying to determine how the courts will decide between privacy interests.

***California v. Ciraolo* (1986)**

Summary: Officers attempted to see into Ciraolo's yard after receiving a tip that marijuana was being grown in the backyard, but multiple fences blocked the view. The officer used a private plane to fly over the backyard at an altitude of 1,000 feet, which was within the FAA's definition of public navigable airspace (McNeal, 2014).

Issue: Did the fly-over constitute a warrantless search and violate Ciraolo's right to privacy?

Holding: The naked-eye aerial observation of the backyard did not violate the Fourth Amendment. The Court reasoned that just because an individual has taken steps to protect his or her backyard from the view of others does not stop a police officer from observing the area from a public vantage point. The Court's decision rested on the fact that the plane was in a publicly navigable airspace and performed the fly-over in a physically non-intrusive manner (*California v. Ciraolo*, 1986).

***Florida v. Riley* (1989)**

Summary: Riley was suspected of growing marijuana in a greenhouse on his property. Some attempts had been made to hide the greenhouse from observation at ground levels. However, the sides and roof of the greenhouse were left partially open. Police flew a helicopter over Riley's land at approximately 400 feet and observed marijuana plants growing in the greenhouse (McNeal, 2014).

Issue: Was the use of helicopter fly-over a violation of Riley's expectation of privacy and in violation of the Fourth Amendment?

Holding: The Court found no violation of the Fourth Amendment. This decision rested greatly on the fact that law enforcement committed no actual physical intrusion on the Riley's land and used only publicly navigable airspace (McNeal, 2014).

The *California v. Ciraolo* and *Florida v. Riley* decisions allowed law enforcement to make observations from publicly accessible areas and use any information from those observations to then obtain a search warrant (McNeal, 2014). Because drones are able to fly at much lower altitudes, the question now remains how to define air space as private or public.

There are very few guiding cases on this issue. One of the few comes from 1946 in *United States v. Causby.* In this case, a farmer raised chickens adjacent to a small airport that was used by the military during World War II. Military flights were 67 feet above Causby's home and 83 feet above the land. Noise from the airplanes caused the chickens to fly into the wall of the coop and die. Causby's sued the government on the grounds of the Fifth Amendment (McNeal, 2014). The Supreme

Court held that a landowner owned "at least as much of the space above the ground as he can occupy or use in connection with the land" (McNeal, 2014, p. 19) Although an owner's interest in the airspace directly above his or her property was recognized in this decision, no definitive altitude was established (McNeal, 2014). Thus the question is left open to vigorous debate by privacy rights advocates and law enforcement alike.

Future Technology

Technology has been used by agencies across the country to increase agency efficiency, provide real-time data, promote public and officer safety, and increase offender accountability. Commonly used today is equipment that was unthinkable 5, 10, or 20 years ago. Many officers now regularly wear body cameras, police vehicles are often equipped with computers, and programs provide license plate reading, facial recognition, and mobile consoles for fingerprint reading (Avalos, 2016).

David Roberts, senior program manager for the technology center at the International Association of Chiefs of Police, described an agency in Lincoln, Nebraska, using map-based apps that can alert them to locations of known criminal offenders. "Officers can drive down the street, and have a smartphone or a tablet device, and have the map app open. The app can tell them the addresses of a person wanted for a crime, known incidents of felonies in the area, someone who is a registered sex offender. It provides situational awareness that is integrated with records management and emergency call systems" (Avalos, 2016, para. 10).

Three-dimensional crime-scene imaging is a forensic technology method that uses scanners to capture a 3D model of a crime or accident scene (Gasior, 2017). This information is later used by officers to reconstruct the scene and create impactful exhibits at trial (Gasior, 2017). Because the scene must only be maintained for the duration of the scan, scenes can be more quickly cleared, resulting in more efficient use of law enforcement resources, as well as increased public and officer safety (Gasior, 2017).

Some have also suggested holding prosecutors accountable by monitoring their work based on the impact they have on the community they serve (Titlow, 2016). Adam Foss, a former Boston prosecutor and cofounder of Prosecutor Integrity states, "We can start collecting data so that when prosecutors get evaluated, it's not about how many trials we've won, but about how many people's lives you've made better because they're no longer in the system" (Titlow, 2016, para. 13).

Obstacles

Many law enforcement agencies operate in rural areas, meaning they don't have uniform or consistent access to wireless service. These areas may struggle with systems when service drops or is not easily accessible (Avalos, 2016).

Concerns about mass incarceration continue to grow as criminal actors work in concert throughout the nation with the use of technology. Speaking on a panel about criminal justice reform panel in 2016, John Legend said, "There's nobody that's better at locking people up than we are. We lock up people for a longer time than any other country. Why is that?" (Titlow, 2016, para. 2).

And perhaps most importantly, data must not be used only to improve the criminal justice system, but to recognize the human struggles victims and their loved ones face every day.

Conclusion

Police face an incredibly difficult balancing act as officers move through the technological jungle. Law enforcement must plan their actions with the knowledge that new technology will raise new legal issues. Any policies or procedures must be created with an eye toward protecting the rights of those they have sworn to serve while successfully investigating criminal acts. Agencies must also understand the political nuances that are part and parcel of every decision and how those nuances change with the people in power. These unknown factors can make it extremely difficult for agencies to guess which policies and procedures the courts may require.

Marc Goodman, a former police officer, now considered a leading authority on global security, speaks for many when he states,

> Frankly, I'm afraid. I've spent a career in law enforcement and that has informed my perspective on things. ... We consistently underestimate what criminals and terrorists can do. ... Every time a new technology is being introduced, criminals are there to exploit it. ... More connections to more devices means more vulnerabilities. Criminals understand this. ... If you control the code, you control the world. (Goodman, 2012)

Goodman (2012) identifies 3D printers and synthetic drugs, both the result of technological advances, as two of the most pressing dangers in our world today and presents law enforcement with perhaps the most important question they face: "In the Sony Hack, 100 million people were robbed. When in the history of humanity has it ever been possible for one person to rob 100 million. ... The ability of one to affect many is scaling exponentially. And it's scaling for good and it's scaling for evil. How can we prepare?"

Key Terms

Combined DNA Index System (CODIS): The United States national DNA database created and maintained by the Federal Bureau of Investigation.

Dark Web: World Wide Web content that is generally inaccessible by the general public because it requires the use of specific software or authorizations to access it. Because of this, it has become a central location for criminal activity.

Daubert standard: From *Daubert v. Merrell Dow Pharmaceuticals, Inc.* (1993). In this case, the court required that the admissibility of scientific evidence be determined by (a) whether the theory or technique employed by the expert is generally accepted in the scientific community, (b) whether the technique has been subjected to peer review and publication, (c) whether the technique can be and has been tested, (d) whether the known or potential rate of error is acceptable, and (e) whether the research was conducted independent of the litigation.

Frye standard: From *Frye v. United States* (1923). In this case, the court ruled that scientific evidence must be sufficiently established to have gained general acceptance in the scientific field.

Internet Crimes Against Children Task Force (ICAC): A working group that involves collaboration between multiple law enforcement agencies on the local, state, federal, and international levels, allowing for specialized technical training in identifying, tracking, investigating, and arresting perpetrators to enforce child pornography and other laws involving the protection of children.

"John Doe" warrants: Warrants used when the offender is unknown but an identifiable DNA sample has been collected.

warrant requirement: The requirement, found in the Fourth Amendment to the United States Constitution, that a warrant is needed whenever the government wants to seize a person or property or search a private place.

Discussion Questions

- What do you think about the effect technology has on an individual's reasonable expectation of privacy after reading the chapter?
- What impact has technology had on contemporary American policing? Has that impact been good or bad?
- Why do you think criminals are more adept at using technology to meet their ends? What can the police do to reverse this?
- How has legal concept of a "reasonable expectation of privacy" evolved over time? Is there even a "reasonable expectation of privacy" in the era of modern technology?
- Which "trending topic" do you think is most important to the police? Explain your answer.
- What is your opinion on the decision in *Riley v. California* (2014)? Do you favor the privacy that it protects, or would you prefer that police be allowed to search cells phones after arrest to protect evidence?
- What are your thoughts on the use of drones to gather intelligence? Do you think they present a threat to privacy, or do you like the ease with which they are able to be used to gather intelligence?
- In your opinion, what will be the most important future technology for policing?

References

Alderton, M. (2018, April 13). To the rescue! Why drones in police work are the future of crime fighting. *Autodesk.* Retrieved from https://www.autodesk.com/redshift/drones-in-police-work-future-crime-fighting/

Avalos, G. (2016, January 18). Police use new technologies to fight crime. *Digital Communities*. Retrieved from http://www.govtech.com/dc/articles/Police-Use-New-Technologies-to-Fight-Crime.html.

California v. Ciraolo, 476 U.S. 207 (1986).

Carpenter v. United States of America, 585 U.S. ____ (2018).

Daubert v. Merrell Dow Pharmaceuticals, 509 U.S. 579 (1993).

Dillon, N. (2018, June 14). Golden State Killer suspect cleared by DNA in 1978 murders of mom and young son, disappointing man wrongly convicted in case. *New York Daily News*. Retrieved from http://www.nydailynews.com/news/ny-news-golden-state-killer-suspect-cleared-in-1978-rhonda-wicht-murders-20180614-story.html

Florida v. Riley, 488 U.S. 445 (1989).

Frye v. United States of America, 54 App. D.C. 46, 293 F.1013 (1923).

Gasior, M. (2017, September 26). New technology in law enforcement. *PowerDMS*. Retrieved from https://www.powerdms.com/blog/new-technology-in-law-enforcement/

Geberth, V. (2017, March 13). 30 years of DNA technology. *Forensic Magazine*. Retrieved from https://www.forensicmag.com/article/2017/03/30-years-dna-technology

Goodman, M. (2012, June). A vision of crimes in the future. *TED*. Retrieved from https://www.ted.com/talks/marc_goodman_a_vision_of_crimes_in_the_future

Hodge, C. (2017, June 9). DNA: The shifting science of DNA in the courtroom. *CNN*. Retrieved from https://www.cnn.com/2017/06/09/health/dna-technology-forensic-evidence/index.html

Katz v. United States of America, 389 U.S. 347 (1967).

Kim, S. (2015, August 26). Meet the dog investigators say helped catch ex-Subway spokesman Jared Fogle. *ABC News*. Retrieved from https://abcnews.go.com/US/meet-dog-investigators-helped-catch-subway-spokesman-jared/story?id=33330258

Kyllo v. U.S., 533 U.S. 27 (2001).

LexisNexis. (2014, November). *Social media use in law enforcement: Crime prevention and investigative activities continue to drive usage*. Retrieved from https://risk.lexisnexis.com/insights-resources/white-paper/law-enforcement-usage-of-social-media-for-investigations

Mapp v. Ohio, 367 U.S. 643 (1961).

McGovern, A., & Milivojevic, S. (2016, October 16). Opinion: Social media and crime: The good, the bad and the ugly. *The Conversation*. Retrieved from http://theconversation.com/social-media-and-crime-the-good-the-bad-and-the-ugly-66397

McNeal, G. (2014, November). Drones and aerial surveillance: Considerations for legislators. *Brookings*. Retrieved from https://www.brookings.edu/research/drones-and-aerial-surveillance-considerations-for-legislatures/

Miller, S. (2017, April 26). State officials push tech to combat child porn. *GCN*. Retrieved from https://gcn.com/articles/2017/04/26/state-ags-protect-children-tech.aspx

O'Brien, S.A. (2018, April 9). Woman awarded $6.45 million in revenge porn case. *CNN*. Retrieved from http://money.cnn.com/2018/04/09/technology/revenge-porn-judgment/index.html

Parent, A. (2017, December 2). 79 charged in massive N.J. child predator probe. *PhillyVoice*. Retrieved from http://www.phillyvoice.com/79-charged-massive-nj-child-predator-probe/

Park, K. (2018, March 2). New tech helps police in fight against child porn. *Associated Press*. Retrieved from https://www.apnews.com/342f0b80765248c3b10ab6d90a1aecff

Riley v. California v. Brima Wurie, 134 S.C.t. 2473 (2014).

Roufa, T. (2018, May 13, updated). Technologies that are changing the way police do business. *The Balance Careers*. Retrieved from https://www.thebalancecareers.com/technologies-that-are-changing-the-way-police-do-business-974549

Rubin, J., Quelly, J., & Paresh, D. (2016, March 28). FBI unlocks San Bernardino shooter's iPhone and ends legal battle with Apple, for now. *L.A. Times*. Retrieved from http://www.latimes.com/local/lanow/la-me-ln-fbi-drops-fight-to-force-apple-to-unlock-san-bernardino-terrorist-iphone-20160328-story.html

Sadwick, R. (2016, January 11). 7 ways technology is fighting human trafficking. *Forbes*. Retrieved from https://www.forbes.com/sites/rebeccasadwick/2016/01/11/tech-fighting-human-trafficking/#5b66369e6cac

SEASKATE, INC. (1998, July 1). *The evolution and development of police technology*. Retrieved from https://www.ncjrs.gov/pdffiles1/Digitization/173179NCJRS.pdf

Titlow, J. P. (2016, November 17). How technology is helping (and hindering) criminal justice reform. *Fast Company*. Retrieved from https://www.fastcompany.com/3065343/how-technology-is-helping-and-hindering-criminal-justic

U.S. v. Causby, 328 U.S. 256 (1946).

U.S. v. Jones, 132 S.Ct. 945 (2012).

U.S. v. Katzin, No. 12-2548 (2014).

USC Annenberg Center on Communication Leadership and Policy. (2011) Technology and human trafficking: Human trafficking online. *University of Southern California*. Retrieved from https://technologyandtrafficking.usc.edu/report/human-trafficking-online-cases-patterns/

Weeks v. U.S., 232 U.S. 383 (1914).

Wortley, R., & Smallbone, S. (2006) Child pornography on the Internet, guide no. 41. *Arizona State University, Center for Problem-Oriented Policing*. Retrieved from http://www.popcenter.org/problems/child_pornography/print/

Wyoming v. Houghton, 526 U.S. 295, 119 S.Ct. 1297 (1999).

Zhao, C. (2018, April 27). How was the Golden State Killer caught? DNA from relative on genealogy website was key. *Newsweek*. Retrieved from https://www.newsweek.com/how-was-golden-state-killer-caught-dna-relative-genealogy-website-was-key-903590

CHAPTER 4

Black and White Attitudes Toward Police Use of Force

The More Things Change, the More They Stay the Same

By Brian D. Fitch

Opening Questions

Answer the following question before reading this chapter:

> What do you know about the effect of race on attitudes toward police use of force prior to reading this chapter?

Answer the following question while reading the chapter:

> What are some concepts from the chapter that stand out to you? Why do you think they are important?

Introduction

At around 12:30 a.m. on March 3, 1991, Rodney King, accompanied by his friends Bryant Allen and Freddie Helms, was driving a 1987 Hyundai Excel west on the Foothill Freeway (Interstate 210) in the San Fernando Valley at a high rate of speed when King caught the attention of officers Tim and Melanie Singer, husband-and-wife members of the California Highway Patrol (CHP). King, who was intoxicated after spending the evening watching basketball and drinking with his friends, initially tried to outrun the officers. King later admitted that he tried to evade the officers because an arrest for driving under the influence would have violated his parole for a previous robbery conviction (Cannon, 1999). King exited the freeway around the Hansen Dam Recreation Center. The pursuit continued through residential streets at speeds ranging from 55 to 80 miles per hour, with several police cars and a police helicopter joining in the chase.

After approximately 8 miles, officers cornered King in his car near the intersection of Foothill Boulevard and Osborne Street in the city of Los Angeles. The first five Los Angeles Police Department (LAPD) officers to arrive were Sergeant Stacy Koon (the ranking officer on scene) and officers Laurence Powell, Timothy Wind, Theodore Briseno, and Rolando Solano (Whitman, 1993). Officer Tim Singer ordered King and his two passengers to exit the vehicle and to lie face down on the ground. While Allen and Helms both exited the vehicle, King remained inside the car. When he finally emerged from the car, King grabbed his buttocks, which Officer Melanie Singer understood as King reaching for a weapon, although King was later found to be unarmed. Singer drew her service weapon, ordered King to lie on the ground, and approached him. Sergeant Koon instructed Officer Singer to stand down. He told Singer that the LAPD was taking command and ordered all the officers to holster their weapons (Serrano, 1992).

Koon ordered the four LAPD officers—Powell, Wind, Briseno, and Solano—to subdue and to handcuff King using a technique called a "swarm." This technique uses several officers to grab a suspect with empty hands to quickly overcome any potential resistance. As the four officers attempted to restrain King, he resisted, by standing, to remove officers Powell and Briseno from his back. The officers later testified that they believed King was under the influence of phencyclidine (PCP), although King's toxicology report showed no signs of the drug in his body (Cannon, 1993). As King rushed toward Officer Powell, he was tasered twice by Sergeant Koon. In the now-famous video of the beating, which was captured on a video camcorder by George Holliday from his apartment near the intersection of Foothill Boulevard and Osborne Street in Lake View Terrace, taser wires can be seen hanging from King's body.

Officer Powell used his baton to knock King to the ground. King was struck several more times with batons. Reportedly, it was at this point that Sergeant Koon told the officers, "That's enough." King continued to try to get back to his feet and was struck a total of 33 times by batons and kicked six times before he was eventually subdued and handcuffed by officers. Officers then dragged King on his abdomen to the side of the road to wait for emergency services personnel. King was transported to Pacifica Hospital, where he was found to have suffered a broken ankle, fractured facial bone, and multiple lacerations and bruises (Cannon, 1999). King later sued the city of Los Angeles for damages and a jury awarded him $3.8 million, as well as an additional $1.7 million in attorney's fees. The city did not pursue criminal charges against King for driving while intoxicated and evading arrest, citing insufficient evidence for prosecution (Ford, 1992).

Two days after the incident, Holliday called LAPD headquarters at Parker Center. He advised the police department of the video, but he could not find anyone who was interested in watching it. He then went to KTLA television, who aired the tape. The footage of King's beating quickly went viral, transforming what would have been a violent, yet soon-forgotten encounter between LAPD officers and King into one of the most widely watched and transformative incidents in police history (Winston, 2016). In fact, the video of the beating was broadcast so often that Ed Turner, executive vice president of *CNN*, referred to it as "wallpaper" (Cannon, 1998).

On March 15, 1991, Sergeant Koon and the four officers were indicted by a Los Angeles grand jury in connection with the beating. Despite the videotape, the sergeant and officers were acquitted of all charges by a majority White jury in Semi Valley in April 1992. Within a few hours of the jury's verdict, frustration spilled into the streets (Sastry & Bates, 2017). The city of Los Angeles erupted into 5 days of riots, with smaller riots occurring in other

U.S. cities, including San Francisco, Las Vegas, Seattle, Atlanta, and New York. By the time law enforcement and the California National Guard restored order, 63 people had lost their lives, over 5,000 people had been arrested, and an estimated $1 billion in financial losses had been reported (*Koon v. U.S.*, 1996).

In August 1992, a federal grand jury returned indictments against Sergeant Koon and officers Powell, Wind, and Briseno on the charge of violating King's civil rights. A federal jury convicted Officer Powell on one count of violating King's constitutional right to be free from an arrest made with "unreasonable" force. As the ranking officer on scene, Sergeant Koon was convicted of permitting the civil right violation to occur (Zeidler, 2012). Officers Wind and Briseno were acquitted of all charges. No riots followed the verdicts.

Soon after the incident, the **Christopher Commission**, an independent group, was founded to conduct an unparalleled investigation and examination of the LAPD, including its **use-of-force** policies and training (Stewart, 2012). Among its findings, the commission noted a significant number of LAPD officers who repeatedly used excessive force against the public and persistently ignored the written guidelines of the department. The commission recommended that LAPD leadership give priority to curbing the use of excessive force. The commission further concluded that police violence was not confined to the Los Angeles Police Department, but rather was part of the organizational culture found in many law enforcement agencies throughout the nation (Independent Commission on the LAPD, 1991).

George Holliday's video did more than merely capture the beating of Rodney King by members of the LAPD. It changed LAPD force policy and training by banning the use of the police baton, a tool, which for many, had come to symbolize police abuse of authority. The Rodney King beating not only changed the LAPD, but also the basic practices of police agencies across the nation (Cannon, 1999). However, and more importantly, by being one of the first incidents of its kind to be broadcast into homes across the nation and around the world, the Rodney King beating changed forever the conversation about police and race in America (Taylor, 2012)—and, by doing so, highlighted stark and long-standing differences in the ways that Black and White Americans view the criminal justice system and civil rights in the United States, especially police use of force.

The Racial Divide: Just How Real Is It?

For more than 50 years, surveys of citizens' attitudes toward police have consistently identified a deep-rooted racial divide in the amount of confidence that Black and White citizens express toward police. Following the 1967 race riots, the **Kerner Commission** report pointed to racism and economic inequality as the causes of civil unrest. The commission recommended a number of reforms, including more Black police officers in neighborhoods, more training for police, an end to "abrasive" police practices, and higher levels of police protection in Black neighborhoods (National Advisory Commission on Civil Disorders, 1968). Despite advances in many of these areas—for example, increases in the numbers of minority police officers—many of the same concerns and recommendations highlighted in the Kerner report appeared again in the **Ferguson report** (U.S. Department of Justice, 2015). These included issues of accountability, unreasonable use of force, training, and inadequate protection of citizens.

A Gallup survey following the August 9, 2014, death of Michael Brown, a Black teenager shot to death by a White police officer in Ferguson, Missouri, found that combined 2011–2014 data measuring American's confidence in police showed that while 50% of Whites expressed a "great deal" or "quite a lot" of confidence in police, only 37% of Blacks expressed a similar opinion (Newport, 2014). The same survey found that Blacks view police officers as less honest than do Whites, that younger Black males are more likely to report being treated unfairly by police, and that Blacks are more than 2.5 times as likely as Whites to attribute the higher rate of incarceration among Black than White men as the result of discrimination.

Confidence in the criminal justice system, and law enforcement in particular, matters. **Legitimacy** refers to the extent that members of the public trust and have confidence in police, believe that officers are honest and competent, and think that officers treat people fairly and respectfully (Tyler, 2006). When citizens accept police authority as legitimate, they are more likely to concede to an officer's authority (Tyler & Huo, 2002), obey the law (Jackson et al., 2012), and support law enforcement efforts to fight crime (Tyler & Fagan, 2008). Distrust of law enforcement, on the other hand, has serious negative consequences. It reduces confidence in police, decreases voluntary cooperation, and lessens the public's willingness to report a crime. A 2016 survey, for example, found that Blacks and Latinos were more than 20 points less likely than Whites to "definitely" report a crime (Ekins, 2016).

The tension between police and Blacks in the United States has a long history. The first Blacks were brought to the fledgling United States by slave traders, where they were bought and sold as property. Slaves were not regarded as citizens within the meaning of the U.S. Constitution, thus the special rights and immunities guaranteed to citizens did not apply to them (*Scott v. Sandford*, 1856). The Fugitive Slave Act of 1850, which was passed as part of the compromise between the southern slave states and northern free states, required that all escaped slaves be returned to their masters and that officials and citizens of free states were required to cooperate. Early police focused much of their effort on maintaining economic order and assisting wealthy landowners in recovering and punishing runaway slaves (Turner, Giacopassi, & Vandiver, 2006). At the end of the Civil War, violence against Blacks continued with the rise of vigilante groups and lynch mobs, with little interference from police. In 1871, Congress passed the Ku Klux Klan Act, which prohibited state officials from violating the civil rights of citizens, in part because of police involvement with the Klan (Kappeler, 2014).

The mistreatment of minority groups, and, in particular, Blacks, continued well into the 20th century. Between 1882 and 1951, it is reported that 3,437 Blacks and 1,293 Whites were the victims of lynch mobs, with most of these **lynching** occurring in smaller towns and isolated rural communities of the South (Guzman, 1952). In many cases, Blacks were lynched for offenses that would not have been considered crimes at all had they been committed by a White man.

To further marginalize Blacks and to keep them separate from Whites, many states in the South passed Jim Crow laws. These laws prevented Blacks from using the same public facilities as Whites and from living in many of the same towns or from going to the same schools as Whites. Interracial marriage was also illegal. During the civil rights movement of the 1960s, Americans watched footage of Blacks being beaten by police officers, attached by police dogs, and sprayed with water cannons during peaceful marches and sit-ins in the South (Nodjimbadem, 2017). On March 7, 1965, the civil rights movement turned especially violent as roughly 600 peaceful protestors clashed with police officers during the Selma to Montgomery march to protest the killing of a Black civil rights activist by a White police officer and to encourage legislators to enforce the 15th Amendment.

Despite significant progress in minority civil rights initiatives, a number of recent high-profile abuses and shootings of young Black men have continued to strain the already difficult relations between police and Blacks in many communities. The torture of Abner Louima by New York City police officers; the shooting death of Tamir Rice, a 12-year old Black boy carrying a toy gun; and the death of Antwon Rose, a Black teenager who was shot in the back three times and killed by a White police officer as he fled on foot after being pulled over in a car believed to have been connected to an earlier drive-by shooting, have all contributed to heighten and to reinforce perceptions of racial disparities and unreasonable force directed against Blacks.

Racial Disparity: Fact or Fiction?

In 2015, police officers killed at least 965 people in the United States, according to a report in the *Washington Post* (Kindy, Fisher, Tate, & Jenkins, 2015). The *Post* concluded that race remained the most volatile factor in any accounting of police shootings. While Black men make up only 6% of the U.S. population, they accounted for 40% of the unarmed men shot to death by police in 2015. And although the majority of people killed by police after attacking another person with a weapon or brandishing a gun were White, a largely disproportionate number of those killed (60%) for less-threatening behavior were Black or Latino.

Police use of force, especially **deadly force**—including the role of race—has been the subject of research for decades, while allegations concerning the disparate treatment of minorities by police continue to be vigorously debated by all sides. It can be difficult to measure the number of police shooting in the United States because there are no mandatory or uniform reporting procedures to record such incidents. Although the federal government collects data on a variety of topics, there is still no reliable government data on how many people are shot by the police each year. Rather, the FBI operates a voluntary program where law enforcement agencies can choose to submit their data on "justifiable homicides" each year (Swaine & Laughland, 2015). The system—the subject of considerable debate—has been criticized by a number of activist groups, along with proposed legislature from two U.S. senators, demanding that all states submit mandatory reports to the Department of Justice.

Early research characterized the "police personality" as cynical, aggressive, and prejudiced (Balch, 1972; Niederhoffer, 1967; Skolnick, 1977). In 1951, William Westley wrote of his observations with the Gary, Indiana police: No white police with whom I had contact "failed to mock the Negro, to use some type of stereotyped categorization, and to refer to the Negro in exaggerated dialect, when the subject arouse" (Westley, 1951, p. 168). Little imagination, on the other hand, is required to deduce how Blacks felt about the police (Skolnick, 2007). Whether prejudice affects officer decision making and discretion, however, is less clear.

In a 1966 study on police sponsored by the President's Commission on Law Enforcement and the Administration of Justice, 36 field observers accompanied police in their patrol cars on random 8-hour shifts in Boston, Chicago, and Washington, DC. The researchers found overwhelming evidence of widespread prejudice against Blacks by police (Reiss, 1966). Thirty-eight percent of officers expressed "extreme" prejudice, while another 34% expressed "considerable" prejudice. However, despite the large percentage of officers who admitted to prejudice against Blacks, officer conduct was found to be "prejudiced" in only 2% of cases, with "some signs" of prejudice identified in another 6% of cases. Reiss (1966) concluded that while many of the officers surveyed harbored prejudice, those same officers responded primarily to citizen behavior, not race.

A more recent study funded by the National Institute of Justice on police officer decision making and discretion found similar results (Albert et al., 2006). During the summer of 2002, trained field observers accompanied police officers in each of the four precincts and across all three shifts in Savannah, Georgia. Observers participated in a total of 132 ride-alongs with officers. The study found that citizens are more likely than officers to demonstrate a negative attitude or to show disrespect at the beginning of a police-citizen encounter and that officers then react to that negativity. The same study concluded that officers form the majority of their suspicions based on citizen behavior, not race.

Other evidence of police prejudice against Blacks is less favorable. For example, following the shooting death of Michael Brown, the U.S. Department of Justice conducted an extensive investigation of the Ferguson Police Department's policies and practices. Investigators found wide disparities in the treatment of White versus Black residents with regard to stops, searches, citations, arrests, and use of force. According to the final report, issued by the Civil Rights Division of the U.S. Department of Justice, while Blacks accounted for 67% of the city's residents, a full 86% of all vehicle stops involved Blacks. Blacks also accounted for 93% of all arrests, 90% of all citations, and 96% of all warrant arrests. Even more noteworthy, however, were the disparities in searches and use of force. According to data collected and maintained by the Ferguson Police Department, despite the fact that the "hit" rate for contraband was 58% higher for Whites—in other words, officers were 58% more likely to uncover contraband during the search of a White subject than a Black subject—Blacks were more than twice as likely to be searched as White residents. Moreover, 90% of all force used by officers and 100% of all K9 bites were directed against Blacks (U.S. Department of Justice, 2015).

Similar racial disparities have been found with other law enforcement agencies as well. Dolores Jones-Brown and her colleagues at the Center on Race, Crime, and Justice at John Jay College conducted an analysis of data collected and complied by the New York City Police Department on the police practices of stopping, questioning, and frisking pedestrians in New York City. For the years 2003 through 2009, Blacks and Latinos made up a substantial majority of the persons stopped. In 2009, Blacks and Latinos combined were stopped 9 times more than Whites (Jones-Brown, Gill, & Trone, 2010). **Stop-and-frisk** data, available from the New York Civil Liberties Union (NYCLU), reports that in the year 2011, a total of 685,724 New York City residents were stopped by police. Of those, only 9% (61,805) were White, while 34% were Latino (223,740) and another 53% were Black (350,743). Although the total number of people who were stopped and frisked dropped significantly in 2017, the percentages of Blacks, Latinos, and Whites remained fundamentally unchanged: 58% of those who were stopped and frisked were Black, 32% were Latino, and only 9% were reported as White (NYCLU, 2018). These numbers are further exacerbated by the fact that Blacks account for only 24% of the city's population, according to U.S. Census Bureau (2017) records.

Comparable results were found in an analysis of more than 700,000 stop-and-frisk cases involving Los Angeles Police Department officers between July 2003 and June 2004. Of every 10,000 residents, about 3,400 more Black people were stopped than Whites, and 360 more Latinos were stopped than Whites. Additionally, stopped Blacks were 127% more likely to be searched—and stopped Latinos were more than 43% more likely to be searched—than stopped Whites (Ayres, 2008). An analysis published in the *Toronto Star* found that race, age, and gender were significant factors in determining who gets stopped by police in Canada (Rankin, 2010). Male Blacks aged 15–24, according to the analysis, were stopped and documented 2.5 times more than White males the same age. Moreover, in each of the city's 74 police patrol zones, Blacks were stopped and documented at a considerably higher rate than their overall census population—and, in several zones, the same pattern held true for "Brown" people, mostly people of South Asian, Arab, and West Asian backgrounds.

The question of whether these disparities are justified by legitimate public safety concerns—for example, whether the police should use more aggressive enforcement tactics in high-crime neighborhoods—remains a hotly debated topic. One problem is that many of the highest rates of violent crime are in minority neighborhoods, communities occupied by Blacks, Latinos, and new immigrants. According to a recent DOJ report, the homicide rate for White men peaks at age 20 (11.4 homicides per 100,000 White males), while the homicide rate for Black men peaks at age 23 (100.3 homicides per 100,000 Black males). The highest murder rate for Black men is nearly 9 times higher than the rate for White men (Smith & Cooper, 2013). This creates the impression that race or ethnicity are linked with serious crime and that crime in America is particularly a "Black problem" (Braga & Brunson, 2015). This line of reasoning has led some scholars—for instance, James Q. Wilson—to argue that police stop and search residents of minority neighborhoods more often than Whites, not because of **racial profiling**, but rather because that is where violent crime, including high murder rates of minorities, is occurring (Wilson, 1994). A second line of reasoning suggests that the disproportionate stops of racial minorities may not necessary reflect racial bias by police, but rather may imply an honest, good-faith effort by police to increase the success rate of searches (Harcourt, 2014). In other words, police search minorities more often than Whites based on the mistaken belief that minorities are more likely to carry weapons and contraband than Whites. A third perspective contends that the practice of racial profiling by police is both immoral and illegal, regardless of the circumstances or reasons (Martin & Glaser, 2012). It undermines fundamental civil rights while failing to promote public safety.

Regardless of the position, there is strong and compelling evidence that people of color are stopped and searched by police more often than Whites (Ayres, 2008). These racial disparities seem to be reflected in many of the attitudes that minority groups, including Blacks, hold toward the police, and, in some, cases, toward the government more generally. Surveys across time have consistently identified pervasive differences in the ways that Black and White Americans view police. Moreover, the racial divide over policing has not changed much over the past five decades (Harris & Brink, 1967), including attitudes toward police use of force.

Attitudes Toward Police: What's Different?

Police are the most numerous and visible component of the American justice system (Kappeler, Sluder, & Alpert, 1998). More importantly, the actions of police can significantly influence our daily lives. However, much of what the police do cannot be accomplished without public cooperation. Police cannot compel people to report crimes, cooperate with investigators, or defer to an officer's authority. Poor attitudes toward the police negatively affect the ability of police to prevent crime and to apprehend criminals (Task Force on the Police, 1967). Therefore, the attitudes that citizens hold toward the police are important. And, while no group is "anti-police," Black and White Americans express different feelings toward police on a number of issues.

A 2014 *CBS News* poll found that while four in five Whites expressed confidence in their local police to make them feel mostly safe, that number dropped to only 52% among Blacks (De Pinto, Dutton, Salvanto, & Backus, 2014). Forty-three percent of Blacks surveyed indicated that local police make them feel mostly anxious. The same study found that Whites and Blacks also hold different views on police use of deadly force. While 84% of Blacks surveyed say that police are "most likely" to use deadly force against a Black person, none of the Blacks surveyed (0%) believe that police are "most likely" to use deadly force against a White person. In comparison, 57% of the Whites surveyed consider that race is not a factor in police use of deadly force. And while a majority of both Blacks and Whites oppose the practice of racial profiling, Blacks are far more likely to say they have been targeted by police because of their race, with 54% of Blacks—including 66% of Black men—reporting they have been personally discriminated against by police, compared to only 10% of Whites.

A 2015 NORC Center for Public Affairs Research poll found a similar divide among Blacks and Whites. While nearly three-quarters of the Blacks surveyed identified violence against civilians by police officers as an "extremely" or "very serious" issue, less than 20% of White respondents felt the same way (AP-NORC Center for Public Affairs Research, 2015). Additionally, an overwhelming majority of Blacks said that, in general, police are too quick to use deadly force and that they are more likely to use it against a Black person. Most Whites, on the other hand, thought that police officers typically use deadly force only when necessary, and that race is not a factor. The Black and White respondents were also sharply divided on the question of whether police officers who injure or kill civilians are treated too leniently by prosecutors and how much that contributes to use of force against members of the public. Despite overwhelming opposition to racial profiling, half of the Black Americans surveyed reported being treated unfairly by police because of their race, compared with only 3% of Whites who reported being treated unfairly because of their race.

One explanation for the negative attitudes that many Blacks hold toward police is individual experiences of unfair treatment (Zinni, 1995). Differences in attitudes toward police can be the result of either direct or indirect experience. Direct experiences are the result of unfair treatment by police officers. Blacks tend to have a higher number of negative contacts with the police than do Whites (Alpert, Dunham, & Smith, 2007), as well as higher arrest and incarceration statistics than Whites (Federal Bureau of Investigation, 2016). Indirectly, the treatment of family members and friends by police officers can cause people to "experience vicariously" those interactions. Indeed, significantly fewer Black Americans (31%) than Whites Americans (64%) express a high degree of confidence in the ability of local police officers to treat all racial groups equally (Ekins, 2016). These problems are compounded by the finding that a bad experience is significantly more likely than a good experience to shape a person's attitude toward police (Skogan, 2006).

A second explanation is based on differences in the power structure that underlies social order. These differences predict that members of disadvantaged groups—for example, Blacks and young adults—are more likely to be the target of law enforcement efforts, both in terms of the relative frequency of their arrests and the quality of their treatment (Erez, 1984). Blacks, especially in lower socioeconomic areas where many crimes occur, tend to perceive police as lacking concern or compassion. Thus, many Blacks view police as "occupying armies" in Black neighborhoods whose main job it is to protect the status quo and to serve the interests of those in power (Cashmore, 1991). This is consistent with the finding that race influences views of police even after controlling for demographic factors, including income. Indeed, survey data reveals that higher-income Blacks (48%) are not much more likely than lower-income Blacks (41%) to have a positive view of police (Ekins, 2016).

Victimization also affects Black attitudes toward police. While Blacks are more often the victims of both violent and property crime than Whites, many crimes in Black communities go unsolved (Morgan & Truman, 2018). High victimization rates and low clearance rates create the impression among many Blacks that the police are generally ineffective at solving crimes and keeping citizens safe. A 2016 Pew Research Center study found that only 14% of Blacks expressed "a lot of confidence" in their local police, compared with 42% of Whites who say they have "a lot of confidence" (Morin & Stepler, 2016). This has caused some researchers (see, for example, Frank, Brandl, Cullen, & Stichman, 1996) to posit that attitudes toward the police may actually be part of a larger negative attitude toward government authority.

Moving Forward: What's Next?

Despite different attitudes on the current state of policing in the United States, there appears to be widespread agreement among both Black and White Americans on a number of proposed solutions (Newport, 2014). To begin with, both Black and White Americans are interested in public safety, with both groups equally unwilling to decrease the number of officers to lower taxes. Rather, Black communities are interested in improving public safety with more, not fewer, police officers (Newport, 2014). Blacks and Whites also agree on how police should prioritize their time. Americans generally agree that the top three priorities for police should be first investigating violent crimes, such as murder, assaults, and domestic violence (78%); second, protecting individuals from property crimes and robbery (64%); and third, investigating property crimes and robbery (58%). Slightly less than a third of Americans believe that police should make enforcing drug laws a top priority

(Ekins, 2016). While Blacks, Whites, and Latinos all prioritize the same three tasks for police, they differ significantly in support. For instance, Blacks and Latinos (45%) are 18 times less likely than White Americans (63%) to prioritize the police investigating property crimes and robbery. On the other hand, Blacks and Latinos (27%) are about twice as likely as Whites (15%) to support the police "providing guidance and social services to troubled young adults" (Ekins, 2016, p. 20)

In addition to similarities in how police should prioritize their time, there is agreement across racial and ethnic groups on a path toward police reform, according to a Cato Institute 2016 criminal justice survey (Ekins, 2016). For example, the majority of Americans (89%) support police body cameras and a slim majority (51%) are willing to raise taxes pay for them. A narrow majority of people (51%) also believe that police should be able to review the footage before making official statements. Three-fourths of those surveyed think body cameras protect both officers and citizens equally. On the subject of officer misconduct, a full 79% of Americans support outside law enforcement agencies conducting investigations of police misconduct, while 21% prefer police departments to handle such investigations internally. A full 68% support additional training for police officers to deal with confrontations, while 73% want police to notify citizens if they may refuse to submit to a stop or search. Another 77% of Americans support prohibiting police officers from using profanity with citizens.

The confidence gap that Blacks express toward police is significant for citizens and officers alike. Effective policing depends on mutual trust and respect between police and community members. To solve crimes and keep citizens safe, police and their communities must work together. As Sir Robert Peel, widely regarded as the father of modern policing, laid out in his "Nine Principles of Police Work," "The ability of the police to perform their duties is dependent upon public approval of police actions" (Peel, 2014, para 3). The police are best able to serve and protect their communities when citizens cooperate freely with the police, for example, when residents are willing to report a crime they witness. This includes eliminating race or ethnicity as a factor when deciding whom to stop, question, and search, except in cases where race is part of a reliable suspect description tied to a specific crime (Means, 2014). While police need the authority and resources to do their jobs, they also require training and oversight to ensure proper accountability, as well as to ensure that everyone, regardless of race or ethnicity, is treated with the same levels of professionalism and respect.

Key Terms

Christopher Commission: A commission formed in 1991 to examine any aspect of the law enforcement structure in Los Angeles (LAPD) that might cause or contribute to the problem of excessive force.

deadly force: A level force that may result in the death of the person against whom the force is applied.

Ferguson Report: A 2015 report from the United States Department of Justice outlining the findings from its investigation of the Ferguson, Missouri police department in the wake of the Michael Brown shooting and the civil unrest that followed.

Kerner Commission: A commission established by President Lyndon B. Johnson to examine the causes of the 1967 race riots in the United States.

legitimacy: A concept that refers to the extent that members of the public trust and have confidence in police, believe that officers are honest and competent, and think that officers treat people fairly and respectfully.

lynching: Premeditated extrajudicial killing by a group.

racial profiling: Being suspicious of or targeting of persons of a racial group because of assumptions about that racial group.

stop and frisk: A temporary detention for purposes of investigation wherein the subject in question may also have a limited search of the exterior of their clothing (a pat down) performed for the purpose of determining if the subject is armed. Also called a "Terry stop." (See *Terry v. Ohio*, 1968).

use of force: Amount of effort required by police to compel compliance by an unwilling subject.

Discussion Questions

- What do you think about the effect of race on attitudes toward police use of force after reading the chapter?
- Why is there a racial divide in perception of police use of force?
- Black men make up what percent of the United States population? What percent of unarmed men shot and killed by police are Black men?
- Is there a racial disparity in use of force? What accounts for that disparity?
- Discuss the arguments surrounding the racial disparity discovered in stop-and-frisk data. Which argument do you see having the most merit?
- What effects do communities experience when they do not trust or have confidence in their police? What do police in those jurisdictions experience?
- What do you think holds the most promise in improving attitudes toward police moving forward?

References

Albert, G. P., Dunham, R. G., Stroshine, M., Bennett, K., & MacDonald, J. (2006). *Police officers' decision making and discretion: Forming suspicion and making a stop*. Washington, DC: U.S. Department of Justice. Retrieved from https://www.ncjrs.gov/pdffiles1/nij/grants/213004.pdf

Alpert, G. P., Dunham, R. G. and Smith, M. R. (2007). Investigating racial profiling by the Miami-Dade police department: A multimethod approach. *Criminology and Public Policy, 6*(1), 25–56.

AP-NORC Center for Public Affairs Research (2015). *Law enforcement and violence: The divide between Black and White Americans*. Retrieved from http://www.apnorc.org/projects/Pages/HTML%20Reports/law-enforcement-and-violence-the-divide-between-black-and-white-americans0803-9759.aspx

Ayres, I. (2008, October 23). Racial profiling: The numbers don't lie. *Los Angeles Times*. Retrieved from http://articles.latimes.com/2008/oct/23/opinion/oe-ayres23

Balch, R. W. (1972). The police personality: Fact or fiction. *Journal of Criminal Law and Criminology, 63*(1), 106–119.
Barlow, D., & Barlow, M. (2000). *Police in a multicultural society: An American story.* Prospect Height, IL: Waveland.
Braga, A., & Brunson. R. I. (2015). The police and public discourse on "Black-on-Black" violence. *New Perspectives in Policing Bulletin*. Washington, DC: U.S. Department of Justice. Retrieved from https://www.ncjrs.gov/pdffiles1/nij/248588.pdf
Cannon, L. (1993, March 16). Prosecution rests case in Rodney King beating trial. *Washington Post*. Retrieved from http://tech.mit.edu/V113/N14/king.14w.html
Cannon, L. (1998, January 25). The King incident: More than met the eye on videotape. *Washington Post*. Retrieved from https://www.washingtonpost.com/archive/politics/1998/01/25/the-king-incident-more-than-met-the-eye-on-videotape/2248e35e-178b-47e9-a8db-0734f88b46e0/?utm_term=.1bfff4e94ffa
Cannon, L. (1999). *Official negligence: How Rodney King and the riots changed Los Angeles and the LAPD*. Boulder, CO: Westview Press.
Cashmore, E. (1991). Black cops, Inc. In E. Cashmore & E. McLaughlin (Eds.), *Out of order: Policing black people* (pp. 97–108). New York, NY: Routledge.
De Pinto, J., Dutton, S., Salvanto, A., & Backus, F. (2014, December 10). Michael Brown and Eric Garner: The police, use of force and race. *CBS News*. Retrieved from https://www.cbsnews.com/news/michael-brown-and-eric-garner-the-police-use-of-force-and-race/
Ekins, E. (2016). *Policing in America: Understanding public attitudes toward the police: Results from a national survey.* Washington, DC: Cato Institute. Erez, E. (1984). Self-defined desert and citizens' assessment of the police. *Journal of Criminal Law and Criminology, 75*(4), 1276–1299.
Federal Bureau of Investigation. (2016). *Crime in the United States*. Washington, DC: U.S. Department of Justice. Retrieved from https://ucr.fbi.gov/crime-in-the-u.s/2016/crime-in-the-u.s.-2016/topic-pages/tables/table-21
Ford, A. (1992, December 23). Charges against King belatedly dropped: Law enforcement: Incidents allegedly occurred in March 1991, from beating. *Los Angeles Times*. Retrieved from http://articles.latimes.com/1992-12-23/local/me-2180_1_rodney-king-incident
Frank, J., Brandl, S. G., Cullen, F. T., & Stichman, A. (1996). Reassessing the impact of race on citizen's attitudes toward the police: A research note. *Justice Quarterly, 13*(2), 321–334.
Guzman, J. P. (Ed.) (1952). *1952 Negro yearbook*. New York, NY: Tuskegee Institute.
Harcourt, B. E. (2014). Henry Louis Gates and racial profiling: What's the problem. In B. D. Fitch (Ed.), *Law enforcement ethics: Classic and contemporary challenges* (pp. 295–324). Thousand Oaks, CA: SAGE.
Harris, L., & Brink, W. (1967). *Black and white: A study of United States racial attitudes today.* New York, NY: Simon and Schuster.
Independent Commission on the Los Angeles Police Department (1991). *Report of the Independent Commission on the Los Angeles Police Department (Christopher Commission report)*. Retrieved from https://archive.org/stream/ChristopherCommissionLAPD/Christopher%20Commission%20LAPD_djvu.txt
Jackson, J., Bradford, B., Hough, M., Myhill, A., Quinton, P., & Tyler, T.R. (2012). Why do people comply with the law? Legitimacy and the influence of legal institutions. *British Journal of Criminology, 52*(6), 1051–1071.
Jones-Brown, D., Gill, J., & Trone, J. (2010). *Stop, question and frisk policing practices in New York City: A primer.* New York, NY: Center on Race, Crime, and Justice at John J. College of Criminal Justice. Retrieved from http://www.atlanticphilanthropies.org/wp-content/uploads/2015/09/SQF_Primer_July_2013.pdf

Kappeler, V. E. (2014, January 7). A brief history of slavery and the origins of American policing. *Police Studies Online*. Retrieved from http://plsonline.eku.edu/insidelook/brief-history-slavery-and-origins-american-policing

Kappeler, V. E., Sluder, R. D., & Alpert, G. P. (1994). *Forces of deviance: Understanding the dark side of policing* (2nd ed.). Long Grove, IL: Waveland.

Kindy, K., Fisher, M., Tate, J., & Jenkins, J. (2015, December 26). A year of reckoning: Police fatally shoot nearly 1,000. *Washington Post*. Retrieved from https://www.washingtonpost.com/sf/investigative/2015/12/26/a-year-of-reckoning-police-fatally-shoot-nearly-1000/?utm_term=.53171b7f6d8b

Koon v. U.S., 116 S. Ct. 2035 (1996).

Martin, K. D., & Glaser, J. (2012). The indefensible problems with racial profiling. In J. Gans (Ed.), *Society and culture: Debates on immigration* (pp. 491–508). Thousand Oaks, CA: SAGE.

Means, R. R. (2014). *The law of policing: Federal constitutional principles* (2nd ed.). Portland, OR: LRIS Publications.

Morgan, R. E., & Truman, J.L. (2018). *Criminal victimization, 2017*. Washington, DC: Bureau of Justice Statistics.

Morin, R., & Stepler, R. (2016, September 29). *The racial confidence gap in police performance*. Washington, DC: Pew Research Center. Retrieved from http://www.pewsocialtrends.org/2016/09/29/the-racial-confidence-gap-in-police-performance/

National Advisory Commission on Civil Disorders (1968). *Report of the National Advisory Commission on Civil Disorders*. Washington, DC: National Institute of Justice. Retrieved from https://www.ncjrs.gov/pdffiles1/Digitization/8073NCJRS.pdf

Newport, F. (2014, August 20). Gallup review: Black and White attitudes toward police. *Gallup*. Retrieved from https://news.gallup.com/poll/175088/gallup-review-black-white-attitudes-toward-police.aspx

Niederhoffer, A. (1967). *Behind the shield: The police in urban society*. New York, NY: Anchor Books.

Nodjimbadem, K. (2017, July 27). The long, painful history of police brutality in the U.S. *Smithsonian.com*. Retrieved from https://www.smithsonianmag.com/smithsonian-institution/long-painful-history-police-brutality-in-the-us-180964098/

Peel, R. (2014, April 15). Sir Robert Peel's nine principles of policing. *New York Times*. Retrieved from https://www.nytimes.com/2014/04/16/nyregion/sir-robert-peels-nine-principles-of-policing.html

Rankin, J. (2010, February 6). Race matters: Blacks documented by police at high rate. *Toronto Star*. Retrieved from https://www.thestar.com/news/crime/raceandcrime/2010/02/06/race_matters_blacks_documented_by_police_at_high_rate.html

Reiss, A. J., Jr. (1966). *Patterns of behavior in police and citizen transactions: Boston, Chicago, and Washington, DC, 1966*. Ann Arbor, MI: Inter-university Consortium for Political and Social Research.

Sastry, A., & Bates, K. G. (2017, April 26). When LA erupted in anger: A look back at the Rodney King riots. *NPR*. Retrieved from https://www.npr.org/2017/04/26/524744989/when-la-erupted-in-anger-a-look-back-at-the-rodney-king-riots

Scott v. Sandford, 60 U.S. 393 (1856)

Skogan, W. G. (2006). Asymmetry in the impact of encounters with police. *Policing & Society, 16*(2), 99–126.

Skolnick, J. H., (1977). A sketch of the policeman's "working personality." In D. B. Kennedy (Ed.), *The dysfunctional alliance: Emotion and reason in justice administration* (pp. 10–25). Cincinnati, OH: Anderson.

Skolnick, J. H. (2007). Racial profiling—then and now. *Criminology & Public Policy, 6*(1), 65–70.

Serrano, R. A. (1992, March 18). Bid for officer's acquittal fails: King case. *Los Angeles Times*. Retrieved from http://articles.latimes.com/1992-03-18/local/me-3983_1_sufficient-evidence

Smith, E. L., & Cooper, A. (2013). *Homicide in the U.S. known to law enforcement, 2011*. Washington, DC: Bureau of Justice Statistics. Retrieved from https://www.bjs.gov/content/pub/pdf/hus11.pdf

Stewart, A. W. (2012, June 12). 5 ways the Rodney King beating and LA riots changed America. *CNN*. Retrieved from http://inamerica.blogs.cnn.com/2012/06/18/5-ways-the-rodney-king-beating-and-la-riots-changed-america/

Swaine, J., & Laughland, O. (2015, June 2). US senators call for mandatory reporting of police killings. *The Guardian*. Retrieved from https://www.theguardian.com/us-news/2015/jun/02/us-senators-call-for-mandatory-reporting-police-killings

Task Force on the Police (1967). *Task force report: The police (1967)*. Washington, DC: U.S. Government Printing Office.

Taylor, M. (2012, June 17). Rodney King case changed perceptions of police brutality. *ABC News*. Retrieved from https://abcnews.go.com/US/rodney-king-case-changed-perceptions-police-brutality/story?id=16589385

Terry v. Ohio, 392 U.S. 1 (1968)

Turner, K. B., Giacopassi, D., & Vandiver, M. (2006). Ignoring the past: Coverage of slavery and slave patrols in criminal justice texts. *Journal of Criminal Justice Education, 17*(1), 181–195.

Tyler, T. R. (2006). *Why people obey the law*. Princeton, NJ: Princeton University Press.

Tyler, T.R., & Fagan, J. (2008). Why do people cooperate with the police? *Ohio State Journal of Criminal Law, 6*, 231–275.

Tyler, T. R., & Huo, Y. J. (2002). *Trust in the law: Encouraging public cooperation with the police and courts*. New York, NY: Russell-Sage Foundation.

U.S. Census Bureau. (2017, July 1). *Quick facts: New York City, New York*. Washington, DC: Department of Commerce. Retrieved from https://www.census.gov/quickfacts/fact/table/newyorkcitynewyork/PST045217

U.S. Department of Justice. (2015). *Investigation of the Ferguson Police Department*. Washington, DC: Author. Retrieved from https://www.justice.gov/sites/default/files/opa/press-releases/attachments/2015/03/04/ferguson_police_department_report.pdf

Whitman, D. (1993, May 23). The untold story of the LA riot. *US News*. Retrieved from https://www.usnews.com/news/articles/1993/05/23/the-untold-story-of-the-la-riot

Wilson, J. Q. (1994). Just take away their guns. *New York Times Magazine*. Retrieved from https://www.nytimes.com/1994/03/20/magazine/just-take-away-their-guns.html

Winston, R. (2016, March 2). How the Rodney King beating 'banished' the baton from the LAPD. *Los Angeles Times*. Retrieved from http://www.latimes.com/local/california/la-me-rodney-king-baton-20160303-story.html

Zeidler, S. (2012, June 17). Timeline: Rodney King from 1991 to 2012. *CNN*. Retrieved from http://news.blogs.cnn.com/2012/06/17/rodney-king-what-happened-in-1991/

Zinni, F. P. (1995). The sense of injustice: The effects of situation, beliefs, and identify. *Social Science Quarterly, 76*(2), 419–437.

CHAPTER 5

Leadership and Leaders

Frontline Leadership in Law Enforcement Organizations

By Danny L. McGuire, Jr.

"Leadership is practiced not so much in words as in attitude and in actions."

—Harold S. Geneen

"I think that in any group activity—whether it be business, sports, or family—there has to be leadership or it won't be successful."

—John Wooden

Opening Questions

Answer the following question before reading this chapter:

> What do you know about the role of frontline leadership in policing prior to reading this chapter?

Answer the following question while reading the chapter:

> What are some concepts from the chapter that stand out to you? Why do you think they are important?

Introduction

To understand the dynamic of the **frontline leader** we must first understand **leadership** and if there is a difference between leadership and leaders. There are several different definitions of leadership, just as many (if not more) descriptions of leaders, and several theories thereof. Northouse (2019) described some history of defining leadership and provided some insight to past descriptions. One such explanation is "the ability to impress the will of the leader on those led and induce obedience, respect, loyalty, and cooperation" (Moore, 1927, p. 124).

More definitions provided that leadership was an individual's behavior while involved in directing group activities (Hemphill, 1949). At the same time, leadership by persuasion was distinguished from drivership or leadership by coercion (Copeland, 1942). In the 1960s, leadership was defined by Seeman (1960) as "acts by persons which influence other persons in a shared direction" (p. 53).

In the 1970s and 1980s, defining leadership grew and, according to Burns (as cited in Northouse, 2019), leadership was defined as "when one or more persons engage with others in such a way that leaders and followers raise one another to higher levels of motivation and morality" (p. 83).

Additionally, Burns (as cited in Northouse, 2019) state that "leadership is the reciprocal process of mobilizing by persons with certain motives and values, various economic, political, and other resources, in a context of competition and conflict, in order to realize goals independently or mutually held by both leaders and followers" (p. 425).

Northouse (2019) contended that the debate as to whether leadership and management are separate practices continues; however, research has emphasized the process of leadership as "an individual influenc[ing] a group of individuals to achieve a common goal" (p. 4).

Northouse (2019) explained that leadership is a process that involves influence and occurs within a group context that attends two common goals: While leaders and followers are involved together, they need each other, and often times leaders initiate and maintain the relationships yet are never above or better than followers (Heller & Van Til, 1983; Northouse, 2019).

More descriptions indicated that leadership involves influence and is concerned with how the leader affects followers through communication that occurs between leaders and followers (Ruben & Gigliotti, 2017).

Leaders have a tremendous amount of power as it relates to the work environment. Leaders utilize the leadership process to influence others to get the mission accomplished. That power can become intoxicating and may negatively impact leaders' decisions (Maner & Case, 2013).

Understanding how power is used in leadership is instrumental, and understanding the dark side of leadership that sees leaders using their position to achieve their own personal ends and lead in toxic, destructive ways (Krasikova, Green, & LeBreton, 2013) is as important as understanding the positives of leadership.

Kellerman (2012) stated that there has been a shift in leadership power from the leader to the follower over the past 40 years. Innovations such as technology have given followers access to information, which has leveled the playing field and contributed to more leader transparency. This change also makes followers more demanding of their leaders. This dynamic expressed a decline in respect for leaders, which made power no longer synonymous with leadership.

Posner (2015) found that volunteer leaders, such as board members of nonprofit organizations, do not have positional authority in the organization; however, they were able to influence leadership. Essentially, volunteer leaders engaged more frequently in leadership behaviors than did paid leaders. One school of thought surrounding Posner (2015) is someone who volunteers for a leadership role may be more passionate about that role than his or her paid counterparts in an organization in which he or she does not believe.

Managers Versus Leaders

"The manager accepts the status quo; the leader challenges it."

—Warren G. Bennis

Kotter (1990) compared the tasks of management with the functions of leadership and argued that they are quite dissimilar. The dominant function of management is to provide order and consistency to organizations, whereas the principal function of leadership is to produce change and movement. Management is about seeking order and stability; leadership is about seeking adaptive and constructive change.

Management and leadership are essential if an organization is to prosper, which means if an organization has strong management without leadership, the outcome can be unproductive and bureaucratic. On the other hand, if an organization has strong leadership without management, the outcome can be worthless or without direction. To be effective, organizations need to nurture both management and skilled leadership.

Kotter (1990) contended that leadership and management are distinct constructs, which Bennis and Nanus (2007) continued. Managing means accomplishing activities and mastering routines, where leading means influencing others and creating visions for change. Bennis and Nanus (2007) often stated that "managers are people who do things right and leaders are people who do the right thing" (p. 221).

Rost (1991) has also been a supporter of differentiating between leadership and management. His contention was that leadership is a multidirectional influence relationship and management is a unidirectional authority relationship. He went on to say that leadership is concerned with the process of developing mutual purposes; management is directed toward coordinating activities to get a job done. Leaders and followers work together to create real change whereas managers and subordinates join forces to sell goods and services (Rost, 1991).

Simonet and Tett (2012) examined how leadership and management are best conceptualized. The study found 22 competencies descriptive of both leadership and management and also found several unique descriptors for each. They found that leadership was distinguished by motivating intrinsically, creative thinking, strategic planning, tolerance of ambiguity, and being able to read people, while management was synonymous with rule orientation, short-term planning, motivating extrinsically, orderliness, safety concerns, and timeliness.

Zaleznik (1977) offered that leaders and managers themselves are separate and that they are basically different types of people. Zaleznik (1977) contended that managers are reactive and prefer to work with people to solve problems but do so with little to no emotional contribution. He proposed that leaders are emotionally active and involved and seek to shape ideas instead of reacting to them. He went on to say that leaders expand the available options to solve long-standing problems, which essentially helps change the way people think.

In relation to the difference between managers and leaders, Northouse (2019) suggested

> there are clear differences between management and leadership[;] the two constructs overlap. When managers are involved in influencing a group to meet [] goals, they are involved in leadership. When leaders are involved in planning, organizing, staffing, and controlling, they are involved in management. Both processes involve influencing a group of individuals toward goal attainment. For purposes of our discussion in this book, we focus on the leadership process. In our examples and case studies, we treat the roles of managers and leaders similarly and do not emphasize the differences between them. (p. 14)

Shifting over to law enforcement, Lee (2017) and Powalie (2013) argued there are distinct characteristics between leaders and managers. In particular, Lee (2017) details that managers plan the details; minimize risks; instruct employees; have objectives; meet expectations; see problems; and give approval, while leaders set the direction; take risks; encourage people; have vision; chart new growth; and see opportunities.

Powalie (2013) also made a comparison with regard to leaders and managers by saying that law enforcement has taken a "customer service" stance where managers thrive; however, leaders are necessary to make decisions because in law enforcement things are not cookie-cutter type scenarios.

Additionally, Powalie (2013) also made reference to managers as individuals who focus on making themselves look good while leaders conversely are there to make their charges shine and follow the mission of the organization rather than their individual focus.

McGuire, Jr. (2010a) made a parallel between leadership and leaders by contending that

> leadership is a talent that must be practiced and honed like all other skills in law enforcement. [T]he illiterates of the future are those who cannot change their stances, viewpoints, and/or positions on topics related to new experiences. A true leader puts his charges, and their needs, before his/her own. A true leader is one that leads by example. (p.19)

The Frontline Leader

"The difference between a boss and a leader: a boss says, 'Go!'[;] a leader says, 'Let's go!'"

—E. M. Kelly

Understand that law enforcement has a paramilitary-type structure that includes a chain of command. **Chain of command** is defined by the Cambridge Dictionary as "the way that people with authority in an organization, especially in the military, are ranked, from the person with the most authority to the next one below, and so on."

After reviewing the aforementioned information regarding leadership, leaders, and the difference between a leader and a manager leads us to our next phenomena: the law enforcement frontline leader.

Frontline leadership is a dynamic that exists in many different aspects of the world. From banking to education, law enforcement to the military, even sports teams have a chain of command and leadership. The frontline leader is the first tier of leadership and of the organization; often referred to as the immediate supervisor, the frontline leader is the person who passes orders down from middle management as well as handles the concerns of the people in their charge. These are just some of the contributing factors that make frontline leaders of police the most stressful job in America according to Giang (2013).

In law enforcement in particular, the frontline leader is the person who will, more often than not, be handling the business of street operations and interacting with his or her charges by fielding questions about operations, doling out discipline for transgressions, fielding complaints from citizens, and ensuring that the mission of the executive arm of the police department is being followed.

The fronline leader has many different monikers, depending on the individual police department and its rank structure. Some of the names frontline leaders are referred to as are corporal, sergeant, and/or shift leader; whatever the name is that goes with the distinction, the frontline leader is one of the most important leadership roles in any law enforcement agency.

McGuire, Jr. (2010b) contended that "the [f]rontline leader, also known as Corporal or Sergeant and in some cases Team Leader, is one of the most important leadership roles in Law Enforcement. Arguably the sergeant is the most effective at turning the proverbial 'battleship' when it comes to morale and other issues of personnel for law enforcement agencies" (p. 32).

Some frontline leaders have issues with getting respect, as the shift in leadership power has diminished as a cultural phenomenon according to Kellerman (2012) and Rowe (2006) who argued that "frontline officers place great value on being led by senior officers who have considerable direct experience of street level police work. Those officers who have rapidly climbed the promotion ladder, without "serving their time" on the streets, are regarded with some suspicion" (both quotes Rowe, 2006, p. 757).

McGuire, Jr. (2010b) stated that [t]he [f]ront line leader is a powerful person in the leadership realm today because [he or she has] direct contact, or at least should have direct contact with [his or her] charges. It is more than just a manager and/or supervisor; it is a leader, a coach, and a mentor" (p. 32).

Frontline Leadership Discussions

"Seek first to understand, then to be understood."

—Stephen R. Covey

Prior to having discussions about leadership, it was necessary for leadership tiers to be identified and defined. Based on the author's experiences, discussions with officers and detectives from various law enforcement agencies, and reviewing organizational charts from police departments, there are three tiers of leaders:

- **Frontline leader:** Also referred to as "immediate supervisor"
- **Middle management leader:** Next rung up from frontline leader in the leadership ladder and may have more than one rank in this tier depending on department size
- **Executive leader:** Final and highest step in the leadership tiers, which is the agency's highest executives

The formal titles are not consequential in this matter and vary from department to department depending on size, structure, and organizational charts.

Over the past 11 years, the author of this chapter has been investigating the phenomenon of frontline leadership through informal qualitative analysis by conducting interviews, generating, distributing, and collecting surveys, as well as writing articles regarding leadership utilizing said resources for law enforcement-centric magazines and other periodicals. In addition to the aforementioned qualitative information, the author spent several years as a frontline leader in the Chicago Police Department.

In 2013, an unpublished study was generated by this author to gauge the importance of a frontline leader based on information gathered through contacts the investigator developed over several years of teaching public safety professionals and law enforcement professionals going back to school to earn their undergraduate or graduate degrees. These individuals represented multiple police agencies from the greater Chicagoland area.

This study received 262 responses from law enforcement personnel of the rank of detective and police officer. The result of this survey saw that officers who work the street on a daily basis see their frontline leader the most during their daily tour. This information was presented to police departments during training sessions as well as in presentations at professional conferences centric to law enforcement and its leadership.

This unpublished study revealed that 88% of police officers and detectives saw their executive leader or chief of police zero times during their daily tour of duty while 100% of them saw their frontline leader at least two times or more during their tour of duty.

Based on this information, the investigator followed up in 2018 by conducting informal interviews with 83 law enforcement professionals from the Chicago Police Department with a rank of detective and/or police officer, asking several questions regarding information that was based on earlier interviews, surveys, and focus groups.

Many of the participants of the follow-up interviews did not wish to disclose their name or identity in fear that the information they provided would be used against them because of the sensitivity of leadership issues within Chicago Police Department. Please note that all the participants were off duty and their perceptions of the situation, which resonate with their feelings and opinions, made this a qualitative phenomenological research model.

According to Waters (2016), the goal of qualitative phenomenological research such as this is to describe a "lived experience." This research presentation employs a method to study the experiences of individuals in the first person, in other words, people who have firsthand experience in an area that others may not have experienced (Roth, 2012) Policing is a closed craft that does not lend itself well to direct observation; to understand policing fully, one has to have lived it. Extracting that "lived" data was the goal of these interviews.

One of the questions asked of the participants was with regard to interaction with the rank structure during their daily tour.

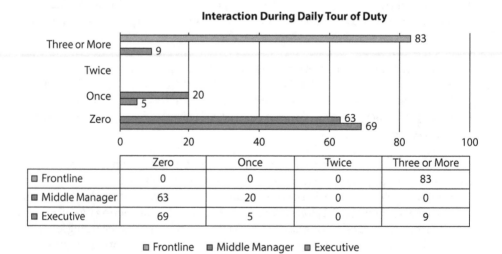

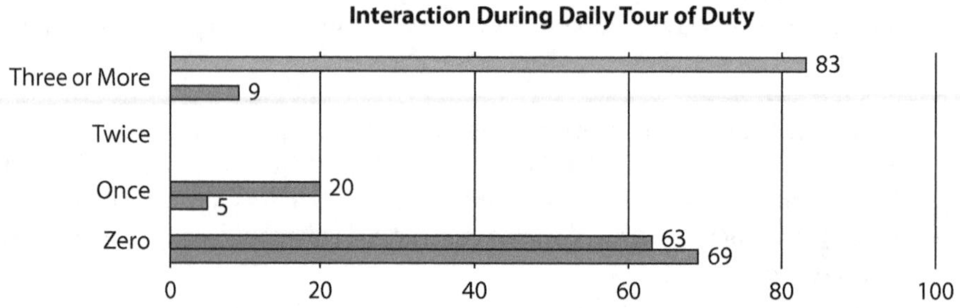

	Zero	Once	Twice	Three or More
Frontline	0	0	0	83
Middle Manager	63	20	0	0
Executive	69	5	0	9

Frontline ■ Middle Manager ■ Executive

FIGURE 5.1: Interaction of police officers and detectives during their daily tour of duty.

Figure 5.1 illustrates that 83 of the 83 (100%) participants saw their frontline leader (in this case their sergeant) three or more times during their daily tour and 69 of the 83 (83%) officers and detective saw the executive leadership zero times during their daily tour.

This established that the frontline officer had the most interaction with the frontline leader, as stated by McGuire (2010). This information also reaffirms the information gathered in the 2013 surveys that the frontline leader is seen the most during officers' daily tour of duty.

To further express the importance of the frontline leader, the participants were asked about who in leadership rank they would approach first with professional questions as they relate to their job duties.

As figure 5.2 demonstrates, frontline police officers and detectives would first approach their frontline leader before middle management or executive command. Once again, this demonstrates the importance of the frontline leader role in law enforcement.

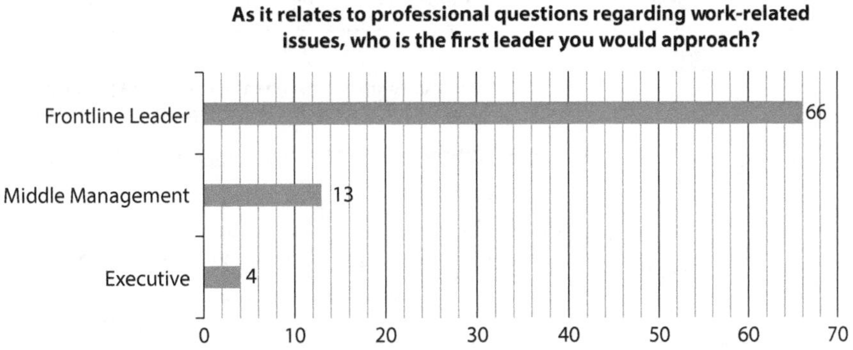

	Executive	Middle Management	Frontline Leader
■ As it relates to professional questions regarding work-related issues, who is the first leader you would approach?	4	13	66

FIGURE 5.2: Illustrates who frontline police and detectives would approach first regarding professional questions.

In particular, participants, when asked why particular leadership tiers were approached instead of others, the respondents overall responses resonated with comfort levels and approachability. Some of the participants stated they had personal relationships with middle managers from years of experience working with them so they felt more comfortable going to the middle manager or executive level than a newer sergeant.

Additional questions were asked in follow-up, such as "Have you ever gone to a department leader with questions or issues of a personal matter?" and "Which leader would you go to first?" The responses were as follows:

As illustrated by figure 5.3, 100% of the officers and detectives reported that they have approached a department leader regarding personal issues. Figure 5.4 illustrates which leader officers were more likely to approach regarding those personal issues.

As with the professional question, the follow-up was regarding why officers felt more comfortable going to certain leadership tiers than other (see Figure 5.5). Once again, police officers and detectives stated personal relationships and "comfort" with particular leadership tears in lieu of newer frontline supervisors they did not know.

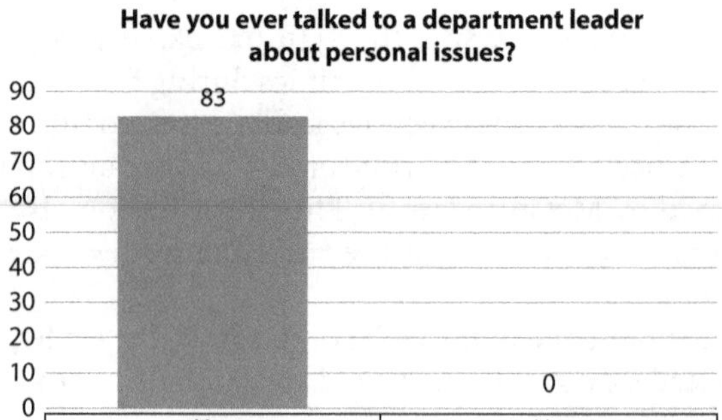

	Yes	No
■ Have you ever talked to a department leader about personal issues?	83	0

FIGURE 5.3: How many officers approached department leaders to talk about personal issues.

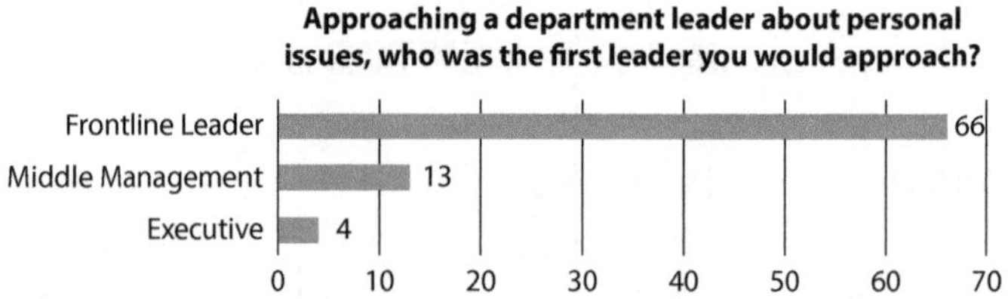

	Executive	Middle Management	Frontline Leader
■ Approaching a department leader about personal issues, who was the first leader you would approach?	4	13	66

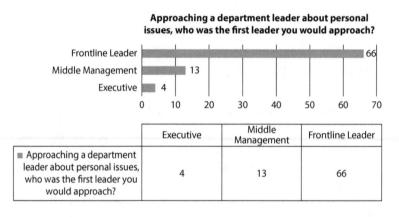

FIGURE 5.4: Illustrates which leadership tier officers and detectives would first approach with personal matters.

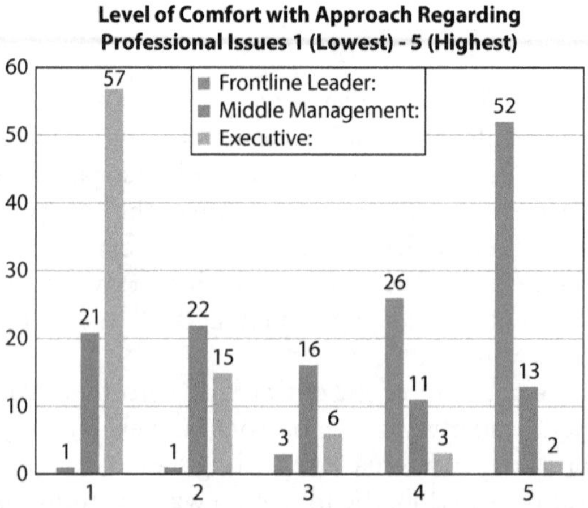

FIGURE 5.5: Level of comfort police officers reported when approaching leadership regarding professional questions.

Expanding on the dynamic of "comfort," participants were asked follow-up questions were asked regarding comfort levels with individual rank structures (see Figure 5.6). Responses parallel the aforementioned data.

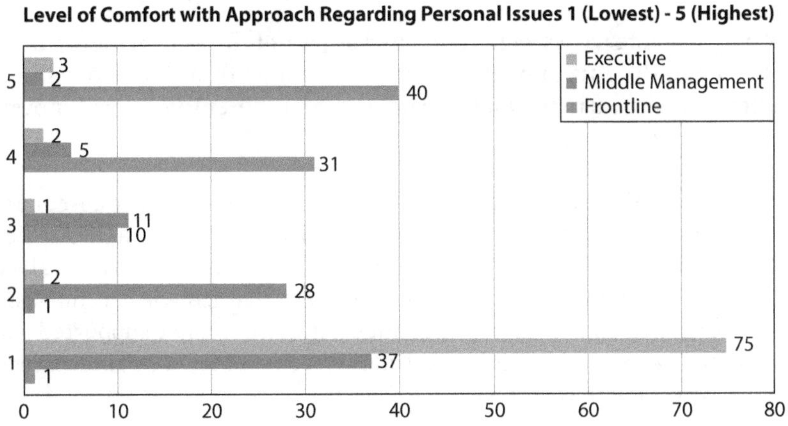

FIGURE 5.6: Level of comfort police officers reported when approaching leadership regarding personal questions.

As it relates to approachability, within leadership tiers and according to the data collected, the frontline leader is the most important leadership tier on a daily basis within the rank and file of a law enforcement agency. Comfort and approachability directly relate to people's willingness to ask questions of their leaders. When officers and detectives are comfortable with approaching their frontline leader, they will do so regarding professional and personal issues.

The key element to approachability is ensuring that the frontline leader has the tools to address the situations and/or questions brought to his or her attention. If the frontline leader does not have the tools to address these issues or the support of the executive level or middle management level, then the frontline leader will not be able to adequately handle the questions or issues brought to his or her attention. This points, once again, to having frontline leaders as highly trained and educated individuals serving in law enforcement agencies.

Effective Frontline Leadership

"A good leader inspires others with confidence in him; a great leader inspires them with confidence in themselves."

—Unknown

As we established previously, law enforcement follows a chain of command, which is representative of military-style leadership. You have police officers and detectives, in many departments, who answer to an immediate supervisor who can be referred to as many different formal titles, which we have established is the frontline leader.

The question has been asked, "What makes an effective frontline leader"? The effectiveness of frontline leaders resonates with the frontline leader's ability to lead. Many different theories of leadership have been discussed in the past: servant, authentic, team leadership, etc., and often times opinions such as "rank has its privileges" have been expressed.

Several personal interviews were conducted as part of the information-gathering process as follow-up to the 2013 unpublished study regarding frontline leadership. During a personal interview with an individual who has served in law enforcement for over 25 years, the participant stated,

> I have had several different sergeants in my 25 years of experience. The best ones never had to tell you that they were in charge or never had to follow up in order 'because I'm the sergeant and I said so'; rather, they just le[d] by example and if I really think hard, years ago the best sergeants I had were those that led with enthusiasm and made you believe in what you are doing out on the street. They supported you and were passionate about your success. At times it seemed they were more concerned about your success than their own.

In another interview with a participant who had over 30 years of experience, the individual stated the following:

> Rank doesn't have its privileges[;] it has more responsibilities. As you move up the ladder of influence and leadership, in my opinion, you have more responsibilities to do the right thing. I have had sergeants that I have zero respect for because they did nothing and I had sergeants that had far less time than me on the job and had all my respect because they le[d] by example, follow[ed] through with what they said they were going to do, and always were right next to you in the field. Those days are few and far between[;] leaders now seem to be more concerned about the next step up th[a]n leading men and women on the street.

In both of the excerpts from the interviews, the term "rank" seems to play a role. As it relates to the term "rank," Murphy & Drodge (2003) contend,

> You don't have to have rank. Rank means nothing in the RCMP when it comes to actual leadership because that person sitting in that chair may have 3 stripes, 4 stripes or whatever, but they will get bypassed to go to the person that actually comes up with the solid decisions. It doesn't really matter whether or not they're a staff sergeant or a corporal, or you can be a constable with 2 or 3 years' service. I can see [leadership emerging] with people that I work with, you know, the younger officers, which we have a lot of in this detachment. You can see them emerging, because they're the ones that'll take the bull by the horns and realize that there is a problem. And I hate using the corny words but they take ownership of it and say 'yeah I care'. They're the leaders of the future as well." (p. 7)

To understand what an effective frontline leader is, we must first understand effectiveness. McGuire (2009) established six characteristics of poor leadership that frustrate the most productive employees. The author establishes this as SALLID, which stands for the following:

- Self-serving agenda
- Acceptance of mediocrity

- Lack of communication
- Lack of transparency
- Indecision
- Disorganization

McGuire, Jr. (2009) contends that the aforementioned characteristics only contribute to the frustration of your most productive employee. He describes each of these elements as (a) self-serving agenda, putting one's own interests before their followers; (b) acceptance of mediocrity, letting employees do the minimum to get by and celebrating the fact that they are just mediocre; (c) lack of communication, leader does not communicate effectively or convey his or her directions properly; and (d) their communication skills do not allow them to listen effectively either.

In addition, McGuire, Jr. (2009) described the next three characteristics as (a) lack of transparency, described as a leader who is not honest or completely transparent; (b) indecision, "the bobble head syndrome" or someone who can not make a decision; and (c) disorganization, someone who is not organized.

In an article for the Illinois *Tactical Officers Association* magazine, McGuire (2010a) identified characteristics of leadership that were appealing to followers. He interviewed 15 retiring police officers who had between 20 and 35 years of service. These attributes included following through, leading by example, being left alone, teaching/mentoring, being empathic, being balanced, providing friendship, and showing confidence. The results were as follows (see figure 5.7):

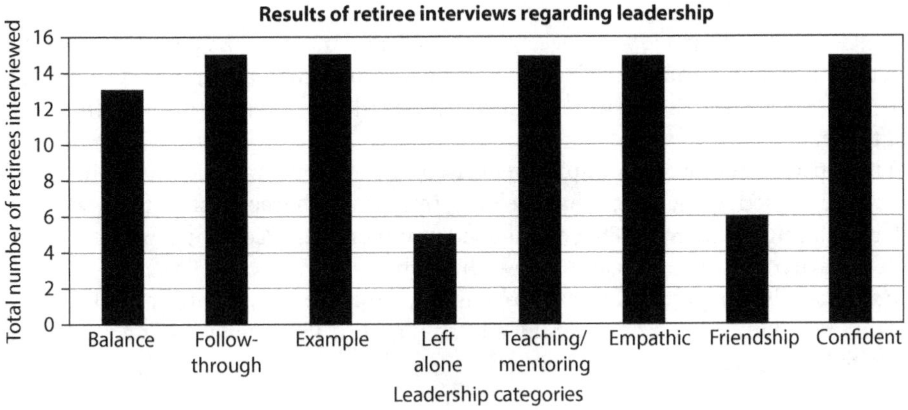

FIGURE 5.7: Results of retirees interviews on leadership

Source: McGuire (2010a)

"Balance" was described as a leader who did not let his or her personal life or mood impact his or her leadership style. "Following through" described a leader who, if he or she announced he or she would do something, he or she would follow through. One retiring officer stated he had a supervisor who promised to put him in for department recognition for jobs well done and never "followed through."

"Characteristic of example" was explained as leadership or leading by example while "teaching/mentoring" meant that the leader took on the role of teacher or mentor to help coach officers through situations. "Left alone" was described as someone who did not want to be bothered by supervisors, and the respondents stated that if they did not want to be bothered, they were probably doing something they should not be doing. "Friendship" was self-explanatory, and many of the retiring officers reported they did not want a friend; they wanted a leader.

Lastly, was confidence, which at many times can be confused with cockiness or arrogance. At times a confident leader may come off as somewhat of a know-it-all; however, a confident leader is one whose confidence is contagious and can help his or her charges become the best professional officers they can be. Confidence in later interviews would also pose issues with being misconstrued as arrogant.

During follow-up interviews in 2018, 83 officers and/or detectives were queried regarding these characteristics of a frontline leader in addition to other attributes such as passion and transparency. The rank order of characteristics of effective frontline leaders was as follows:

1. Example
2. Mentor/coach
3. Communication
4. Follow-through
5. Passionate
6. Transparent
7. Empathic
8. Balance
9. Confidence
10. Friendship

The issue of confidence was once again raised, and many of the participating officers/detectives concluded that confidence could be misconstrued as arrogance. The respondents also stated they did not want a friend they needed a leader at times when situations were tense.

The top attributes were example, mentor/coach, communication, follow-through, and passionate. A participant stated that the most important characteristic of a good frontline leader is leading by example. That overlapped into mentoring/coaching, which overlapped into effective communication and follow-through.

Additionally, during the follow-up phase in 2018, the investigator asked the 83 participants for their opinion on several leadership issues. The questions and responses are illustrated in Figures 5.8, 5.9, and 5.10.

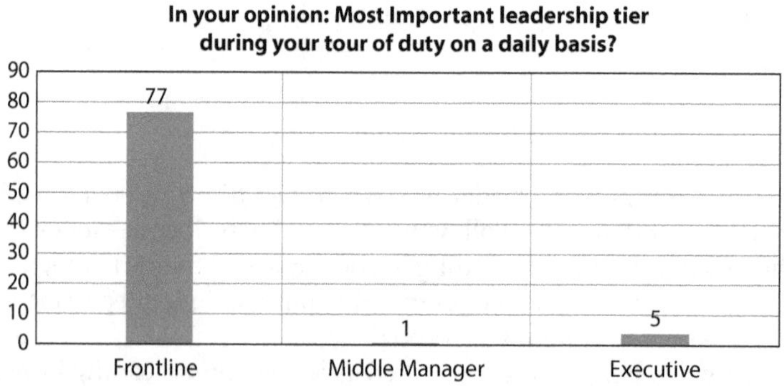

FIGURE 5.8: Responses from 83 detectives/police officers regarding their opinion of which leadership tier is most important during their daily tour.

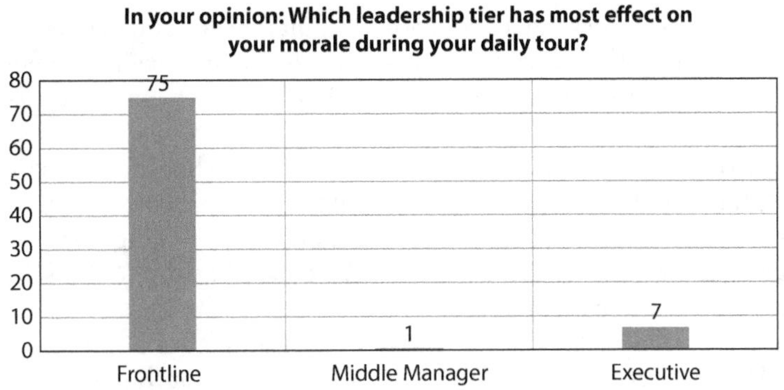

FIGURE 5.9: Participants' opinions on which leadership tier has the most effect on their morale during their daily tour.

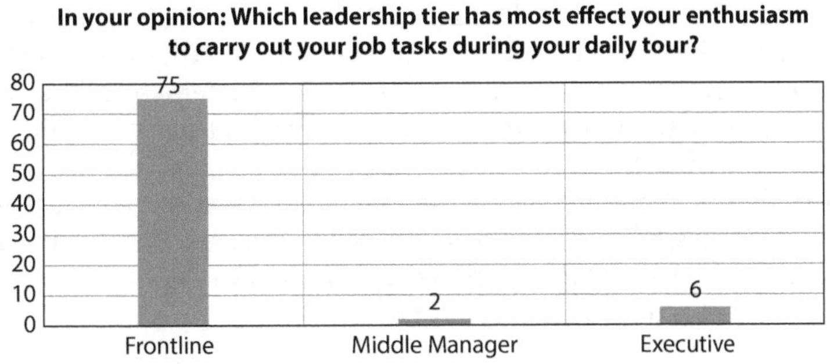

FIGURE 5.10: Participants' opinions on which leadership tier has the most effect on their enthusiasm to carry out their job tasks during their daily tour.

As demonstrated, the frontline leader once again has the most effect on frontline law enforcement professionals on a daily basis, according to the information gathered.

Becoming a Frontline Leader

"The illiterate of the 21st century will not be those who cannot read and write, but those who cannot learn, unlearn, and relearn."

—Alvin Toffler

The information presented in this chapter explains the difference between a leader and manager, tells us what leadership is, and talks about the effectiveness of a frontline leader.

Becoming a frontline leader may be a challenge for some; however, Murphy & Drodge (2003) contended that

> it is clear that leader behavior must be authentic, that there must be genuine concern for people's needs and aspirations. All of us are leaders and followers at various

> moments so we all share some fundamental human needs and desires concerning those roles: the need to feel trust in others, the desire for recognition when we do good deeds or perform well, a need for belonging to a group, goal or cause (p. 13)

Doh (2003) says that leadership can be taught and learned while McGuire (2010a) contends that the **CAPER** method will help a leader who may not be proficient in his or her assignment or who may be uncomfortable in the leadership role by being aware of deficiencies and by preparing to close the gap in deficiencies by educating him- or herself on his or her new role through education and research.

In closing, leaders have different ranks, styles, traits, and internal currency. These are all factors in leadership effectiveness; however, it could be said that the frontline leader in law enforcement is the most important leadership tier in the whole agency. This individual is the person collectively responsible for keeping morale high and overseeing street operations, and often times may be the only leadership rank working at particular shift.

Based on this information, it is suggested to department executive leadership to provide the highest level of training, education, and support to the frontline leader. This is a twofold process because the first fold will see the frontline leader and his or her charges offering the best service to the municipality and the citizens they serve. The second fold will even the playing field for all frontline leaders in the way of education and training; the department executives can identify who the future middle managers and even executives will be.

Frontline leadership is a phenomenon that is not only law enforcement centric, it exists in all aspects of business, education, and even sporting cultures. The best frontline leaders have the respect and support of the charges they lead, and whatever their field of services, they will have the best results on the front line.

Summary

"Success is not final, failure is not fatal: it is the courage to continue that counts."

—Winston Churchill

Frontline leadership is not just a dynamic that occurs in law enforcement. Frontline leadership is the first tier of leadership, often referred to as "immediate supervisors." The phenomenon of law enforcement frontline leadership is a dynamic that exists due to the nature of work in law enforcement. Law enforcement professionals consistently deal with stressful, dangerous, deadly, and emotional situations on a daily basis.

This chapter has established that the frontline leader is the most visible leadership tier to the frontline officers in the field on a daily basis. It also established the leadership tier, which provides the most officer morale and effectiveness in officers' willingness to carry out their duties on a daily basis.

Having an effective frontline leader who is a communicator, who leads by example, and who is a coach/mentor who follows through with passion and transparency may provide effective frontline leadership for the people he or she leads and the agency he or she serves.

Key Terms

CAPER: A method of deriving confidence for new leaders or leaders who take on a position with which they do not have familiarity. CAPER stands for confidence is derived from awareness of gaps the leader may have, then through preparation to close those gaps through education and research.

chain of command: The way that people with authority in an organization, especially in the military, are ranked, from the person with the most authority to the next one below, and so on.

executive leader: The final step and highest in the leadership tiers, which is the agency's highest executives.

frontline leader: Also be referred to as an immediate supervisor.

frontline leadership: Performing leadership functions.

leadership: A process whereby an individual influences a group to achieve a common goal.

middle management leader: The next rung up from frontline leader in the leadership ladder; there may be more than one rank in this tier, depending on department size.

Discussion Questions

- What do you think about the role of frontline leadership in policing after reading the chapter?
- According to the information reported by the author, please describe the SALLID theory.
- Explain and describe the CAPER method.
- What is a front-line leader and what are some of the most important attributes of a frontline leader as described by the author?
- Describe the three levels of leadership within a law enforcement agency and explain their roles.
- What are the top five characteristics that people want in their frontline leader?

References

Bennis, W. G., & Nanus, B. (2007). *Leaders: The strategies for taking charge* (2nd ed.). New York, NY: Harper & Row.

Copeland, N. (1942). *Psychology and the soldier.* Harrisburg, PA: Military Service Publications.

Doh, J. P. (2003). Can leadership be taught? Perspectives from management educators. *Academy of Management Learning and Education, 2*(1), 54–67.

Giang, V. (2013, November 15). The 14 most Stressful jobs in America. *Yahoo.* Retrieved from https://finance.yahoo.com/news/the-14-most-stressful-jobs-in-america-171029957.html

Heller, T., & Van Til, J. (1983). Leadership and followership: Some summary propositions. *Journal of Applied Behavioral Science, 18*(3), 405–414.
Hemphill, J. K. (1949). *Situational factors in leadership.* Columbus: OH: Ohio State University, Bureau of Educational Research.
Kellerman, B. (2012). *The end of leadership.* New York, NY: HarperCollins.
Kotter, J. P. (1990). *A force for change: How leadership differs from management.* New York, NY: Free Press.
Krasikova, D. V., Green, S. G., & LeBreton, J. M. (2013). Destructive leadership: A theoretical review, integration, and future research agenda. *Journal of Management, 39*(5), 1308–1338.
Lee, J. (2017, December 18). Leadership vs. management. *Blueline.* Retrieved from https://blueline.news/law-enforcement/leadership/leadership-vs-management/
Maner, J. K., & Case, C. R. (2013, October). The essential tension between leadership and power: Why power corrupts—and how to prevent it. *Psychological Science Agenda.* Retrieved from http://www.apa.org/science/about/psa/2013/10/leadership-power.aspx
McGuire, D. L., Jr. (2009). Leadership part III: The S.A.L.L.I.D. theory. *Illinois Tactical Officers Association Journal, 2009*, 27–30.
McGuire, D. L., Jr. (2010a). Leadership part IV: Things to remember about leadership. *Illinois Tactical Officers Association Journal, 2010*,16–19.
McGuire, D. L., Jr. (2010b). Leadership part V: Request for supervisor; rather, front-line leader or FLL. *Illinois Tactical Officers Association Journal, 2010*, 32–34.
Moore, B. V. (1927). The May conference on leadership. *Personnel Journal, 6*, 124–128.
Murphy, S. A., & Drodge, E. N. (2003). The four I's of police leadership: A case study heuristic. *International Journal of Police Science & Management, 6*(1), 1–15.
Northouse, P. G. (2019). Leadership: Theory and practice. Thousand Oaks, CA: SAGE.
Posner, B. Z. (2015). An investigation into the leadership practices of volunteer leaders. *Leadership & Organization Development Journal, 36*(7), 885–898.
Powalie, A. (2013, April 11). Leader or manager? You make the choice. *PoliceOne.* Retrieved from https://www.policeone.com/police-jobs-and-careers/articles/6193108-Leader-or-manager-You-make-the-choice/
Roth, W. (2012). *First-person methods—Toward an empirical phenomenology.* New York, NY: Springer.
Rowe, M. (2006). Following the leader: Front-line narratives on police leadership. *Policing: An International Journal of Police Strategies & Management, 29*(4), 757–767. doi:10.1108/13639510610711646
Ruben, B. D., & Gigliotti, R. A. (2017). Communication: Sine qua non of organizational leadership theory and practice. *International Journal of Business Communication, 54*(1), 12–30.
Simonet, D. V., & Tett, R. P. (2012). Five perspectives on the leadership-management relationship: A competency-based evaluation and integration. *Journal of Leadership & Organizational Studies, 20*(2), 199–213.
Seeman, M. (1960). *Social status and leadership.* Columbus: OH: Ohio State University, Bureau of Educational Research.
Waters, J. (2016). Phenomenological research guidelines. Retrieved from https://www.scribd.com/document/382096708/Phenomenological-Research-Guidelines
Zaleznik, A. (1977, May–June). Managers and leaders: Are they different? *Harvard Business Review, 55*, 67–78.

CHAPTER 6

Police Training and Education

21st-Century Perspectives

By Marcel F. Beausoleil and Mark H. Beaudry

Opening Questions

Answer the following question before reading this chapter:

> What do you know about police training and education prior to reading this chapter?

Answer the following question while reading the chapter:

> What are some concepts from the chapter that stand out to you? Why do you think they are important?

Introduction

The police today are under more scrutiny than they ever have been before. The police are given power and authority over citizens, with discretion in their use. In addition, police officers have the legal right to use coercive force against citizens (Klockars 1985). These factors demand that those who exercise these powers can do so without abuse, to treat persons with dignity and respect, and to act in accordance with law and the Constitution. There is little tolerance today for acts of corruption and misconduct by police officers as the public demands a fair and impartial justice system. The use of handheld technologies and social media have allowed for an unprecedented capability to monitor and scrutinize police actions.

In addition to increased oversight, police are also being asked to do more. Mediation of disputes, school shootings and mass shootings in general, and the opioid crisis have placed demands on police that didn't exist in past years. **Training** and **education** of police officers has taken on greater significance, yet while this is an area of concern, it is often underfunded and placed behind other items on the priority list. This chapter will look at the training and education of the police through a historical overview and current research and developments, discuss the role of training and education and how they relate, and discuss their future.

Historical Perspective of Police Training

Modern policing in the United States developed in the early 19th century with the advent of industrialization and rapid urbanization. This urbanization brought about social and crime problems that the British system of watchmen and constables were ill equipped to handle. Unlike their British counterparts, policing in the United States developed as a fragmented system organized along municipal lines, was controlled by local politicians, and was known as the political era. This combination of decentralization and political control made it difficult to professionalize the police.

In the political era, there was little to no formalized training. Officers were generally political appointees, and training consisted of learning the job from more senior officers (White, 2007). According to Palmiotto (2003) New York City began police training that in 1853, which was limited to military drill, local ordinance, and criminal law, as well as departmental rules. This initial training originally consisted of 30 days and gradually increased to 6 weeks by 1914, then increased to 12 weeks.

By the early 20th century, in what is known as the reform/professional era of policing, other large cities such as Berkeley, Philadelphia, and Los Angeles began to develop their own training programs for police. The Wichita Police Department under O.W. Wilson created a police training school that eventually grew to 17 weeks and mandated that officers take college courses in certain police topics (Palmiotto, 2003). Instructors in the training program included attorneys from the district attorney's office and professors from Wichita State University.

Another development in training occurred in the 1930s as most states created state police departments (Palmiotto, 2003). Most of these agencies developed their own training programs that generally were 3 months or longer in duration, covered topics ranging from criminal law to investigations, and were run in a paramilitary fashion. They would become models for municipal police agencies to follow.

State-mandated training began in the 1950s, the first with New York State in 1959. This was the result of a state law that required 80 hours of training to become a full-time police officer (Palmiotto, 2003). While police training was administered at the local level, it was overseen by an advisory council and an executive director at the state level. California soon followed suit, with several other states also developing similar laws and policies to mandate training of entry-level police officers.

Civil disorder and riots in the 1960s spurred a number of presidential commissions to study the police and make recommendations for reform (White, 2007). This also heralded the beginning of the community policing era. Two of these commissions were of importance for police training and will be briefly discussed.

The first, in 1965, was the President's Commission on Law Enforcement and Administration. Broken into several study groups, its role was to study the police (Palmiotto, 2003). Titled the "Task Force Report: The Police," it studied police training and made several recommendations. It noted that police training was deficient generally, but this was more pronounced in smaller departments. Among its recommendations were a call for minimum training and curriculum standards, training for instructors, and a call for research by outside agencies to improve police training. Palmiotto (2003) has noted that many of these recommendations have since been achieved.

The Law Enforcement Assistance Administration created the National Advisory Commission on Standards and Goals in 1971, which was to make recommendations to improve the criminal justice system. They made several recommendations for training, which they found was based mostly on crisis. The report stated that training should be based on reality and must emphasize the patrol task (Palmiotto, 2003). It also recommended the creation of program objectives and instructional methods designed to assist recruits in learning. Other recommendations focused on the improvement of training through such things as evaluation and critique of training programs, taking steps to ensure that training programs satisfy state standards, and identifying what measures will be taken to ensure that recruits achieve training objectives for each course. By the 1980s it reported that every state had mandated training through some type of peace officer standards and training (POST) commission (White, 2007).

The Bureau of Justice Statistics (BJS) reported in 2016 that there were 664 state and local law enforcement academies providing training in the United States as of 2013 (Reaves, 2016). In addition to "traditional" police academies, those run by single police agencies or regions for several police agencies, Reaves (2016) noted there are several academies run by, or affiliated with, 2-year and 4-year schools as well as technical schools.

White (2007) maintained that there are three roles fulfilled by the police academy. The first is to provide formal training both in skills such as self-defense and in the knowledge necessary for policing such as criminal law. Next is that the academy is the arena for weeding out recruits who are unprepared or are not qualified to become police officers. Finally, many scholars of policing feel that the academy is where the process of socializing into the police subculture begins. Citing the Center for Accreditation of Law Enforcement Agencies, White (2007) says that the purpose of training is to better prepare officers to act decisively and correctly and to foster greater productivity and effectiveness, as well as for increased cooperation.

Police Training Today

While academies have improved over the years, there remain shortcomings to the current training model. Two are pointed out by White (2007) and others. The first is that many academies do not provide enough, if any, discussion of important police issues such as use of discretion, ethics, and use of informants (White, 2007). Knowledge of these area is important for new police officers as they embark on their careers. Second is the use of the lecture and the pedagogical teaching method rather than the andragogical adult-based teaching method. A third issue is the underfunding of training by the states and municipalities that run these academies. Training is often taken for granted, seen as a last place to allocate funds, or not thought to be important.

The police are facing problems today in community relations and poor public perception due to several factors: use of deadly force; questions of discrimination in arrests and use force; and perception of being out of touch with the public. Recruitment and training are viewed as ways in which to address these issues. The questions then become, "What kind of training? What should be taught? By who? For how long?"

One of the issues currently debated is this: Should police training be done in a stress or a non-stress environment? A **stress-based training academy** is one is one that is based on a military model and has intense physical and psychological demands (Reaves, 2003). Reaves (2003) describes the **non-stress academy** as having a more relaxed atmosphere where academic achievement is stressed and the student–instructor relationship is more supportive and resembles a coaching style. It is also noted that some academies use a combination of styles. Rahr and Rice (2015) have argued that the stress model of training is counterproductive to community policing and produces a warrior mentality that fosters an "us versus them" mentality (p. 4). This is echoed by Weinblatt (2018) who stated that military-type training creates officers who are "rigid and less approachable" and further contributes to a split between the police and the community (para. 33). Rahr and Rice (2015) feel that when recruits are subjected to abuse from those in power, they see that as an acceptable way in which to treat the public.

Weinblatt (2018) describes the new training philosophy as the academic basic training style and says that its goals are to instill individualized thinking and problem-solving abilities in officers. Rahr and Rice (2015) argue that the new type of police training should be geared toward instilling a guardian mind-set, one in which democratic ideals are protected and officers are focused on procedural justice. They describe how this has been put into place in Washington State by eliminating the military-type discipline and moving toward a coaching style. More emphasis has been placed on democratic ideals and teaching a justice-based policing, in which respect and crisis intervention skills are emphasized.

It would be fair to say that there are still many chiefs of police and others who are concerned that the de-emphasis on military-type training could lead to officers who cannot follow orders and who might not be able to effectively act in crisis situations. However, there is a lack of sufficient research in this area to say which style is better. Because of this, there are many academies that try to use a middle approach and incorporate both types of training. Reaves (2016) reports that approximately a third of police academies use this middle-ground training. It is likely that this debate will continue until solid research either way assists in identifying proper training methods.

Historical Perspective of Criminal Justice Education

Numerous studies (see Table 6.1) regarding a college degree requirement for entrance into the police profession has been suggested since the National Commission on Law Observance and Enforcement (known as the Wickersham Commission) (1931), and other committee's since have recognized that police officers *should* be required to have a college degree (Eskridge & Roberg, 1981). Yet, to date, most police agencies only require a high school diploma or equivalent to begin a career in the police profession, even though according to Hickman and Reaves (2006) there are approximately 12,766 local police departments in the United States. The International Association for Chiefs of Police (2008) discovered that 9% of local police departments require a 2-year degree; however, the study also found 2% require a 4-year degree.

In 1908, August Vollmer (1926) established the first educational program for criminal justice at the Berkeley Police School, connected to the University of California (Eastman, 1972; MacQuarrie, 1935; Schanz, 2013). The first recorded involvement of higher education in criminal justice came about at the National Conference on Criminal Law and Criminology, convened in Chicago in 1909 on the initiative of Northwestern University (Stephens, 1976). With that, a new discipline of policing courses was initially inspired by Vollmer (Gault, 1918), and the late 1920s through the 1930s emphasized the administrative aspects of policing (Fike, Harlan, & McDowell, 1977; Southerland, Merlo, Robinson, Benekos, & Albanese, 2007). Criminal justice education programs during the 20th century evolved from individual courses at a few institutions in 1914 to approximately 664 degree programs in 1974 (Brandstatter, 1968; Gault, 1918; Kobetz, 1975; Kuykendall & Hernandez, 1975). The first degree was an associate of arts in police training offered by San Jose State Teachers College in 1930 (MacQuarrie, 1935).

TABLE 6.1 Various national commissions on policing have recommended some years of college be required for appointment and promotions and as an occupational necessity.

Report and/or author	Recommendation made by each commission
National Commission on Law Observance and Enforcement (Wickersham Commission) (1931)	A police reform strategy that all police officers have college degrees
President's Commission on Law Enforcement and the Administration of Justice (1967)	All personnel with general enforcement powers have a baccalaureate degree
Higher Education Programs in Law Enforcement and Criminal Justice, National Institute of Law Enforcement and Criminal Justice (Tenney, 1971)	All personnel with law enforcement powers have a baccalaureate degree
National Advisory Commission on Criminal Justice Standards and Goals (1973)	Recommended raising minimum qualifications by 1978, that all recruits have at least 2 years of college and by 1982 have a baccalaureate degree
American Bar Association Project on Standards for Criminal Justice (Burger, 1973)	Police agencies should require a baccalaureate degree of new recruits
Sherman and National Advisory Commission on Higher Education for Police Officers (1978)	Police agencies should require a baccalaureate degree of new recruits

In 1937, criminology and corrections courses were in many universities in the departments of sociology. By the early 1950s, there were 64 colleges and universities offering educational programs in criminal justice (Adams 1976; Tenney, 1971). Also, due to public criticism, the creation of the President's Commission on Law Enforcement and Administration of Justice in 1967 was formed and determined that the police profession had become more demanding and complex, so the commission recommended that a baccalaureate degree be the minimum requirement for all police officers and emphasized the need for increased critical thinking skills (Krimmel & Tartaro, 1999). Kuykendall (1977) and Landahl (2009) argue that by 1960, criminal justice degree-granting programs existed in 2% of the institutions of higher education. In 1965, Public Law 89-17, the Law Enforcement Act, established the Office of Law Enforcement Assistance (OLEA), which included federal monies for the development of academic programs. Then passage of Public Law 90-35 1, the Omnibus Crime Control and Safe Streets Act, replaced OLEA with the Law Enforcement Assistance Administration (LEAA 1973) and created LEEP (Law Enforcement Education Programs) to make available financial grants and loans to encourage pre- and in-service individuals to continue their education beyond high school (Bennet & Marshall, 1979; Foster, Magers, & Mullikin, 2007; Hoover, 1975; Senna, 1974). An additional impetus was the 1973 reports of the National Advisory Commission on Criminal Justice Standards and Goals that recommended specific degree requirements for practitioners. Chapman (2012) also adds that a report of the U.S. Commission on Civil Rights (2000) noted that "a college degree requirement would help restore public confidence in police with proper training who are less likely to succumb to temptations of deviant behavior" (U.S. Commission on Civil Rights, 2000, p. 16).

Police Education Today

The current literature indicates that police officers who have a 4-year college degree display the following: They are more adaptive to their profession; generally use more initiative; understand human behavior and diversity; are capable of analyzing problems; tend to value ethical conduct at a higher level; do not express authoritarian behavior; have a greater sense of intellectual capacity; exhibit an increase with motivation and self-confidence; exercise better written and oral communication skills; display more tolerant views; result in less disciplinary actions, including citizen complaints; and tend to interact with the public much easier than non-college educated officers (Alpert & Dunham, 1988; Carlan & Byxbe, 2000; Carter & Sapp, 1990; Carter, Sapp, & Stephens, 1988; Cascio, 1977; Delattre, 2002; Douglas, 2005; Finckenauer, 2005; Hall, Ventura, & Lambert 2007; Kelly, 1998; Mahony & Prenzler, 1996; Scott, 2010; Sherman & National Advisory Commission on Higher Education for Police Officers, 1978; Shernock, 1992; Smith, Locke, & Fenster, 1970; Worden, 1990). Some have suggested that better-educated police officers could rely on communication and problem-solving skills instead of force to defuse volatile criminal engagements (Aamodt, 2004; Holbert & Rose, 2004; Kelly, 1998; McElvain & Kposowa, 2008; Paoline & Terrill, 2007).

This research further indicates that a college education generally has a positive effect on the job performance and attitudes of police officers. Further, Wood (1998) argues that law enforcement has long sought to be recognized as a profession, and higher education arguably provides that body of knowledge as the cornerstone of professionalism and adds value and benefit to communities that they serve (Sherman & McLeod, 1979). Emphasis on quality management and community-policing sees benefits with their well-developed communications skills, racial and ethnic awareness, and a professional demeanor that enhances the likelihood of agencies' success in these endeavors (Bumgarner, 2002; Schneider, 2009; Vodicka, 1994).

The nature of policing has forced issues such as recruitment, selection, and training to become critically important for the complex police profession, resulting in the need for significant changes in the philosophy of the job's mission. In addition, greater society has become increasingly educated, and it is necessary for police to keep pace with the larger public. This exposure to others from varied cultures and customs will teach people to learn a greater tolerance and understand others different from them. Many police departments have moved toward a problem-oriented style of policing, requiring critical thinking and analytic skills, communication, and writing, and these skills are generally learned in college. The expectations placed on police officers today are greater than they have ever been before, as are the skills necessary to protect the public. Quite simply, a college education makes applicants more attractive, and once hired, promotion and salary increases are often tied to achievement of undergraduate and graduate degrees (Brereton, 1961; Gardiner, 2015; Paoline, Terrill, & Rossler, 2015; White & Escobar, 2008).

Research evidence on the benefits of higher education for police officers in the United States is equivocal and can be split into two distinct bodies of literature. The first body of research on the impact of higher education on police attitudes was built during the 1970s and demonstrated that university-educated police officers were less authoritarian than non-university-educated police officers (Parker, Donnelly, Gerwitz, Marcus, & Kowalewski 1976; Roberg, 1978) and less cynical (Regoli, 1976) and that the higher the level of education attained, the more flexible the officers' value system became (Guller, 1973). This evidence also expressed improved attitudes toward minority groups and higher professional behavior for ethnicity and cultural awareness (Parker et al., 1976; Paterson, 2011; Roberg & Bonn, 2004; Sanders, 2008). The second body of literature emerged during the 1990s and questioned the reforming zeal of the new university-educated police recruits (Austin & Hummer, 1994) and reinstated questions about the value of higher education beyond the legitimacy and credibility provided to the police by accreditation.

Research also demonstrates that higher education can improve officer knowledge, skills, and problem-solving techniques to utilize noncoercive strategies to resolve a situation (Brandstatter, 1970; Carlan, 2007; Paoline & Terrill, 2007; Worden, 1990). The differences between education and training, and the future needs of the law enforcement profession can offer some guidance for creating a stronger link between education, training, and a result of improved police services (Buerger, 2004; Carlan & Lewis, 2009; Friedmann, 2006; Johnson, 2012; Landhal, 2009; Molden, 1999; Buerger 2004; Nelson 2006). Perhaps the way to approach education is from the top down (Jenkins & DeCarlo, 2014; MacNamara, 1950). Despite significant progress, the policing field has still fallen well short of meeting a recommendation made 25 years ago by the national commissions (LaGrange, 2003; Maguire & King, 2004; Maggard, 2001; Pascarella & Terenzini, 2005; Patzius, 2011; Sherman & National Advisory Commission on Higher Education for Police Officers, 1978).

Research undertaken by the author shows that a few Massachusetts police departments selected using a random number generator and drawn from a list provided by the Massachusetts Major City Police Chief Association consisted of full-time officers working in a city with at least 40,000 residents or least 75 officers. This sample is from 30 police departments grouped by three population profiles. A total of 352 surveys were completed or returned. The survey instrument was partially a replication of the Minnesota police education study conducted by Hilal and Erickson (2010), as well as questions developed by the authors.

Interestingly, there are 74% of respondents that either agree or strongly agree that they still would have entered law enforcement if a 2-year degree had been required when they entered the profession. Furthermore, 58% of respondents agree or strongly agree that they still would have entered law enforcement if a 4-year degree had been required upon entry. At the same time, 49% of respondents agree that a 2-year degree should be a requirement to become a police officer, while only 29% disagree. In addition, 28% of the respondents agree that a 4-year degree should be a requirement to become a police officer, while 43% disagree. Also, as the level of responsibility rises, the survey respondents increasingly agree that a 4-year degree should be required for promotion to the specific supervisory ranks.

Conclusion

Today, it appears that police officers are becoming more educated and the degree does matter for the good of the profession and to make better decisions (Chappell, McDonald, & Manz, 2006; Worden 1990). Both the literature and the data collected from this research indicate that a 2-year college degree should be required for entry into the police profession. The results of this study also add to the police higher education debate by looking at the opinions of police officers in a state that only requires a high school diploma to enter the police profession. Considering that two-thirds of the respondent police officers think it should be higher than a high school diploma still speaks favorably for higher education in law enforcement.

This lends support to the idea that people who really want to be police officers will invest the time, money, and resources necessary to pursue the requisite qualifications to be eligible to apply. The theory is that future police officer recruits will be better prepared for and committed to life in law enforcement because they invest substantial time and resources up front. Such an approach enables agencies to better distinguish between job applicants, but also delivers substantial savings for the police agency in salary costs per officer during their training period, which is appealing in these tough economic times. Finally, meeting the changing needs of the police in the next century cannot be left to chance. A coordinated effort between higher education, law enforcement, and states will nurture the development of police professionalism in the years to come.

Key Terms

education: Gaining theoretical or academic knowledge in a formal classroom setting. Can occur before or after hire.

Non-stress academy: A police training academy with a more relaxed atmosphere, where academic achievement is stressed and the student–instructor relationship is more supportive and resembles a coaching style.

stress-based training academy: A police training academy based on a military model and has intense physical and psychological demands.

training: Developing specific, job-related skills in officers. Usually occurs after hire.

Discussion Questions

- What do you think about police training and education after reading the chapter?
- The history of police education is similar to other disciplines such as psychology, sociology, and others. Discuss some of the changes during its growth.
- The LEAA funded many law enforcement programs and assisted many people to obtain a degree in law enforcement. Discuss how such a program contributed to the policing profession.
- Some committees recommend that a college degree for entrance into law enforcement. Discuss why none have been implemented.
- Discuss how and why the training of police has evolved over the years and what further changes you foresee taking place.
- Reflecting on the debate between stress versus non-stress training for police, what are thoughts as to which is the best method? Support your answer.

References

Aamodt, M. (2004). *Research in law enforcement selection.* Boca Raton, FL: Brown Walker Press.

Adams, R. (1976). Criminal justice: An emerging academic profession and discipline. *Journal of Criminal Justice, 4*(4), 303–314.

Alpert, G., & Dunham, R. (1988). Analysis of police use-of-force data, (NIJ) 95-IJ-CX-0104, Washington, DC: National Criminal Justice Reference Service.

Austin, T., & Hummer, D. (1994). Has a decade made a difference? Attitudes of male criminal justice majors towards female police officers. *Journal of Criminal Justice Education, 5*(2), 229–239.

Bennett, R., & Marshall, I. (1979). Criminal justice education in the United States: A profile. *Journal of Criminal Justice Education, 7*(2), 147–172.
Brandstatter, A. (1968). History of police education in the United States. In, *Police science degree programs: Report of the Conference on Development of Degree Programs in Police Science* (pp. 9–19). Washington, DC: U.S. Government Printing Office.
Brandstatter, A. (1970). A career concept for police. *Journal of Criminal Law and Criminology, 61*(3), 438–445.
Brereton, G. (1961). The importance of training and education in the professionalization of law enforcement. *Journal of Criminal Law and Criminology, 52*(1), 111–121.
Buerger, M. (2004). Educating and training the future police office. *FBI Law Enforcement Bulletin, 73*(1). 26–32.
Bumgarner, J. (2002). An assessment of the perceptions of policing as a profession among two-year and four-year criminal justice and law enforcement students. *Journal of Criminal Justice Education, 13*(2), 313–334.
Burger, W. E. (1974). The ABA Standards for Criminal Justice. *Am. Crim. L. Rev., 12*, 251.
Carlan, P. (2007). The criminal justice degree and policing: Conceptual development or occupational primer? *Policing: An International Journal of Police Strategies and Management, 20*(4), 608–619.
Carlan, P., & Byxbe, F. (2000). The promise of humanistic policing: Is higher education living up to societal expectation? *American Journal of Criminal Justice, 24*(2), 235–245.
Carlan, P., & Lewis, J. (2009). Dissecting police professionalism: A comparison of predictors within five professional subsets. *Police Quarterly, 12*(4), 370–387.
Carter, D., & Sapp, A. (1990). The evolution of higher education in law enforcement: Preliminary findings from a national study. *Journal of Criminal Justice Education, 7*(1), 59–85.
Carter, D., Sapp, A., & Stephens, D. (1988). Higher education as a bona fide qualification (BFOQ) for police: A blueprint. *American Journal of Police, 7*(2), 1–27.
Cascio, W. (1977). Formal education and police officer performance. *Journal of Police Science and Administration, 5*, 89–96.
Chapman, C. (2012). Use of force in minority communities is related to police education, age, experience, and ethnicity. *Police Practice and Research, 13*(5), 421–436.
Chappell, A., MacDonald, J., & Manz, P. (2006). The organizational determinants of police arrest decisions. *Crime & Delinquency, 52*(2), 287–306.
Delattre, E. J. (2002). *Character and cops: Ethics in policing* (4th ed.). Washington, DC: AEI Press.
Douglas, J. (2005). *John Douglas's guide to landing a career in law enforcement*. New York, NY: McGraw-Hill.
Eastman, E. (1972). *Police education in American colleges and universities: A search for excellence*. Washington, DC: Bureau of Research.
Eskridge, C., & Roberg, R. (1981). A new paradigm for criminal justice education: Some reflections on a crime management approach. *Journal of Contemporary Criminal Justice, 2*(1), 19–25.
Fike, L., Harlan, J., & McDowell, C. (1977). Criminal justice curricula: A reflective glance. *Journal of Police Science and Administration 5*(4), 456–464.
Finckenauer, J. (2005). The quest for quality in criminal justice education. *Justice Quarterly, 22*(4), 413–426.
Foster, J., Magers, J., & Mullikin, J. (2007). Observations and reflections on the evolution of crime-related higher education. *Journal of Criminal Justice Education, 18*(1), 123–136.
Friedmann, R. (2006). University perspective: The policing profession in 2050. *Police Chief, 73*(8), 23.
Gardiner, C. (2015). College cops: A study of education and policing in California. Policing: An *International Journal of Police Strategies & Management, 38*(4), 648–663.

Gault, R. (1918). A progressive police system in Berkeley, California. *Journal of American Institute of Criminal Law & Criminology, 9*(3), 319–322.
Guller, I. (1973). Higher education and policemen: Attitudinal differences between freshman and senior police college students. *Journal of Criminal Law and Criminology, 63*(3), 396–401
Hall, D., Ventura, L., & Lambert, E. (2007). Factors influencing the higher education decision of criminal justice professionals. *American Journal of Criminal Justice, 32*(1–2), 116–128.
Hickman, M., & Reaves, B. (2006). Local police departments, 2003 (NCJ210118). Washington, DC: Bureau of Justice Statistics.
Hilal, S., & Erickson, T. (2010). The Minnesota police education requirement: A recent analysis. *FBI Law Enforcement Bulletin, 79*(6), 17–21.
Holbert, S., & Rose, L. (2004). *The color of guilt and innocence: Racial profiling and police practices in America*. San Ramon, CA: Page Marque Press.
Hoover, L. (1975). *Police educational characteristics and curricula*. U. S. Department of Justice, Law Enforcement Assistance Administration, Grant 73-N1-99-1004, 2-91.
International Association of Chiefs of Police. (2008, September). *Improving 21st century policing through priority research: The IACP's national law enforcement research agenda*. Retrieved from https://www.ncjrs.gov/pdffiles1/nij/grants/237968.pdf
Jenkins, M., & DeCarlo, J. (2014, May 6). *Educating police executives in a new community problem-solving era*. Retrieved from https://leb.fbi.gov/articles/featured-articles/educating-police-executives-in-a-new-community-problem-solving-era
Johnson, R. (2012). Police officer job satisfaction: A multidimensional analysis. *Police Quarterly, 15*(2), 157–176.
Kelly, P. (1998). *College education as an entry-level requirement in law enforcement*. Tallahassee, FL: Criminal Justice Standards and Training Commission.
Klockars, C. (1985). The idea of police. Thousand Oaks, CA: SAGE.
Kobetz, R. (1975). Law enforcement and criminal justice education directory, 1975–76. Gaithersburg, MD: International Association of Chiefs of Police.
Krimmel, J., & Tartaro, C. (1999). Career choices and characteristic of criminal justice undergraduates. *Journal of Criminal Justice Education, 10*(2), 276–289.
Kuykendall, J. (1977). Criminal justice programs in higher education: Course and curriculum orientations. *Journal of Criminal Justice, 5*(2), 149–163.
Kuykendall, J., & Hernandez, A. (1975). Undergraduate justice systems education and training at San Jose State. *Journal of Criminal Justice 3*, 11–30.
LaGrange, T. (2003). The role of police education in handling cases of mental disorder. *Criminal Justice Review, 28*(1), 88–112.
Landahl, M. (2009). Want to get ahead: Stop stalling and go get your degree! *Sheriff, 1*(1), 26–28.
Law Enforcement Assistance Administration (LEAA). (1973). *Fifth annual report of the LEAA*. Washington, DC: U.S. Government Printing Office.
MacNamara, D. (1950). American police administration at mid-century. *Public Administration Review, 10*(3), 181–189.
MacQuarrie, T. (1935). San Jose State College Police School. *Journal of Criminal Law and Criminology, 26*(2), 247–54.
Maggard, D. (2001). Higher education and law enforcement: Past and present perspectives. *Journal of California Law Enforcement, 35*(2), 1–7.
Maguire, E., & King, W. (2004). Trends in the policing industry. *The ANNALS of the American Academy of Political and Social Science, 593*(1), 15–41.
Mahony, D., & Prenzler, T. (1996). Police studies, the university and the police service: An Australian study. *Journal of Criminal Justice Education, 7*(2), 284–303.

McElvain, J., & Kposowa, A. (2008). Police officer characteristics and the likelihood of using deadly force. *Criminal Justice and Behavior, 35*(4), 505–521.
Molden, J. (1999). College education for police officers. Law & Order, March 1999, 47 (3), 17–18.
National Advisory Commission on Criminal Justice Standards and Goals. (1973). *A national study to reduce crime*. Washington, DC: U.S. Government Printing Office.
National Commission on Law Observance and Enforcement. (1931). *Report on police*. Washington, DC: U.S. Government Printing Office.
Nelson, K. (2006). Police education for the 21st century. *FBI Law Enforcement Bulletin, 75*(7), 14–16.
Palmiotti, M. (2003). *Policing and training issues*. Upper Saddle River, NJ: Prentice Hall.
Paoline, E., & Terrill, W. (2007). Police education and experience, and the use of force. *Criminal Justice and Behavior, 34*(2), 179–196.
Paoline, E., Terrill, W., & Rossler, M. (2015). Higher education, college degree major, and police occupational attitudes. *Journal of Criminal Justice Education, 2*(1), 49–73.
Parker, L., Donnelly, M., Gerwitz, D., Marcus, J., & Kowalewski, V. (1976). Higher education: Its impact on police attitudes. *The Police Chief, 43*(7), 33–35.
Pascarella, E., & Terenzini, P. (2005). *How college affects students*, Vol. 2. San Francisco, CA: Jossey-Bass.
Paterson, C. (2011). Adding value? A review of the international literature on the role of higher education in police training and education. *Police Practice and Research, 12*(4), 286–297.
Patzius, B. (2011, September 21–23). Dogmatism and higher education among urban police officers in a midwestern state. Midwest Research-to-Practice Conference in Adult, Continuing, Community and Extension Education, Lindenwood University, St. Charles, MO.
President's Commission on Law Enforcement and Administration of Justice. (1967). *The challenge of crime in a free society*. New York, NY: Avon.
Rahr, S., & Rice, S. K. (2015, April). From warriors to guardians: Recommitting American police culture to democratic ideals. *Harvard Kennedy School of Government*, 1–16.
Reaves, B. A. (2016). State and local law enforcement training academies, 2013. Washington, DC: Bureau of Justice Statistics.
Regoli, R. (1976). The effects of college education on maintenance of police cynicism. *Journal of Police Science and Administration, 4*(3), 340–345.
Roberg, R. (1978). An analysis of the relationships among higher education, belief systems, and job performance of patrol officers. *Journal of Police Science and Administration, 6*, 336–344.
Roberg, R., & Bonn, S. (2004). Higher education and policing: Where are we now? *Policing: An International Journal of Police Strategies & Management, 27*(4), 469–486.
Sanders, B. (2008) Using personality traits to predict police officer performance. *Policing: An International Journal of Police Strategies & Management, 31*(1), 129–147.
Schanz, Y. (2013). Perception of undergraduate students on criminology and criminal justice education in the United States: An empirical analysis. *International Journal of Criminal Justice Sciences, 8*(2), 105–119.
Schneider, J. (2009). In pursuit of police professionalism: The development and assessment of a conceptual model of professionalism in law enforcement (Unpublished dissertation). University of Pittsburgh, Pittsburgh, PA.
Scott, M. (2010). Policing and police research: Learning to listen, with a Wisconsin case study. *Police Practice and Research, 11*(2), 95–104.
Senna, J. (1974). Criminal justice higher education: Its growth and direction. *Crime and Delinquency, 20*, 389–397.

Sherman, L., & McLeod, M. (1979). Faculty characteristics and course content in college programs for police officers. *Journal of Criminal Justice, 7*(3), 249–267.

Sherman, L. W., & National Advisory Commission on Higher Education for Police Officers. (1978). *The quality of police education: A critical review with recommendations for improving programs in higher education*. San Francisco, CA: Jossey-Bass.

Shernock, S. (1992). The effects of college education on professional attitudes among police. *Journal of Criminal Justice Education, 3*(1), 71–92.

Smith, A., Locke, B., & Fenster, A. (1970). Authoritarianism in policemen who are college graduates and non-college police. *Journal of Criminal Law and Criminology, 61*(2), 313–315.

Southerland, M., Merlo, A., Robinson, L., Benekos, P., & Albanese, J. (2007). Ensuring quality in criminal justice education: Academic standards and the reemergence of accreditation. *Journal of Criminal Justice Education, 18*(1), 87–105.

Stephens, G. (1976). Criminal justice education: Past, present and future. *Criminal Justice Review, 1*(1), 91–120.

Tenney, C. (1971). *Higher education in law enforcement and criminal justice*. Washington, DC: National Institute of Law Enforcement and Criminal Justice.

U.S. Commission on Civil Rights. (2000). *Police practices and civil rights in New York City*. Washington, DC: Author.

Vodicka, A. (1994, March). Educational requirements for police recruits. *Law and Order*, 91–94.

Vollmer, A. (1926). The prevention and detection of crime as viewed by a police officer. *ANNALS of the American Academy of Political and Social Science*, 125–148.

Weinblatt, R. (2018). The paramilitary vs. academic training debate. *Police Link*. Retrieved from http://policelink.monster.com/training/articles/1996-the-paramilitary-vs-academic-training-debate

White, M. (2007). *Current issues and controversies in policing*. Boston, MA: Pearson.

White, M., & Escobar, G. (2008). Making good cops in the twenty-first century: Emerging issues for the effective recruitment, selection and training of police in the United States and abroad. *International Review of Law Computers & Technology, 22*(1–2), 119–134.

Wood, R. (1998). *College educational requirements and the impact on the recruitment of minority officers*. Sacramento, CA.: California Commission on Peace Officer Standards and Training.

Worden, R. (1990). A badge and a baccalaureate: Policies, hypotheses, and further evidence. *Justice Quarterly, 7*(3), 565–592.

CHAPTER 7

Police Discretion

Encounters with Mental Health Issues

By Paul R. Gormley

Opening Questions

Answer the following question before reading this chapter:

> What do you know about police discretion prior to reading this chapter?

Answer the following question while reading the chapter:

> What are some concepts from the chapter that stand out to you? Why do you think they are important?

Introduction

Effective use of **discretion** allows a police force to enforce the law while protecting lives and property and maintaining a balance of powers and actions to build strong communities. When vested in a trained and experienced officer, the exercise of discretion is a powerful ability that takes into consideration the totality of the circumstances in a range of actions from stop to arrest and far more. The breadth of discretion allows the officer to consider aggravating or mitigating factors, whether further investigation is needed, and the additional circumstances that only the eyes and experience of the onsite officer can evaluate. This gathering of information provides the opportunity for the officer to weigh the best response to the facts and events presented and to take action. The acts of discretion, regardless of whether the exercise is tilted to the soft or hard side of action, are premised on encounters with rational individuals. When the encounters are between police and individuals with mental illness, the facts of the encounter can no longer be trusted as mutually visible, tangible, or even the subject of rational dispute. This turns the police decision-making process into a tangle of uncertain meaning, words, and motivations, forcing the officer into a corner that limits the ability to use discretion. This limitation means that the officer loses the softer options and relies on harder options to assert and maintain control of the circumstances.

Broad Concepts of Police Discretion

Examining the concept of discretion more clearly, a police officer has discretion whenever the limits on the officer's power leave that officer free to make a choice among a range of possible actions, degree and nature of action, or even inaction. Years of research into policing document that the policing task and duties always involve discretion, as every police action involves a decision whose authority and force are fully vested in the officer at the scene (Bronitt & Stenning, 2011).

From the moment a police officer receives a call for service, the officer is making moment-to-moment decisions of large and small unsupervised authority: the method and speed of response, direction of approach and actions on arrival, mode and scope of investigation and inquiry, making an arrest, seeking alternate process, or closing out the call with an alternate resolution. Discretion in the criminal justice system is not found only in policing; all steps of the American criminal justice system reflect ranges of discretion in the ability to make decisions based on the information presented and on limits on those decisions through policies, procedure, guidelines, and statutes for charges filed, bail decisions, calendars, trials, motions, sentencing, probation, and parole (Bronitt & Stenning, 2011).

Beyond the organizational objectives and day-to-day issues of police discretion, in the absence of police discretion, there is no officer accountability and no opportunity for experiential learning and development and it would force all officers to consult a voluminous policy manual that would determine and mandate every action of every hour. This undesired result would preclude the actions of any officer to provide a more *just* outcome to an encounter than would be mandated by policy. At the same time, on the larger scale, absence of discretion would hobble police officer training and professional development while eliminating any criteria for promotion or recognition. The role of superior officers would be limited to mindless monitoring of compliance with the policies and procedures, with no ability to creatively solve problems absent a command from the policy manual (Pepinsky, 1984).

The broad view of discretion throughout the criminal justice system assumes that the exercises of discretion will be made according to longstanding concepts of justice, equal protection, and due process unimpaired by anger, short temper, racism, or other forms of bias (Bronitt & Stenning, 2011). The process of making the decisions that are the province of discretion requires some form of inquiry and analysis, even if that process occurs in a fraction of a second to identify a lethal threat that justifies response with lethal force. This process, regardless of the time involved, level and detail of inquiry possible, and information available, means that the officer forms an opinion supported by the time, inquiry, and evidence that the circumstances are within the authority and responsibility of the officer to act. It is only from that opinion, transformed by action into a judgment through the training and experience of the officer, that the full force of discretionary action is brought to bear (Bronitt & Stenning, 2011).

There are countless areas where the discretion of an officer is guided or restrained by the statutory authority, departmental policy, or local practice. In most states, once a prima facie case of operating a motor vehicle under the influence of an intoxicating liquor (Mass. Gen. Laws ch. 90, § 24, et seq. [2018]), the officer, in his quest for evidence in the case, must seek to administer field sobriety tests and a breathalyzer examination. The driver can refuse both sets of tests, but refusing the breathalyzer carries a statutory consequence (Mass. Gen. Laws ch. 90, § 24, et seq. [2018]). An officer's failure to administer field sobriety tests, in the absence of contravening circumstances, would be viewed as incompetent. The failure to attempt administration of the breathalyzer, independent of driver's refusal, is a violation of law (Mass. Gen. Laws ch. 90, § 24, et seq. [2018]). The range of discretionary options for the officer is that area between incompetence and legal consequences.

Considering this in the circumstances of a report of domestic violence, many police departments have mandatory arrest policies as a limitation on officer discretion. Here, again, the actions available to the officer require that a judgement, as discussed, be reached to some action that meets the level of a domestic violence offense. There are many potential observations and inferences for the officer to evaluate in making this judgment; according to the Seattle Police Department (2018), this includes indications of injuries, marks, redness, disheveled clothing, lack of clothing, smeared makeup, evidence or report of neck compression, victim's demeanor or emotional state of mind, damage to property or signs of a struggle, presence of alcohol or drugs, and signs of animal neglect. If the responding officer reaches the judgment that no domestic violence offense occurred, the officer must be prepared to justify that finding to a superior officer. If probable cause exists to believe that one did occur, the officer is mandated to arrest by department policy or, in some regions, state law (Mass. Gen. Laws ch. 209A, § 7 [2018]).

There are ethical considerations beyond the mere mechanical aspects of discretion exercise for police officers. While the view of this chapter is that officers exercise discretion for reasons that are just and lawful, that view is premised on the assumption that the officers have the legal authority to act in the manner chosen and do so in good faith. The lawful and good faith exercise of discretion is vested in every police officer, starting with the fresh-from-the-academy patrolman to the highest superior officer. Discretion is a crucial part of the department's function and operation of the criminal justice system and in the relationship between the department and the communities served. Every day, the lowest officer, operating autonomously and without immediate supervision on patrol in the community, can exercise more public-facing discretion than superior officers (McCartney & Parent, 2015).

Good faith errors in discretion cause tension in police agencies. Command officers must find a path between allowing officers unfettered discretion in the performance of their duties and assertion of control by superior officers over endless minutiae and daily operational decisions. Efforts to control patrol officer discretionary decision making through restrictive policies frequently breed resentment and decreases in department morale. In contrast, greater liberty in discretionary authority is correlated to higher morale, greater efficiency, and a more professional demeanor, appearance, and perception of police departments by the communities served (McCartney & Parent, 2015).

As an organization, granting and supporting a broader range of discretionary authority to police workforce allows for greater development of leadership skills in middle management officers and increases the ability of departments to prioritize and allocate resources to higher concern and priority cases. Police departments cannot apprehend every wrongdoer, and society does not benefit from seeing every minor offense prosecuted to the maximum extent of the law. Full apprehension and prosecution of every offense would overwhelm the rest of the criminal justice system with every case that could be pursued but does not merit such attention. The discretionary choices, ethically exercised, to allow offenses to go unpunished sets priorities and allows for the effective allocation of police resources in a manner that reflects the values and concerns of both the agency and the community (McCartney & Parent, 2015).

In reaching a judgment that a set of circumstances justifies spontaneous police in the absence of a call for service, officer decision making is based on broadly described categories of appearance, behavior, time and place, and other information. *Appearance* described an individual and/or vehicle with factors of distinctive dress, incongruent indicators of socio-economic class, vehicle type, color, condition, etc. *Behavior* described outwardly observed actions an individual or vehicle that seemed inconsistent with environmental circumstances, inappropriate, or illegal. *Time and place* referred to the officer's knowledge of a specific area or neighborhood and the activities that are inconsistent with combination of the locale and hour of the day. Last, *other information* refers to information provided at roll call, by dispatch, or fellow officers and departments. A sufficiently strong combination of these indicators, most commonly initially flagged by behaviors, prompts inquiry by officers (Alpert, Dunham, Stroshine, Bennett, & MacDonald, 2004).

Police carry out a combination of duties in their daily activities. The common motto to *protect and serve* includes not only protection of society from crime, but also, under the ***parens patriae*** doctrine, protection of members of society who cannot care for themselves for a variety of reasons (Thomas, 2016). The factors (appearance, behavior, time and place, and other information) can combine to indicate criminal activity or, in other circumstances, mental illness.

Police Discretion and Mental Illness: Scope of the Problem

In routine patrol or in response to a dispatched call for service, police officers frequently encounter members of society in a mental health crisis. As an example, in correspondence to other city officials, the New York City Police Department reported approximately 150,000 calls annually for service for people in some form of mental health crisis (Byrne, 2017). Around the nation, agencies estimate that 7% of all police contacts involved mentally ill citizens; the substantial number of persons with mental illnesses in the community are a growing proportion of the criminal offender population. This increases the probability that mentally ill persons will have encounters with local law enforcement (Sellers, Sullivan, Veysey, & Shane, 2005).

Nationally, mental illness strikes approximately 1 in 5 adults annually; further, 1 in 25 adults will experience serious mental illness each year that substantially interferes with more major life activities. Approximately 26% of the homeless population suffer from serious mental illness and 20% of state prisoners and 21% of local jail prisoners have a recent history of mental health issues (NAMI, n.d.). The homeless are a population that police regularly encounter and, while the prison and jail populations are incarcerated for their offenses, their incarcerated status means that there were police encounters during the investigation and apprehension of these offenders.

In police encounters with the mentally ill, officer discretion supports an array of formal and informal options to resolve the incident. Where no treatment option or safe institutional non-arrest placement is available, officers are likely to resolve cases informally: releasing mentally ill offenders of minor offenses to family or friends; ignoring the incident; or, in some cases of a minor offender with no ties to the community, transporting the mentally ill person to another community or section of the city. This may place mentally ill citizens in greater risk with no proportional benefit because the citizen does not end up in the custody of an appropriate person but is now in a potentially new and unknown location. This increases the possibility that the problematic behaviors that prompted transport will be aggravated and that the mentally ill citizen will not gain access to appropriate treatment (Wells & Schafer, 2006).

For those circumstances where informal outcomes are not within reach, officer discretion forces a decision between emergency mental health commitment (see Baker Act issues) or arrest and entry to the criminal justice system. If the officer understands the existence and scope of the mental illness, engaging the subject with trained mental health services is the desirable solution, but police find chronic shortages of resources, and the search for clinicians takes more time than a simple arrest. This shortage of resources, combined with a limited grasp of the mental health issues presented, means that many mentally ill citizens are arrested during police encounters (Wells & Schafer, 2006). The exercise of police discretion in good faith and in appropriate scope is defeated by a lack of resources.

The prevalence of mental health issues in America means that police across the nation will encounter persons whose serious mental illnesses will present the combination of factors described (appearance, behavior, time and place, and other information) in a manner that appears to indicate criminal activity or cause for police concern. The officers analyze the factors of appearance, behavior, time and place, and other information to discern the severity of symptoms exhibited. The large number of encounters between police and the mentally ill is a direct cause of the high proportion of people diagnosed with mental illnesses held in police lock ups and incarceration. Police discretion, when circumstances permit, supports dispositions other than arrest and prosecution. Alternate dispositions consume disproportionate police resources compared to most other police-citizen interactions. The police are forced to choose between navigating a range of impediments or plunging the mentally ill citizen into a system of further criminal justice entanglements (Godfredson, Ogloff, Thomas & Luebbers, 2010).

Further aggravating the problem of mentally ill citizens in society is a series of court decisions that increased the procedural protections for persons facing forced commitment to a mental health facility. These decisions created procedural obstacles to the placement of mentally ill individuals in secure facilities or involuntary treatment. It is not expected that police officers will be the first line of treatment or become field psychologists; however, officers have a high frequency of contact with people with mental illness. Police officers responding to or identifying citizens with mental health issues are properly wary, and legitimate safety concerns exist in all such encounters. As a result, officers need to have at least a basic understanding of encounters with mentally ill people and how the exercise of discretion to deescalate difficult encounters can save the lives of both the citizen and officer (Eldridge, 2012).

The circumstances that police now face are such that, in 2015, of 462 people shot and killed by police, 124 (26.8%) were in a mental health crisis and were attempting suicide, suicide by cop, or were otherwise irrational in their response to circumstances. The deaths occurred within a few minutes of police arrival on the scene (Lowery, et al., 2015). The problem is so great that mental illness makes it 16 times more likely that a mentally ill person is killed by police than other civilians (Szabo, 2015).

For centuries, police response to mentally ill persons was grounded in the common law principles of protecting the safety and welfare of the public and *parens patriae*. The second duty dictates protection for the disabled, including mentally ill persons. Mental health codes allow for police involvement with mentally ill persons and instruct police to initiate a psychiatric emergency apprehension when the person is a danger to self or others. Although these legal provisions authorize police powers to intervene, it cannot dictate the officer's response. For all law enforcement decisions, police must exercise discretion to choose the "best" disposition under the circumstances. Officers encountering an irrational person have three choices: transport that person for treatment, make an arrest, or find an alternate and informal resolution. The responding officer's options are limited by resources, obstacles, and legal difficulties (Teplin, 2000). It comes as no surprise, given the constraints of time and treatment options, that officers feel that their discretion to act is hemmed in and allows for a limited range of resolutions.

Police Agency Discretion and Mental Health

In 2017, as Hurricane Irma closed in on South Florida, in an exercise of police discretion at the executive level, combined with local agencies serving the homeless, police searched across Miami and gave the homeless people a choice: voluntarily accept placement in a storm shelter or face immediate emergency commitment for a mental health evaluation on the basis that their refusal to seek shelter in the face of a coming hurricane was evidence of a mental health issue. Refusal to accept shelter was evidence that these homeless people were a danger to themselves (Licon, 2017).

Drawing on the specific factors of appearance (manner of dress, cleanliness of the individual), behavior (failure to seek shelter), time and place (sleeping in parks, streets, etc.), and other information (approach of coming hurricane) provided a way to identify the homeless and act on the police command to save the homeless from themselves. Officers exercised their discretionary authority to determine who was homeless and invoke the Baker Act. Used as a verb, to "Baker Act" someone is to invoke a specific legal provision that enables specific actors, including police officers, to institutionalize individuals who present a danger to themselves or others (Licon, 2017). Florida's Baker Act is matched by similar statutory authority in other states and nations and allows for detention on an emergency basis of potentially mentally ill individuals (Godfredson et al., 2010).

The police duty as community caretaker and under the *parens patriae* doctrine supports this exercise of discretion in that there is no mandated course of action by policy, practice, or law to force homeless citizens off the street in advance of a powerful hurricane's landfall (Thomas, 2016). The issue of discretion was that it allowed, but did not command, the police and local homeless agencies to act to protect the homeless from committing suicide by riding out a hurricane in the streets (Licon, 2017).

Police Discretion on the Line

It is a common event in the call for service police to arrive to find a distraught individual in the throes of crisis bent on self-harm or, for unfathomable reasons, on harming another person.

In April 2017, police arrived at a home in Kansas City and found a woman who threatened the officers with a knife and a hammer while beginning to slice her own wrists. Instead of using force or attempting to overpower her, the officers used their discretion, supported by training and experience, to deescalate the circumstance and ultimately convinced her to surrender the weapons. The officers chose to disengage tactically, protecting themselves against harm and diminishing the urgency and threat posed by the woman—all in the space a of a few seconds. In prior years, choosing not to act immediately and assert physical control was considered cowardice. These new tactics, encouraging and supporting the officers in their acts of discretion based on their perception and understanding of the circumstances, save lives and reduce lawsuits over police use of force. The tactics include concepts of "tactical disengagement and redeployment" to back the officer off or slow down the encounter to increase the time an officer can use to assess a situation make better decisions. This exercise of discretion is countered against the reality that the officer may be able to tactically disengage but cannot abandon the encounter or fully retreat (Rice, 2015).

In contrast, in June 2014, officers acting within the scope of traditional training and without the benefit of mental health training to enhance their discretion encountered an agitated and mentally ill man in Dallas. Jason Harrison's mother called police to help get her son to the hospital due to medication noncompliance for his schizophrenia and decompensation. Upon arrival, officers were told that Harrison was making violent threats. The officers ordered Harrison to drop the screwdriver and he became aggressive. The police officers yelled at Harrison and his agitation increased. Officers knew of his mental illness and were in a tightly confined space. When Harrison moved toward the officers with the screwdriver, both officers fired and killed him (Martin, 2015).

If the officers had the training to tactically disengage and redeploy, with room to move and redeploy the officers, the perception of Harrison's threat would be less urgent, and Harrison might have lived. However, the officers lacked the resources to expand their range of discretionary actions and were forced to act as dictated by their training and experience. The actions of the officers, given the events, their training, and police practices in Dallas, were legally justified (Martin, 2015). The frustrations of all parties, Harrison's family, the officers, and police department, are understandable. However, limiting the choices available to the officers impaired their exercise of discretion to the degree that Harrison died for this lack of training.

Perceptions of Police Discretion by Mentally Ill Subjects

The population of mentally ill subjects and police officers will continue to encounter each other. There are ways for the police to improve the perceptions formed by mentally ill subjects such that the "next" encounter be better than the last. The exercise of discretion is a large part of the past and future encounters.

Procedural justice theory holds that a primary factor shaping perceptions about police officers is whether the individual forms a belief that his or her treatment during personal encounters with police are just and fair. Research on the beliefs of mentally ill citizens shows that the actions, the exercise of discretion by police officers, determines whether the encounters are perceived by mentally ill citizens as procedurally just and fair. Further and just as important, treatment by police in a manner that is not just and fair forms a belief of injustice. These are crucial factors when police consider that future compliance by mentally ill citizens with police actions and decisions is substantially guided by their perceptions and beliefs from prior encounters. Further, fair treatment by the police is viewed as more important to future compliance and obedience to police directions and law-abiding behavior than whether the full process was fair or the outcomes just. For all citizens, not just the mentally ill, three strongest predictors of future compliance with police and law-abiding behavior were quality of treatment by police, police decision making, and police performance (Livingston, 2012).

Enhanced Discretion Through Crisis Intervention Model

Police discretion can be enhanced with training relevant to mental illness to improve outcomes for police, their agencies, and mentally ill subjects. The **crisis intervention team model** is a program designed to enhance officer interactions with mentally ill subjects that improves outcomes for all parties. The program provides officers de-escalation training, and these officers are designated as primary responders to deal with individuals with mental illnesses. The officers are trained and provided resources to get mentally ill individuals into treatment services where appropriate and the justice system when necessary. There are other analogous models that involve mental health professionals who are immediately available for police consultation or, in some instances, ride with police to respond to such calls for service. These mental health professionals improve on the range of choices available to the officer in fulfilling duties and improve the exercise of discretion (Compton, Bahora, Watson & Oliva, 2008).

Research on the outcomes of these police-mental health models found that officers felt more prepared to respond and appropriately exercise their discretion in handling an encounter involving mental illness, that their departments were better prepared to respond to such circumstances, that the referrals to local treatment providers were qualitatively more appropriate by ultimate diagnosis and for treatment, and that earlier mental health intervention is reducing morbidity for that segment of the community. Organizationally, the police-mental health models made fewer arrests of mentally ill individuals and placed fewer individuals into the criminal justice system, more subjects were transported for voluntary psychiatric treatment while decreasing the number sent for involuntary treatment, and the time and cost of calls for service involving a mentally ill subject decreased dramatically (Compton et al., 2008).

Conclusion

The exercise of discretion is not merely how the officer responds and what happens to the person the police find. Officers who improve their knowledge and skills with mental health training exercise their discretionary authority more effectively. Their decisions reduce time on calls, costs of calls for service, and related criminal justice costs; arrest fewer people; and obtain treatment for more citizens with a serious mental illness while decreasing officer injuries, sick time, and civilian injuries and deaths without any compromise to ethical practices or safe and effective police operations (Butler, 2014).

Police discretion is a key factor in the fulfillment of police duties, both effectively and efficiently. However, it is far from the only factor. Training and experience, combined with the totality of the circumstances that only the officer on the scene can observe in that moment, is what will keep the officer alive and alert to carry out the sworn duties in that time and place.

Key Terms

crisis intervention team model: A program designed to enhance officer interactions with mentally ill subjects that improves outcomes for all parties. The program provides officers de-escalation training, and these officers are designated as primary responders to deal with individuals with mental illnesses.

discretion: Official decision-making capacity. The ability of officers to choose what they do at work and how they handle situations.

***parens patriae*:** Literally "parent of the country," is the government's power and responsibility, beyond its police power over all citizens, to protect, care for, and control citizens who cannot take care of themselves (Clark, 2000).

procedural justice: The concept the criminal justice process itself should be fair. It includes not only the concept of due process, but also transparency of the system.

Discussion Questions

- What is discretion? Why is it so very important to the criminal justice system?
- Why would state legislatures and individual departments create policies limiting officer discretion, for example, mandatory arrest laws and policies in instances of domestic violence? What do you think of these laws and policies?
- Why is there an increased probability that mentally ill persons will have encounters with local law enforcement?
- How much more likely is a mentally ill person to be shot and killed by police? Why?
- Why were police in Miami able to place mental health holds on the homeless in advance of Hurricane Irma? Do you agree with this strategy?
- What has research found about the crisis intervention team model? Can you think of applications outside of just dealing with mentally ill subjects?
- What do you think about police discretion after reading the chapter?

References

Alpert, G., Dunham, R., Stroshine, M., Bennett, K., & MacDonald, J. (2004). *Police officers' decision making and discretion: Forming suspicion and making a stop.* Washington DC: National Institute of Justice.

Bronitt, S. & Stenning, P. (2011). Understanding discretion in modern policing. *Criminal Law Journal, 35*(6), 319–323.

Butler, A. (2014). *Mental illness and the criminal justice system: A review of global perspectives and promising practices*. Vancouver, BC: International Centre for Criminal Law Reform and Criminal Justice Policy, School of Criminology, Simon Fraser University. Retrieved from https://icclr.law.ubc.ca/wp-content/uploads/2017/06/Mental-Illness-and-the-Criminal-Justice-System_Butler_ICCLR_0.pdf

Byrne, L. (2017, April 18). City of New York Police Department, legal matters. *NYPD Response to CIT Report.* Retrieved from https://www1.nyc.gov/assets/doi/oignypd/response/2017-4-18-NYPD_Response_to_CIT_Report_FINAL.pdf

Clark, N. L. (2000). Parens patriae and a modest proposal for the twenty-first century: Legal philosophy and a new look at children's welfare. *Michigan Journal of Gender & Law, 6*(2), 381.

Compton, M. T., Bahora, M., Watson, A. C., & Oliva, J. R. (2008). A comprehensive review of extant research on crisis intervention team (CIT) programs. *Journal of the American Academy of Psychiatry Law, 36*(1), 47–55.

Eldridge, L. (2012, February 12). EDPs and cops: Knowledge can go a long way. *PoliceOne.* Retrieved from https://www.policeone.com/emotionally-disturbed-persons-edp/articles/5017987-EDPs-and-cops-Knowledge-can-go-a-long-way/

Godfredson, J. W., Ogloff, J. R., Thomas, S. D., & Luebbers, S. (2010). Police discretion and encounters with people experiencing mental illness: The significant factors. *Criminal Justice and Behavior* 37(12), 1392–1405.

Licon, A. (2017, September 8). Miami shelters homeless against their will as Irma closes in. *Associated Press*. Retrieved from https://apnews.com/c4d3a9f4151340a9bbb86e473ed1262e/AP-Exclusive:-Miami-homeless-removed-against-their-will

Livingston, J. D., Desmarais, S. L., Greaves, C., Parent, R., Verdun-Jones, & Brink, J. (2014). What influences perceptions of procedural justice among people with mental illness regarding their interactions with the police? *Community Mental Health Journal, 50*(3), 281–287.

Lowery, W, Kindy, K., Alexander, K. L., Tate, J., Jenkins, J., & Rich, R. (2015, June 30). Distraught people, deadly results. *Washington Post*. Retrieved from https://www.washingtonpost.com/sf/investigative/2015/06/30/distraught-people-deadly-results/?utm_term=.ee3fab7b56ab

Martin, N. (2015, Mar 17). Dallas cops fatally shoot mentally ill man wielding screwdriver. *PoliceOne*. Retrieved from https://www.policeone.com/police-products/body-cameras/articles/8459038-Video-Dallas-cops-fatally-shoot-mentally-ill-man-wielding-screw-driver/

Mass. Gen. Laws ch. 90, § 24, et seq. (2018). *Section 24: Driving while under influence of intoxicating liquor, etc.; second and subsequent offenses; punishment; treatment programs; reckless and unauthorized driving; failure to stop after collision*. Retrieved from https://malegislature.gov/Laws/GeneralLaws/PartI/TitleXIV/Chapter90/Section24

Mass. Gen. Laws ch. 209A, § 7 (2018). *Section 7: Abuse prevention orders; domestic violence record search; service of order; enforcement; violations.* Retrieved from https://malegislature.gov/Laws/GeneralLaws/PartII/TitleIII/Chapter209A/Section7

McCartney, S. & Parent, R. (2015). *Ethics in law enforcement.* Victoria, BC: BCcampus. Retrieved from http://opentextbc.ca/ethicsinlawenforcement

Pepinsky, H. (1984). Better living through police discretion. *Law and Contemporary Problems, 47*(4), 249–267. Retrieved from https://scholarship.law.duke.edu/cgi/viewcontent.cgi?article=3785&context=lcp

Rice, G. E. (2015, May 8). KC police learning to "tactically disengage" to avoid violent confrontations. *Kansas City Star.* Retrieved from http://www.kansascity.com/news/local/crime/article20561061.html

Seattle Police Department. (2018). *15.410-TSK-1 Patrol Officer Primary Investigation of a Domestic Violence Incident.* Seattle WA: City of Seattle, Washington. Retrieved from http://www.seattle.gov/police-manual/title-15---primary-investigation/15410---domestic-violence-investigation

Sellers, C. L., Sullivan, C. J., Veysey, B. M., & Shane, J. M. (2005). Responding to persons with mental illnesses: Police perspectives on specialized and traditional practices. *Behavioral Sciences & the Law, 23*(5), 647–657.

Szabo, L. (2015, December 10). People with mental illness 16 times more likely to be killed by police. *USA Today.* Retrieved from https://www.usatoday.com/story/news/2015/12/10/people-mental-illness-16-times-more-likely-killed-police/77059710/

Teplin, L. A. (2000). *Keeping the peace: Police discretion and mentally ill persons.* Washington, DC: National Institute of Justice. Retrieved from https://files.eric.ed.gov/fulltext/ED465938.pdf

Thomas, M. S. (2016). Parens patriae and the states' historic police power. *Louisiana State University Law Center, 69*, 759–810. Retrieved from https://digitalcommons.law.lsu.edu/cgi/viewcontent.cgi?article=1417&context=faculty_scholarship

Wells, W., & Schafer, J. A. (2006). Officer perceptions of police responses to persons with a mental illness, *Policing: International Journal of Police Strategies & Management, 29*(1), 578–601.

CHAPTER 8

Police-Minority Relations and Police Subculture

History, Context, and a Hopeful Future

By Jeffrey S. Czarnec and Darren K. Stocker

Opening Questions

Answer the following question before reading this chapter:

> What do you know about the effect of the police subculture on police-minority relations prior to reading this chapter?

Answer the following question while reading the chapter:

> What are some concepts from the chapter that stand out to you? Why do you think they are important?

Introduction

This chapter illustrates the relationship between law enforcement and minorities throughout the history of the criminal justice system in America through the lens of the police **subculture**. Prior to the inception of contemporary policing, those afforded enforcement power were enlisted and employed to track down and detain law breakers and instill some form of perceived justice. That avowed righteousness was often fractional to persons depending on their race, ethnicity, or gender. While policing evolved and moved from decade to decade and into the 21st century, events during each era provides a lens into the challenges that minority citizens faced between themselves and governmental officials. As Donahue and Levitt (2001) suggest, race is a polarizing feature in American society and is no more evident than in the criminal justice system.

Also included in this chapter are various cultural concepts that explore the nature of human experiences. Specific cultural events allow the reader to reflect on how society has transformed, but also why there is a need to continue to consider how historical events have affected the relationship between police and citizens. Lastly, interview excepts are included from two well-noted police leaders who provide candid insight into successes and failures of the police in recent times. Delrish Moss began a lengthy police career in Miami, Florida. In May 2016, Moss became the chief of police of the Ferguson (Missouri) Police Department after the city faced civil and racial unrest. Sheryl Victorian serves as the deputy chief of the Houston Police Department, where she has held various leadership positions and administrative assignments. This will serve to offer a unique perspective on the issues, causes, as well as solutions in which they have been directly and indirectly involved.

Early Police Interventions

Interactions between law enforcement and minority citizens (and noncitizens) have a noted and debated history of bias, racism, and brutality. The informal system of policing prior to the Civil War were the slave patrols that were tasked with preventing the escape of southern slaves and controlling race-based conflict in southern states (Durr, 2016; Walker, 1980). Further, people had a desire to protect themselves and their property (Reichel, 1992). With the passage of the 13th Amendment, freed slaves migrated to the North to find work, support their families, and escape the continued discrimination and intolerance. When Blacks found employment in northern urban municipalities, they remained segregated in separate and distinct neighborhoods, similar to the Irish, Italian, Polish, and German populations. What separated former slaves from other ethnic groups was their southern accents and the color of their skin. Remarkably however, while racial tension was apparent in the Deep South and in the major U.S. cities, the first known Black police officer was in 1861 in Washington, DC, and a decade later in the city of Chicago in 1872 (Kuykendall & Burns, 1980).

During the period of reconstruction (1866–1877), civil rights protections were being granted to those who had been former slaves and those who had been recognized as free before the Civil War. However, some states chose not to recognize the principles of the 13th (abolish involuntary servitude), 14th (equal protection), and 15th Amendments (voting rights to Black males), and instead, Black Codes implemented immediately after the war were being enforced by southern state and local governments (Chin, 2004). The purpose of these "codes" was to control the behavior of newly freed slaves by restricting their movement and their ability to work independently (Forte, 1998). This restricted the ability of Blacks to vote, own property, and engage in other societal activities that were afforded Whites. As Forte (1998) suggests, Black Codes were intended to reestablish involuntary servitude under a dissimilar appearance and epitomized the South's unwillingness to admit the unrestricted status of African Americans. The standing of a minority group may have changed constitutionally, but not the negative and oppressive attitudes toward their members. These arrogances were widespread in the South and existed in northern cities where the fear of losing jobs to Blacks during northern migration was rampant.

Beginning in 1881, **Jim Crow laws** were having a tremendous impact on Blacks in the South. They were used to segregate and treat Blacks as second-class citizens. Blacks were expected to treat Whites with a higher level of respect than what was afforded to themselves. Social inequality toward Blacks was expected and encouraged. Separate hotels, restaurants, and bathrooms were the norm. In the landmark case of *Plessy v. Ferguson* (1896), separate but equal was upheld constitutionally, as long as there were an equal number of public facilities for Whites and Blacks (Roche, 1954). Incidents in the Deep South against Blacks were investigated by state and local sheriff departments, with little to no success in the apprehension or conviction of White offenders. This absence of law enforcement, prosecution, and judicial protections maintained the subjugation in a legal and ethical sense. Although laws were established to eliminate the oppression of a minority group, the enforcement of such laws were found in many instances to be morally and ethically void.

While more contemporary race issues between African Americans and the police are discussed later in this chapter, historical legal misconduct on the part of the criminal justice system could no more effectively be illustrated than in the case of the Scottsboro Boys in 1931, when nine teenage Black males were wrongfully accused of raping two White women on a train in Alabama. This highly discussed tragedy in jurisprudence encompassed the complexities of bias and prejudice in the Deep South and the failures of applying constitutional protections under the issues of the right to a fair trial, the right to be represented justly, and the shields afforded under due process. The injustices in this case are not limited to wrongful convictions, death sentences, the trial of a 13-year-old, exonerating evidence, mistrials, and the failure of victims to appear in court, and ineffective counsel. Pitts (2001) believes this case is important in civil rights history and in the evolution of constitutional law. It furthers the protections under the 14th Amendment and expands a defendant's right to counsel under the Sixth Amendment and sets a requirement that no one shall be excluded from a jury based on their race or ethnicity. As Rizer (2003) purports, the publicity produced from this case drove an investigation of the effect of race in the judicial system, which concluded that race was one of the foremost problems in reaching an impartial and unbiased proceeding.

Future cases involving race and ethnicity continued to plague the history of how African Americans were treated in the criminal justice system. Most noted was the murder of Emmett Till, a 14-year-old African American who was lynched in Money, Mississippi, in 1955 by two Whites. Till was accused of whistling at a White woman while she was working at a grocery store. Till was from a middle-class family in Chicago and was visiting relatives in the small Mississippi town. He was kidnapped, beaten, and later shot in the head before his body was attached to a metal fan and mutilated. Till was then thrown in the Tallahatchie River. His body was pulled from the river 3 days later and identified by the initials "L. T." that were found on his father's ring that he was wearing. Roy Bryant, the husband of the woman who accused Till, and J.W. Milam, the half-brother of Bryant, were arrested and charged with the murder.

In September 1955, a trial was held in Sumner County, Mississippi. The conditions surrounding the trial were indicative of the segregation that existed throughout the criminal justice system and the nearby area. The courtroom was segregated, and the local law enforcement referred to Blacks by racial epitaphs. Two witnesses for the prosecution were arrested in a neighboring town and were kept from testifying. After a 5-day trial, it took the all-White male jury 67 minutes to return with a not guilty verdict. Both Bryant and Milam later admitted to the killing.

Occurring that same year and roughly 280 miles to the east in Montgomery, Alabama, Rosa Parks, a Black female, refused to give up her seat to a White passenger. At the time, segregation laws included public transportation. Parks was sitting in an area designated for African Americans. When the bus began to become increasingly occupied, Parks and other African Americans were told they needed to change seats to accommodate White passengers. Parks refused. Schwartz (2009) describes the complexities and significance of this action—the Montgomery bus protest, not as the first to protest and be arrested, but as the last. Her civil objection not to relinquish her seat was an acknowledgement of the prejudicial treatment of citizens based solely on race. Rosa Parks was arrested in violation of the Montgomery City Code related to the segregation of city buses. She was tried and fine $10.00 and another $4.00 in court costs. However, her stance on the injustice by the government given to her gave way to a boycott of city buses and nation-wide demonstrations against segregation led by a young minister named Martin Luther King, Jr. While her case proceeded through the appellate system in Alabama, the constitutionality of the city ordinance was also being litigated in violation of the 14th Amendment. In 1956, the Supreme Court affirmed a lower court decision and city buses were desegregated.

Although the 1950s shed significant light on the separation and harsh treatment of Blacks throughout America, the decade of the 1960s may have been one of the most tumultuous eras in U.S. history. There was considerable civil unrest, the United States was engaged in a war in Vietnam, marches and sit-ins became the norm in political and social demonstrations, and the burning of flags, bras, and draft cards became the symbols of protest from east to west. In 1963, the 35th president of the United States, John F. Kennedy, was assassinated in Dallas, Texas. In 1968 his brother Bobby was mortally wounded in Los Angeles while campaigning to be the democrat candidate for president, and just 2 months earlier, civil rights leader Martin Luther King, Jr. was shot and killed in Memphis, Tennessee.

Volumes have been written about the leadership and merits of Martin Luther King, Jr., a minister and the most prominent activist during the civil rights era. His ideas of the First Amendment rights were to assemble peaceably. This was remarkably evident during his nonviolent protests in Birmingham, Alabama. In 1963, King actively engaged in the Birmingham campaign, a human rights movement that brought light to the city's segregation laws. He led a march in defiance of a court injunction created to stop the protest. His actions led to his arrest and incarceration, where he was placed in solitary confinement (Oppenheimer, 1992). While imprisoned, King wrote "Letter from a Birmingham Jail" in response to criticism from other clergy members who believed racism was better fought in the courts and not through outward protests in the streets. Included in his writing were statements relative to the injustices toward minorities and the disparagement of the civil rights movement. For King, it was a means of telling society how immoral some laws are, especially those that suppress the rights of all citizens. That same year during a march in Washington, King delivered his famous "I Have a Dream" speech that addressed the issues of civil and economic equality. Though King promoted peace and nonviolence, it was the violent act of another that ended the life of the civil rights leader in 1968. His words and actions, however, made an illustrious impact on the civil rights movement and American history.

Through the 1970s and 80s, turmoil continued to exist in urban industrial areas. There was a need for an increase of minority and women representation in police departments. The consensus was police departments should have a representative depiction of the community in which it served. Martin (2008) suggests that many police departments eliminated discretionary personal policies since the passage of the 1972 amendments to the Civil Rights Act. These policies were often seen as biased and unfair, especially toward women. This era also saw an increase in the crack epidemic and gang affiliation. The widespread increase in crack cocaine was especially problematic in the African American, Latino, and working-class communities (Bourgois, 2003). These areas were seeing increased enforcement from law enforcement, whose mission was to eradicate the drug problem and reestablish the community in an economically sustainable manner. Tactics utilized by the police were often seen as cruel and in violation of civil and constitutional rights. The populace was questioning social and justice institutions such as the government and the police.

As the unbridled events continued, one incident in 1991 provided the world with an awareness into the actual brutality that can exist between minorities and the police. The advent of cable news just a decade before provided viewers the opportunity to see members of the Los Angeles Police Department utilize apparent brutal tactics in their confrontation with Rodney King along a California freeway. A videotape, later released to the news media, captured members of the LAPD kicking and beating King—an African American. The video of the incident was exposed countless times on a world-wide news stage. The videotaping of police officers and their actions by onlookers would become the norm, and, as we see later, another major incident will lead to the call for police body cameras and law enforcement accountability.

Contemporary 21st-Century Police and Race Relations

Weitzer and Tuch (1999) suggest that race is one of the strongest predictors of attitudes toward the police. Race is perhaps a greater predictor of relations between Blacks and the police, even greater than social class. Contemporary challenges include hiring minorities and women in leadership roles in police departments and ensuring the communities in which they serve feel represented and embodied.

In the current national climate of tension and violence between law enforcement and the diverse populations, it is a matter of vital importance that students and criminal justice professionals alike develop and apply the necessary competencies and skills to promote, as well as sustain, positive working relationships with members of the communities they serve. These competencies add to the professionalism of an agency and aid in dissolving issues between the police and the public.

According to Cohen and Caumont (2016) by 2055, the United States will not have a single racial or ethnic majority, Asia will have replaced Latin America and Mexico as the biggest source of new immigrants, and the financial gaps between middle- and upper income Americans will have widened. With law enforcement academies and police agencies operating under increased scrutiny and federal oversight, it is imperative we seek to understand the issues comprehensively and develop effective solutions.

Racism, Trust, and Cultural Sensitivity

It is quite unfortunate to see dialogue commence only after a catastrophic event such those that have occurred in Ferguson, Missouri; Cleveland, Ohio; New York City; and a host of other cities and towns where Black men were shot by White police officers. For those who have examined these cases, the underlying issues, causes and other associated factors are complex and deserve full analysis. It is of great benefit to police agencies, communities, and the nation to develop a complete and thorough exploration and inquiry that sheds light on these complexities.

It is relatively evident that communities are rapidly changing. Out of the United States' estimated total population of 323 million, Latinos represent 17% and growing, Blacks, 13.3%, and Asian, 5%. According to the Pew Research Center (2016), Americans are statistically more ethnically and racially diverse than in prior decades, and this is projected to increase. By the year 2055, the United States will not have a single racial or ethnic majority and much of this will be driven by immigration. In fact, 14% of the country's population is foreign born. In 1965, it was a mere 5%. Change, simply put, is here and America's police agencies and personnel will have to adjust to the multifaceted uniqueness of such a diverse populace. Stepping back from the headline-grabbing events, let's look, however briefly, at other factors, variables, or topics that require examination and discussion. If we are seeking to recruit, train, and deploy police officers that will work well with the people they serve, then what is it that needs to evolve in levels and forms of education and preparation of the law enforcement community?

Cultural Competency

Teaching "cultural diversity" or "cultural sensitivity" has not worked, as it fails to address a core issue: that the police, empowered to maintain and secure the status quo, are serving a diverse public that is seeking empowerment through a political social movement. The development and delivery of training or academic courses aimed at improving relations between the police and the community have not been met with lasting success (Gould, 1997). This begs the question, "What abilities and skills does a police officer need to possess and exhibit to successfully engage with a diverse public?" If we are seeking to build not only knowledgeable and proficient police officers, but police organizations as well, it is significant to understand what this means conceptually to alleviate confusion about what it is that is actually required from the police and what the expectations are from the public they serve. There are four levels to these concepts:

- **"Cultural knowledge"** means that you know about some cultural characteristics, history, values, beliefs, and behaviors of another ethic or cultural group.
- **"Cultural awareness"** is the next stage of understanding other groups—being open to the idea of changing cultural attitudes.
- **"Cultural sensitivity"** is knowledge of the differences that exist between cultures but not assigning values to the differences (better or worse; right or wrong). Clashes on this point can easily occur, especially if a custom or belief in question goes against the idea of multiculturalism. Internal conflict (intrapersonal, interpersonal, and organizational) is likely to occur at times over this issue. Conflict will not always be easy to manage, but it can be made easier if everyone is mindful of the organizational goals.
- **"Cultural competence"** brings together the previous stages—and adds operational effectiveness. A culturally competent organization has the capacity to bring into its system many different behaviors, attitudes, and policies and work effectively in cross-cultural settings to produce better outcomes (Brownlee & Lee, 2017).

Scholars agree that cultural competency has numerous definitions and interpretations, each of them applicable to the various organizations of service delivery. Each definition shares a common focus on organizational change that will allow for better police service (Carrizales, 2017). Cultural competency reflects the deployment of specific activities or policies within an agency that create the foundation for effective police service for the culturally diverse populations they serve. Naturally, the increased diversity of a population may lead to an increase in the number of differences. Cultural differences may play a critical role in police service delivery, as well as enhanced citizen trust and participation in a unified effort to solve problems with the police. Cultural differences among local communities have led some local police agencies to adapt, with efforts for increasing their cultural competency (Benavides & Hernandez, 2007).

If the ultimate goal for a police agency is to hire and retain culturally competent personnel, what are the actions, activities and thinking that defines it? One of the hallmark traits of a culturally competent police agency is to "effectively provide services that reflect the different cultural influences of their constituents or clients" (Benavides & Hernandez, 2007, p. 15). However, neither police agencies nor training academies are capable of accomplishing this on their own, as time and resources are indeed limited to task-oriented job requirements, and the need to put police officers on the street as soon as possible is often vital.

Research has shown that academy learning is based on outdated lectures and simply does not allow trainees or recruits to become effective problem solvers through critical thinking (Pitts, Glensor & Peak, 2015). Further, higher education such as that which may be provided through college-level courses adds significant benefits in the form of advanced problem-based learning, critical thinking, and interpersonal communication skills, all of which are necessary in a multicultural society wherein minor issues can escalate in a matter of seconds (Massinger & Wood, 2016).

The critical competencies of effective, accurate communication and critical thinking, which may be obtained through higher education, are intrinsic to efforts made by several police agencies. There are other excellent examples of agency efforts to help their officers, both new as well as veteran, with the successful development of the necessary competencies. For this, we interviewed Assistant Chief of Police, Sheryl Victorian of the Houston Police Department, along with the chief of the Ferguson, Missouri Police Department, Delrish Moss.

Comments From Deputy Chief Sheryl Victorian, Houston Police Department[1]

What have we learned through analysis (in depth or otherwise) of police failures both recent and past?

> *One of the most important lessons learned of recent and past police failures is that ongoing training and officer accountability are the essential commonalities in critical incidents that affect law enforcement trust and legitimacy. De-escalation, cultural diversity, effective communication, implicit bias, procedural justice, and hand-to-hand combat training should be ongoing and not reserved until after a divisive incident has occurred. Law enforcement agencies must be pro-active in preparing officers to deal with high-risk, low frequency encounters to improve officer's confidence when faced with volatile situations. In addition, when officers perform on their own accord and not within departmental policy, it is critical that the agency is transparent and committed to holding the officers accountable for their actions.*
>
> *Another important lesson learned from recent and past police failures is the importance of building and maintaining community capital prior to a critical incident. When an agency has the respect and trust of the community they serve, the community typically exercises patience and understanding with the agency's policies and processes and is*

1 Comments from Sheryl Victorian republished with permission.

capable of supporting the individual affected of a perceived injustice while trusting that the department will be fair and transparent as the incident is investigated.

What are the limitations of the police when it comes to achieving cultural competency?

There are several limitations of the police when it comes to achieving cultural competency. One limitation is the lack of diversity within police organizations. It is important that law enforcement agencies recruit, retain, and encourage the promotion of minorities. However, it is not enough to support diversity for the sake of diversity. To effectively achieve cultural competency to improve community-police relations, it is essential that the cultural values, goals, and ideas of an agency's diverse workforce are heard and considered when making decisions. Too often police administrators surround themselves with leaders who look like them, think like them, and have similar ideas as they do. When this occurs, we limit ourselves to only those thoughts and ideals which benefit us, instead of considering challenging views and priorities, which compromised with our own, would benefit the majority.

A second limitation of the police when it comes to achieving cultural competency is not acknowledging we all have individual, unintentional, personal biases. As officers, identifying and understanding implicit biases exist is necessary to begin to value cultures different than our own. This also helps us to recognize the significance of developing and maintaining trust and legitimacy within those cultures. Identifying and understanding our own implicit biases do not immediately free us from bias but does help us to comprehend the social barriers which may prevent effective communication and acceptable service to diverse communities.

Finally, to achieve cultural competency, agencies must partner with culturally proficient, and respected, community leaders who are aware of, and support the police mission. Collaborating with these individuals to educate, guide and support officers on how to build trust and legitimacy within culturally diverse communities, provide agencies with advocates for improving relationships and increases the potential to build agency credibility among community members.

Comments From Chief Delrish Moss, Ferguson, MO Police Department[2]

What role does higher education play as it pertains to the police officer of today?

Higher education helps to put people in uncomfortable situations. It serves to challenge their ideas and thoughts. This is just what happens when you are a Police Officer. It helps in their development in order to be able to help a wide variety of people.

In spite of the spate of "bad news" pertaining to officer-minority interactions that have ended poorly, you have made significant strides with your agency. What are some of these?

2 Comments from Delrish Moss republished with permission.

The few bad stories have played over and over. ... [T]hey are front and center. One of the challenges for Law Enforcement is for it to tell its' story. We need to put it out there. For example, two of our Officers took thirty kids to the movies and then have a discussion about it ... and they paid out of their own pockets.

We have always depended on the media ... the six o'clock news to tell the story, but with Social Media such as Facebook and Twitter, we are now starting to master those things—we are able to tell our story a whole lot more and reach a wider variety of audience participants. We need to show all of the positive things we do. ... [T]hat's one of our significant challenges.

Who is your ideal police officer candidate?

We look for people who are powerful communicators who can deal with a wide variety of people. One of the things we are developing is "character-based" hiring. We can teach skills. ... [T]hat's easy. The difficult part is what will your character allow you to do? We ask candidate questions such as, "[W]hen was the last time you did something for a community that you're not a member of? When was the last time you did something for someone and didn't expect anything back?" If we can train the hand and the heart is already developed, we have a good officer.

Conclusion

The issues that appear to remain constant among these and other leaders is that developing strong, authentic relationships with the community helps in case a crisis should occur, ensuring that police officers dismiss their personal biases to be effective service-providers to all, and that personal character is paramount and a critical component of a well-rounded police officer. As society progresses and diversity continues to cultivate within communities, the essential dynamics of policing will be required to change as well.

Key Terms

cultural awareness: Being open to the idea of changing cultural attitudes.

cultural competence: Having the capacity to synthesize many different behaviors, attitudes, and policies and work effectively in cross-cultural settings to produce better outcomes.

cultural knowledge: Exhibiting knowledge about some cultural characteristics, history, values, beliefs, and behaviors, of another ethic or cultural group.

cultural sensitivity: Knowledge of the differences that exist between cultures but not assigning values to the differences (better or worse; right or wrong).

Jim Crow laws: Laws passed in the Southern United States intended to marginalize Blacks and to keep them separate from Whites. These laws prevented Blacks from using the same public facilities as Whites and from living in many of the same towns or from going to the same schools as Whites. They also banned interracial marriage.

subculture: The specialized culture of a group, distinct from the dominant culture yet embedded within it.

Discussion Questions

- What do you think about the effect of the police subculture on police-minority relations after reading the chapter?
- Briefly explain how Jim Crow laws affected African Americans in the southern region of the United States. Provide specific examples that support your comments.
- Identify one event in the 1950s that portrayed the relationship between law enforcement and minorities. Why is this case noteworthy? What, if anything, could have been done to reduce or avoid racial tension during this time period?
- Describe the differences between the terms "cultural knowledge," "cultural awareness," "cultural sensitivity," and "cultural competence."
- What qualities do you believe would make the ideal police candidate? How can a police agency provide an assessment for these qualities?
- Explain how trust can be developed between the police and minority communities.
- Has the media helped or hurt the ability of police agencies to build positive working relationships with the communities they serve?

References

Benavides, A. D. & Hernandez, J. C. (2007). Serving diverse communities: Cultural competency. *Public Management, 86*(6),14–18.

Bourgois, P. (2003). Crack and the political economy of social suffering. *Addiction Research and Theory, 11*(1), 31–37.

Brownlee, T. & Lee, K. (2017). *Building culturally competent organizations.* Retrieved from https://ctb.ku.edu/en/table-of-contents/culture/cultural-competence/culturally-competent-organizations/main

Carrizales, T. (2016). Exploring cultural competency with the public affairs curriculum. *Journal of Public Affairs Education, 14*(4), 593–606.

Chin, G. J. (2004). The voting rights act of 1867: The constitutionality of federal regulations of federal regulation of suffrage during reconstruction. *North Carolina Law Review, 82*(5),1581–1609.

Cohen, D., & Caumont, A. (2016, March 31). 10 demographic trends that are shaping the US and the world. Retrieved from http://www.pewresearch.org/fact-tank/2016/03/31/10-demographic-trends-that-are-shaping-the-u-s-and-the-world/

Donahue, J., & Levitt, S. (2001). The impact of race on policing and arrests. *Journal of Law and Economics, 44*(2), 367–394.

Durr, M. (2015). What is the difference between slave patrols and modern day policing? Institutional violence in a community of color. *Critical Sociology, 41*(6), 873–879.

Forte, D. F. (1998). The spiritual equality, the Black Codes, and the Americanization of freedmen. *Loyola Law Review, 43*, 567–611.

Gould, L. A. (1997). Can an old dog be taught new tricks?: Teaching cultural diversity to new police officers. *Policing: An International Journal of Police Strategies and Management, 20*(2), 339–356.

Kuykendall, J. L., & Burns, D. E. (1980). The Black police officer: An historical perspective. *Journal of Contemporary Criminal Justice, 1*(4), 4–12.
Martin, S. E. (2008). Women on the move? A report of the status of women in policing. *Women Police, 1*(1), 21–40.
Massinger, C. S., & Wood, N. (2016). Linking educational institutions with police officer training programs. *Journal of Education and Learning, 10*(2), 13–146.
Oppenheimer, D. B. (1992). Martin Luther King, *Walker v. City of Birmingham*, and the letter from the Birmingham Jail. *UC Davis Law Review, 26*(4), 791–833.
Pitts, D. (2001). The Scottsboro boys and fundamental rights. *Issues of Democracy, 6*(1), 1–4.
Pitts, S., Glensor, R., & Peak, K. (2015). The police training officer program: A contemporary approach to post-academy recruit training. *Police Chief, 12*(2), 114–121.
Reichel, P. L. (1992). The misplaced emphasis on urbanization in police development. *Policing and Society, 3*(1), 1–12.
Rizer, A. L. (2003). The race effect on wrongful convictions. *William Mitchell Law Review, 29*(3), 846–867.
Roche, J. P. (1954). *Plessy v. Ferguson*: Requiescat at pace. *University of Pennsylvania Law Review, 103*(1), 44–58.
Schwartz, B. (2009). Collective forgetting and the symbolic power of oneness: The strange apotheosis of Rosa Parks, *Social Psychology Quarterly, 27*(2), 123–142.
Walker, S. (1980). *Popular justice*. New York, NY: Oxford University Press.
Weitzer, R., & Tuch, S. A. (1999). Race, class, and perceptions of discrimination by the police. *Crime and Delinquency, 45*(4), 494–507.

CHAPTER 9

Police Suicide

By Christopher James Utecht and Brandy Benson

"Policing is psychologically stressful work filled with danger, high demands, ambiguity in encounters, human misery, and exposure to death."

"For a significant number of cops, the worst part of the job will likely be its long-term negative effect on personal health and wellness."

—Dr. John Violanti and Dr. Bill Lewinski

Opening Questions

Answer the following question before reading this chapter:

> What do you know about police suicide prior to reading this chapter?

Answer the following question while reading the chapter:

> What are some concepts from the chapter that stand out to you? Why do you think they are important?

Introduction

Policing is a dangerous profession. Police operate in a dynamic and sometimes rapidly changing environment that often involves risk or actual violence. The job of police, as portrayed in the news, entertainment, and social media, is regularly depicted in highly volatile and hazardous situations. Despite the inherent risks of policing, officers are expected to place their lives on the line for their community. When considering both felonious and accidental deaths at work, policing regularly ranks in the top 20 most dangerous professions (Johnson, 2016). Despite the shocking number of fatalities that occur as a result of the job, more police officers take their own lives than are killed in the line of duty (Alpert, Dunham, & Stroshine, 2015).

Centers for Disease Control and Prevention (2018) places protective professions, including law enforcement, among the top professions to die by suicide: sixth highest for men, and second highest for women. Most estimates state the police suicide rate is at least twice that of general population (Larned, 2010; Violanti et al., 2009). The National P.O.L.I.C.E. Suicide Foundation estimates that an officer kills him- or herself every 17 hours (Perin, 2007). Police encounter levels of suicide ideation and depression usually associated with the chronically unemployed or institutionalized individuals (Violanti et al., 2009). This should come as no surprise: The police work environment is considered to be unpleasant at best and toxic at worst (O'Hara, Violanti, Levenson, & Clark, 2013; Ramos, 2010).

Identifying and treating police suicide is complicated by the tendency of law enforcement culture to see the world in terms of us versus them, or, more clearly stated, the police versus everybody else (Alpert et al., 2015; Larned, 2010). As such, all officers need to be trained to recognize warning signs in peers who are in an increased state of stress, at high risk for suicide, and are unable to utilize effective coping strategies. However, recognition is insufficient in decreasing the number of officer suicides. Officers also require education on best practices of approaching peers in need and facilitating them by accessing the necessary help (Ramos, 2010). In addition to general education, the availability of **peer support teams**, a cadre of specially trained officers who can actively intervene to help at-risk officers, is equally critical in preventing officer suicides (Larned, 2010; Ramos, 2010).

This chapter will address the phenomenon of police suicide. The history of research into police suicide will be addressed, starting with the foundational work of the New York City–based Committee for the Study of Suicide in the 1930s. The current state of the field and the types of research being done today will also be addressed, with special attention given to the work of the **International Association of Chiefs of Police**, who have taken on the role as the leading and coordinating practitioner in the field today.

History

The relationship between policing and suicide has been known for at least 80 years. "Suicide in police is at epidemic levels" was a headline in the *New York Post* in the late 1930s (quoted in Leenaars, 2010). This headline, written in response to the outrageous number of officer suicides in New York from 1934 to 1940 (93 total), garnered a great deal of attention from the public as well as members of the city government. Owing to the public scrutiny, Mayor Fiorello LaGuardia commissioned a special Committee for the Study of Suicide to study the problem of suicide in New York, including police suicide. The commission was comprised of 10 experts on suicide, the foremost being Gregory Zilboorg (Leenaars, 2010).

Upon analyzing the 93 New York police officer suicides, Zilboorg and the committee found that trying to generalize reasons for suicide was a fruitless endeavor (Leenaars, 2010). Most suicides seem to arise from a "constellation of motivations." He noted that police have a highly complicated psychological component to their occupation. Police are expected to be serene and conscientious while simultaneously being capable of aggressive reactivity in the defense of public safety. This paradox of the police personality, along with the necessity to dam up their internal aggression when it was not needed, led to high levels of stress, which ultimately led to high levels of depression, domestic violence, and ultimately suicide (Leenaars, 2010).

Another issue noted by Zilboorg and the committee were the many reforms that were enacted in the New York Police Department following the election of LaGuardia as mayor (Leenaars, 2010). These reforms were instituted to decrease corruption and police brutality. Measures designed to eradicate corruption involved fundamental changes to the traditional relationship between police officers and the city's politicians. Prior to the implementation of these changes, many city police officers owed their jobs and livelihood to their local politicians and ward bosses. This system of political patronage overlooked many officers' shortcomings and encouraged graft (Leenaars, 2010).

Reforms to reduce police brutality had the effect of cracking down on overly aggressive officers, especially regarding reckless and inappropriate gun use (Leenaars, 2010). One practice instituted during this time was removal of an officer's firearm if the individual was the focus of an Internal Affairs (IA) investigation. At that time, removal of an officer's firearm(s) was viewed as the ultimate disgrace and emasculation. In short, Zilboorg and the committee found a fertile environment for occupation-linked suicide. The generally stressful nature of the police profession, along with the frustration felt in an organization undergoing change, combined to create a milieu in which suicide was an increased likelihood (Leenaars, 2010).

The Zilboorg study also found many issues that are associated with police suicide through present times (Leenaars, 2010). For example, even though almost 30% of the officers who died by suicide had some sort of mental health or substance abuse diagnosis, their comrades were unaware of their personal and emotional struggles. Further, if their colleagues did know, the suffering officer was actively discouraged to receive mental health treatment. Unfortunately, mental health issues for members of the suicidal group were ignored, overlooked, or dismissed by their coworkers. This seems to have been due to police subcultural norms having to do with the effect the stigma associated with mental disorder would have on the career of officer in question. In effect, by trying to save an officer's career by ignoring his mental illness and not encouraging the individual to receive psychological treatment, his coworkers were making it even more likely that the officer would commit suicide (Leenaars, 2010).

Since Zilboorg

In 1978, psychiatrist and police officer Bruce Danto studied a rash of 12 police suicides in the Detroit Police Department, committed from 1968 through 1976 (Leenaars, 2010). He found many of the same issues identified by Zilboorg: a stressful job coupled with outside stressors and untreated mental health problems resulted in officer suicides. Danto also noted the dearth of services available to officers. When services were available, officers generally chose not to use them due to the stigma attached to seeing "Doc Nuts," as well as the possibility that if they were found out they would be stripped of their firearms and their careers would be ruined (Leenaars, 2010, p. 92).

In many cases, the actual extent and damage of police suicide remains unknown (Courts & Mosiniak, 2015). This lack of information may unintentionally mislead the public and members of the police force to believe that police suicide is an isolated or nonexistent problem (Leenaars, 2010). Robert Loo (as cited in Leenaars, 2010) studied police suicide in the Royal Canadian Mounted Police from 1960 through 1983. During that timeframe, there were 35 recorded suicides among Royal Canadian Mounted Police (RCMP) officers, making the suicide rate among RCMP officers half of that for the general public in Canada. A follow-up study of suicide among RCMP officers from 1984 through 1995 found the same result: RCMP officers had a suicide rate at half that of the general public (Leenaars, 2010).

Peter Marzuk (as cited in Leenaars, 2010) studied suicides in the New York Police Department (NYPD) from 1977 through 1996. There were 80 police suicides during that timeframe, resulting in a suicide rate among NYPD officers that was approximately 20% lower than the suicide rate for the larger civilian population of New York (Courts & Mosiniak, 2015; Leenaars, 2010).

Marzuk's study was not without criticism from the readers of the *American Journal of Psychiatry*, where the study was published (Leenaars, 2010). There were two main critiques. First, concerns were expressed that New York police officers conducted the investigations of the police deaths that occurred in the city. It was questioned whether some of these deaths were in fact police suicides but were not recorded as such in an effort to avoid stigma to the deceased officer and his or her family. This is a recurring critique of any data used to analyze the police officer suicide rate through today (Leenaars, 2010; O'Hara et al., 2013; Perin, 2007).

The second critique is equally as observant. Marzuk's data included all members of the general population, including high-risk populations (Courts & Mosiniak, 2015; Leenaars, 2010). This means that substance abusers, the unemployed, the institutionalized and incarcerated, as well as the mentally ill were part of the comparison group. During the time frame under consideration, the NYPD applied psychological screening measures as part of their hiring standards. Sophisticated psychological instruments (i.e., tests) were intended to screen out applicants with a detectable mental illness prior to employment. It is assumed that most of the individuals at high risk for committing suicide should have been removed from the hiring process. As such, the police population would be expected to have a lower proportion of suicides. Presumably, if the general population suicide rate were adjusted, and individuals who would not have passed the NYPD pre-employment psychological examination were removed from the data set, the adjusted general population suicide rate would have been substantially lower than reported. This presents a serious challenge to the validity of the comparison and therefore Marzuk's findings (Courts & Mosiniak, 2015; Leenaars, 2010).

Courts and Mosiniak (2015) outline two major hypotheses regarding occupation-linked suicide, which echo many earlier noted points. The first hypothesis posits that some occupations have a better knowledge of or access to the means of committing suicide. The second is that some occupations have higher levels of occupational stress arising from exposure to trauma, exhaustion, and separation from the rest of society. Police fall under both these conditions. They are familiar with the use of firearms and their effects, are often the subject of intense public scrutiny, and are frequently exposed to the psychological trauma associated with social problems. Given these factors, police are naturally expected to experience a higher rate of occupation-linked suicide (Courts & Mosiniak, 2015).

Current State of the Field

Increasing attention is being paid to address the issue of suicide in policing. In the recent past, one of the most common prevention strategies was to screen out employment candidates through the use of psychological tests (Courts & Mosiniak, 2015). As noted by Leenaars (2010), if this method worked well, the police suicide rate should be a fraction of the general population's suicide rate, not a multiple of it. Fortunately, the situation seems to be improving. Today, agencies and state policies are emphasizing preventative strategies that address occupation-specific factors that result in police suicide (Alpert et al., 2015; Perin, 2007). Factors such as recurring exposure to psychologically traumatic experiences during police work contributes to an increased risk of developing post-traumatic stress disorder

(PTSD) symptomology and substance abusing patterns (Violanti, 2004). The combined risk of PTSD symptoms and substance abuse can increase the occurrence of suicidal ideation among police officers by tenfold (Violanti, 2004). Ramchand and colleagues (2018) conducted a national survey of 110 U.S. law enforcement agencies. These agencies provided feedback on strategies they were implementing in their respective departments to prevent officer suicide, including early intervention measures for conditions such as PTSD. Results support a nationwide trend of active efforts to promote officer wellness and suicide prevention through the implementation of both reactive and proactive measures.

Reactive measures typically fall under the category of psychological or clinical services. These services are utilized by officers on a voluntary or compulsory basis after a problem exists. Resources include employee assistance programs (EAPs), PTSD and substance abuse treatment, and critical incident response procedures and trainings. As previously mentioned, officer's misperceptions and fear of negative recourse often hinder their willingness to access these valuable resources. Berg, Hem, Lau, and Ekeberg (2006) found that police rarely seek help from psychologists or psychiatrists, even when they have serious suicidal ideation. What is more sobering than this finding is that approximately 80% of police suicide victims gave clues of their suicidal intentions but still did not seek clinical help for their problems (Mishara & Martin, 2012). Rather, officers will often seek to disguise their problems to portray themselves in the most positive light (Giddens, Duneier, Appelbaum, & Carr, 2014).

As the need for mental health intervention becomes increasingly dire, access to and promotion of psychological support has been integrated into standard policies and procedures of police administrations. A survey conducted in 1987 of 366 community municipal and county police agencies found that 65% of these agencies offered some form of mental health programming (Rostow & Davis, 2004). The accessibility and variability of mental health services for law enforcement has only continued to expand since that time. Currently, all police agencies possess some form of mental health programming. However, the quality and effectiveness of these programs in preventing PTSD, depression/anxiety, substance misuse, and suicide among officers remains an ever-studied issue.

In recent years, however, there has been a shift away from a purely psychological approach to confronting officer suicide. Sociology is a natural discipline to consider when addressing suicide. The sociological approaches generally fall under symbolic interactionism. Under symbolic interactionism, techniques used to address police suicide attempt to understand how officers define given situations (Giddens et al., 2014). By understanding the various symbols officer use to communicate, one can understand if they are at risk for suicide. This is especially helpful given the lingering stigma in policing associated with mental health issues.

Several interventions are housed under the sociological umbrella. Embedded chaplains, peer-support teams, screening tools, and health and wellness trainings are more frequently being integrated into standard operations for law enforcement agencies (Ramchand et. al., 2018). These measures are considered preventative in nature. An effective way for officers to manage the inherent stress of the job that increases the risk for suicide is through the support of other officers. As previously addressed, police officers are often hesitant to receive assistance, let alone turn to outside help for counseling following a traumatic event (Donnelly, Valentine, & Oehme, 2015). Given the "us-against-them" mentality, officers may be more inclined to communicate candidly with peers about sensitive or highly charged topics. Peer-support teams utilize members of law enforcement to provide informal, nonclinical assistance to officers in need. Peer supporters are specially trained in active listening skills (often present in traditional therapy) and are able to recognize, help prevent, and understand the effects of stress that are unique to police officers. Peer-to-peer sessions allow an officer in distress to receive supportive feedback and guidance from an encouraging counterpart. In addition to helping an officer process an event, peer communication is an opportunity for a trained peer-support officer to identify an officer who is struggling in a way that may require further intervention, such as suicide prevention.

Critical incident stress management (CISM) is an alternative intervention that utilizes peer-support officers immediately following critical incidents, such as an officer death, national disaster, traumatic exposure, etc. CISM is an intervention protocol that is a formalized and highly structured program typically delivered in group format. CISM teams, typically a set of officers who have completed the formalized training protocols, have dedicated their time to supporting their colleagues in need. CISM provides afflicted officers with an understanding of stress reactions and their emotions and commonly offers further referral if help is needed. There are several critical differences between CISM and peer-support programs. First, attendance to a CISM debriefing could be mandated by an officer's department. Officers can discretely seek out assistance from peer-support officers if they so choose. Second, CISM is more structured in appearance. Finally, CISM occurs as needed compared to peer-support interventions, which are more casual and ongoing.

Despite the varied resources available to officers, it is important to recognize that stress can have serious and adverse effects on individuals who do not properly manage their difficulties. Unresolved stressful encounters, marital strain, financial issues, work stress, and sleep deprivation all can contribute to psychological and health problems. CISM, peer-support teams, and professional, clinical services can assist an officer in receiving help and preventing additional tragedies.

Although suicide has been a topic under consideration by the sociologists since the beginning of the discipline, practitioners must be careful not to view the phenomenon of suicide through a purely sociological lens. As acknowledged by Durkheim (1897/2006), "Each victim of suicide gives his act a personal stamp which expresses his temperament, the special conditions in which he is involved, and which, consequently, cannot be explained by the social and general causes of the phenomenon" (p. 306). It is imperative that police suicide is addressed holistically, from a variety of disciplinary viewpoints, to get at the core of the matter and to save as many lives as possible.

Current Leading Practitioner: International Association of Chiefs of Police

While there are many researchers and agencies examining the factors that contribute to and prevent police suicide, the leader and de facto coordinator is the International Association of Chiefs of Police. In July 2013, the International Association of Chiefs of Police and the Department of Justice's Office of Community Oriented Policing Services hosted a symposium to raise awareness of the issue, to identify and evaluate current responses, and to create a strategic plan to guide practitioners in addressing the issue (International Association of Chiefs of Police, 2014). The symposium recognized four main areas that needed to be addressed in a concerted national response: occupational culture change, early warning and prevention protocols, training, and event response protocols.

The symposium acknowledged law enforcement's historic disregard for mental health and wellness (International Association of Chiefs of Police, 2014). There is a persistent and pervasive stigma attached to an officer who asks for help with mental health. In fact, the officer could be found not fit for duty. This shame and fear work to make mental health problems worse. Agencies need to change this culture to keep officers safe. As Acting Assistant Attorney General Tony West said, "Officer suicide and mental wellness needs to be addressed just as directly as officer (ballistic) vests" (International Association of Chiefs of Police 2014, p. 4).

IACP Recommendations

To make this cultural change, the International Association of Chiefs of Police (2014) recommended a three-part approach. First, policy changes are needed to eliminate any adverse repercussions, including threats of termination or reassignment, for officers reaching out for help. Second, after policy changes are made, agencies will need to remove fear of secondary consequences, such as being stigmatized as not being able to cope with the realities of the job. Third, the profession must ensure other officers are conscientious of their coworkers' mental health situations and general wellness. Officers are expected to protect and support each other on the streets; this practice originated early on in the institution of policing to maintain officer safety in physical altercations. Through training and evolving culture, this tradition can naturally be leveraged into officers monitoring and responding to their colleagues' mental well-being (International Association of Chiefs of Police, 2014).

Early warning and prevention protocols must also be developed and put into place (International Association of Chiefs of Police, 2014). Early warning systems are an acknowledgement that mental health problems are easiest to resolve when they are addressed sooner than later. To take advantage of this knowledge, agencies must have early warning and prevention protocols that are well designed and thought out in advance to address officer mental health issues when they are discovered (International Association of Chiefs of Police, 2014).

At their core, early warning systems will help detect stressors related to suicide and mental illness (International Association of Chiefs of Police, 2014). They will also look at officers' behavioral indicators that are generally correlated with suicidal ideation. While intended to help combat the problem of officer suicide, these early warning and prevention protocols can also help identify officers who are experiencing less than suicidal mental health issues, such as depression or anxiety (International Association of Chiefs of Police, 2014).

The International Association of Chiefs of Police (2014) recommend several action items to implement proper early warning and intervention protocols. These include regularly evaluating mental health providers who are conducting police pre-employment psychological screenings, making employee assistance programs (EAP) available at no cost, implementing a wellness program in the workplace, and leveraging technology such as social media, Skype, and text support to help facilitate officers in getting the help they need (International Association of Chiefs of Police, 2014).

One of the most important action items recommended by the International Association of Chiefs of Police (2014) is having specially trained peer support personnel. These officers function as critical mental health resources within the department. Their job is to help officers overcome their reluctance, fear, or shame and to seek out the mental health support they need. These officers will also be formally trained to recognize the stressors and indicators that the early warning system is designed to detect, as well as how to appropriately approach an officer that they, due to their training and experience, believe is at risk for suicide or mental illness (International Association of Chiefs of Police, 2014).

The third area of need identified by the International Association of Chiefs of Police (2014) is individual officer training. This training need focuses on the individual officers and their knowledge of the potential emotional distress that policing carries with it. Unlike the training involved with early warning and prevention protocols, this training concentrates on officers recognizing issues in their own lives and the lives of their co-workers that may indicate an officer is experiencing a mental health issue. This training is not just for line-level officers. To be credible, the agency's leaders must be at the forefront of attending this type of training (International Association of Chiefs of Police, 2014).

Finally, departments need to plan in advance and have event response protocols in place (International Association of Chiefs of Police, 2014). For instance, an appropriate funeral protocol will allow agency personnel to honor the life, service, and successes of a fallen officer, without regard to how they died. This will help reinforce a positive agency culture that does not treat members with mental illness as pariahs (International Association of Chiefs of Police, 2014).

Suicide Prevention Programs

Police suicide poses systemic threats to the individual agency. When a suicide or attempted suicide of a police officer occurs, coworkers experience a higher incidence of mental illness and emotional maladjustment (Bar, Pahlke, Dahm, Weiss, & Heuft, 2004). Therefore, the need for improved suicide prevention measures among law enforcement is not only intended to save the individual, but protect the larger unit. Several agencies have begun to develop and implement formalized educational and preventative trainings. Mishara and Martin (2012) assessed the effectiveness of the Together for Life program in preventing suicide among members of the Montreal Police Force. The goal was to develop the abilities of officers to deal with suicide, develop mutual support and solidarity among members of the force in suicide prevention, provide help for related problems, and develop competencies in using existing resources. This training was distributed annually to both officers and supervisory positions beginning in 1997. Results were astounding: The Montreal police suicide rate decreased by 78.9% from its prior numbers. Comparison to other local agencies that did not have suicide prevention models in place showed slight increases in number of officer suicides during the same timeframe (Mishara & Martin, 2012).

There is a current push in the field of psychology toward the development of evidence-based, suicide prevention programs. However, these programs are being developed in consideration of the general public as opposed to the unique nuances that accompany police work. For law enforcement agencies to effectively integrate behavioral health prevention measures into their mental health programming, several key components need to be addressed. First, officers need to be provided consistent education on ways they can maintain or recognize changes in their basic state of wellness and health. This includes disruptions in sleep quality, irritability, avoidance of pleasurable or usual activities, apathy, and increased substance use. Basic knowledge and familiarity of conditions that commonly afflict police officers, such as PTSD and suicide, is critical. Officers also require training on how to recognize signs of distress in their subordinates or coworkers. However, the ability to recognize distress is insufficient to support positive change. Officers should also be provided training to learn how to approach and properly address peers of whom they are concerned. Finally, readily accessible resources without repercussions is the most critical component of developing a successful suicide prevention model. Officers should be aware of what help is available to them, should they wish to seek assistance. This includes frequent promotion of peer-support officers, EAP services, suicide hotlines, and local mental health resources that can be accessed discreetly by an officer in need.

Conclusion

In any instance, suicide is a complex issue without a simple solution (Durkheim 1897/2006; Violanti et al., 2009). There has been a realization that police suicide is linked to a combination of occupational factors and outside factors. As a survivor said of her husband's suicide, police have the same problems as everyone else, it is just that they also have a job that exacts an incredible mental toll (Films for the Humanities and Sciences, 1992/2006). Any approach that hopes to adequately address police suicide must necessarily include a multi-faceted, multi-disciplinary approach. The classic reliance on psychological methods of addressing suicide must be supplemented with sociological knowledge and thinking.

Suicide is a taboo topic widely viewed with disdain by police personnel (O'Hara et al., 2013). This resistance must be overcome by police practitioners. Suicide prevention in law enforcement is an all-hands responsibility (Larned, 2010). Just as all officers are responsible to each other to be safe when dealing with individuals on the street, so too must they be responsible to each other and look out for each other's mental health (Larned, 2010; Ramos, 2010). Suicide claims the lives of twice as many officers as murder. If the situation was reversed and twice as many officers were killed feloniously while on duty, there would be a national outcry for a solution (Larned, 2010). Only by educating officers, administrators, and the citizens they serve will there be a realization of this tragedy and a concerted move to nationally address this problem.

Key Terms

critical incident stress management: An intervention that utilizes peer-support officers immediately following critical incidents. It is an intervention protocol that is a formalized and highly structured program that is typically delivered in group format.

International Association of Chiefs of Police: An organization of law enforcement professionals dedicated to addressing leadership, policy, and best practices in all aspects of policing.

peer support teams: A cadre of specially trained officers who can actively intervene to help at-risk officers.

Discussion Questions

- What do you think about the phenomenon of police suicide after reading the chapter?
- What was the Committee for the Study of Suicide?
- Why is it so difficult to identify and track police suicide?
- Describe the psychological and sociological approaches to addressing police suicide. Which do you feel would be more successful? Why?
- Why is it important to maintain a holistic approach to police suicide?
- Describe the initiatives recommended by the International Association of Chiefs of Police. Which do you think is most important? Why?
- What is the Together for Life program used by the Montreal police? Why do you think was it so successful?

References

Alpert, G. P., Dunham, R. G., & Stroshine, M. (2015). *Policing: Continuity and change* (2nd ed.). Long Grove, IL: Waveland.

Bar, V. O., Pahlke, C., Dahm, P., Weiss, U., & Heuft, G. (2004). Secondary prevention for police officers involved in job-related psychological stressful or traumatic situations. *Zeitschrift für Psychosomatische Medizin und Psychotherapie, 50*(2), 190–202.

Berg, A. M., Hem, E., Lau, B., Ekeberg, O. (2006). Help-seeking in the Norwegian police service. *Journal of Occupational Health, 48*(3), 145–153.

Centers for Disease Control and Prevention. (2018). Suicide rates by major occupational group—17 states, 2012 and 2015. Retrieved from https://www.cdc.gov/mmwr/volumes/67/wr/pdfs/mm6745a1-H.pdf

Courts, L., & Mosiniak, S. (2015). Police officers and suicide: An international literature review. *Law Enforcement Executive Forum, 15*(4), 81–96.

Donnelly, E., Valentine, C., & Oehme, K. (2015). Law enforcement officers and employee assistance programs. *Florida State University Libraries.* Retrieved from https://diginole.lib.fsu.edu/islandora/object/fsu%3A277447/datastream/PDF/view

Durkheim, E. (1897/2006). On suicide. London, UK: Penguin.

Films for the Humanities and Sciences. (1992/2006). *Suicide and the police officer.* USA: Films Media Group.

Giddens, A., Duneier, M., Appelbaum, R. P., & Carr, D. (2014). *Introduction to sociology* (9th ed.). New York, NY: Norton.

International Association of Chiefs of Police. (2014). *IACP National Symposium on law enforcement officer suicide and mental health: Breaking the silence on law enforcement suicides.* Washington, DC: Office of Community Oriented Policing Services.

Johnson, D. (2016, May 13). The most dangerous jobs in America. *Time.* Retrieved from http://time.com/4326676/dangerous-jobs-america/

Larned, J. G. (2010). Understanding police suicide. *Forensic Examiner, 19*(3), 64–71.

Leenaars, A. A. (2010). *Suicide and homicide-suicide among police.* Amityville, NY: Baywood.

Mishara, B., & Martin, N. (2012). Effects of comprehensive police suicide prevention program. *Crisis, 33*(3), 162–168. doi:10.1027/0227-5910/a000125

O'Hara, A. F., Violanti, J. M., Levenson, R. L., Jr., & Clark, R. G., Sr. (2013). National police suicide estimates: Web surveillance study III. *International Journal of Emergency Mental Health and Human Resilience, 15*(1), 31–38.

Perin, M. (2007). Police suicide. *Law Enforcement Technology, 34*(9), 8–16.

Ramchand, R., Saunders, J., Osilla, K. C., Ebener, P., Kotzias, V., Thornton, E., ... & Cahill, M. (2018, April 12). Suicide prevention in U.S. law enforcement agencies: A national survey of current practices. *Journal of Police and Criminal Psychology*, 1–12.

Ramos, O. (2010). Police suicide—Are you at risk?. *FBI Law Enforcement Bulletin, 79*(5), 21.

Rostow, C. D., & Davis, R. D. (2004). Handbook for psychological fitness-for-duty evaluations in law enforcement. Philadelphia: Haworth Press, Inc.

Violanti, J. M. (2004). Predictors of police suicide ideation. *Suicide and Life-Threatening Behavior, 34*(3), 277–283.

Violanti, J., Fekedulegn, D., Charles, L. E., Andrew, M. E., Hartley, T. A., Mnatsakanova, A., & Burchfiel, C. M. (2009). Suicide in police work: Exploring potential contributing influences. *American Journal of Criminal Justice, 34*(1–2), 41–53.

CHAPTER 10

Policing Behind Closed Doors

Understanding the Complexities and Challenges of Responding to Domestic Violence

By Shelly M. Wagers

Opening Questions

Answer the following question before reading this chapter:

> What do you know about the policing challenges posed to domestic violence prior to reading this chapter?

Answer the following question while reading the chapter:

> What are some concepts from the chapter that stand out to you? Why do you think they are important?

Introduction

Despite numerous policies and intervention efforts, domestic violence continues to be a widespread public health problem and a critical issue for law enforcement. Studies indicate that domestic violence constitutes anywhere from 15–50% of all calls received by police (Kline, 2009). Domestic violence also accounts for the largest category of in-the-line-of-duty deaths, representing an average of 14% of all officer deaths each year (Breul & Keith, 2016). A recent study found that when examining in-the-line-of-duty deaths restricted to calls for service, domestic violence accounted for 22% of officer fatalities, which was the largest single category. In 2017, more officers were shot responding to domestic violence than any other type of firearm fatality (Breul & Keith, 2016). In light of these statistics and other knowledge gained about the complexities of domestic violence over the past 40 years, the International Association of Chiefs of Police (ICAP) recently stated that domestic violence requires a comprehensive approach that factors in the potential danger to officers along with the unique dynamics between the perpetrator and victim. The purpose of this chapter is to provide a better understanding of the complexities and challenges of these cases by reviewing the development of current laws, police practices, and domestic violence theories. This chapter will also present several evidence-based best practices, policies, and programs for effectively policing domestic violence.

Defining Domestic Violence

Most people are familiar with the term "**domestic violence**" but would struggle to specifically define it if asked. Over the past 40 years, various terms have been used interchangeably with domestic violence such as "**wife abuse,**" "**spouse abuse**," and "**intimate partner violence**." These changes in terminology have occurred because of our increased knowledge, along with activist efforts to shift the social recognition of domestic violence from a stigmatized, private matter to a crime and public issue.

As society began to criminalize spousal abuse, reports of domestic violence to police increased, which brought wife beating and other types of **family violence** out from behind closed doors. Family violence includes a range of violent acts that occur within a variety of familial relationships, such as between siblings, cousins, or children hitting their parents. Family violence incidents typically result from situational conflict and are generally discrete or isolated incidents (Johnson, 2005; Johnson & Ferraro, 2000; Straus, & Gelles, 1990). Although it is important for law enforcement to intervene in all incidents of family violence, there is a fundamental difference between wife/spousal abuse, commonly referred to as domestic violence, as compared to other types of family violence. Specifically, domestic violence involves individuals in an intimate, romantic relationship and one person is battering the other. **Battering** is characterized by an ongoing pattern of coercion, intimidation, control tactics, and violence for the purpose of maintaining a relationship of dominance over an intimate partner.

Although research has clearly shown that most incidents of family violence do not involve battering and that not all violence between intimate partners is battering (Pence & Dasgupta, 2006), this knowledge has been slow to impact current police policies. Over time, confusion has occurred and "battering" has become equated with all types of domestic and family violence. For example, the International Association of Chiefs of Police (ICAP) (2018) defines domestic violence as "abusive behavior in any relationship, as outlined by law, that is used to gain or maintain power and control over an intimate partner or family or household member" (para. 2). This broad definition leads to a one-size-fits-all-type approach to intervening in all matters of family violence when wife abuse, or what was originally meant by the term domestic violence, should only encompass one type of violence: battering that occurs between intimate partners.

It is inaccurate and ineffective to continue to consider and respond to all types of violence between family members and all violence by intimate partners as if it follows a similar, systematic, ongoing pattern of intimidation, control, and domination that is characteristic of battering (Pence & Dasgupta, 2006). Grasping the concept that there are important differences in the types of violence that occur between intimate partners is crucial for law enforcement. Importantly, this heightened understanding by law enforcement will guide the development of more effective police polices and interventions. However, to advance best practices, it is important to understand the political historical development of police responses to domestic violence and the theoretical research that has impacted policing domestic violence.

The Battered Women's Movement and Police Responses to Domestic Violence

Although today police acknowledge and regularly intervene when violence occurs between spouses and/or intimate partners, historically wife abuse was not considered a crime. Traditionally, fights between a husband and a wife were viewed socially as a private matter and it was believed the criminal justice system should not get involved (Buzawa, Buzawa, & Stark, 2017; Fagan, 1996). The traditional police response or lack of response was due to the historical social and cultural acceptance of violence against women embedded within a patriarchal system and laws that viewed a wife as the husband's property.

Historically in the United States men were legally allowed to kick and punch their wives in the back as long as they didn't leave marks or bruising. For example, the "rule of thumb" expression comes from the 18th century common law that allowed men to physically beat their wives and children with a switch, provided it was not thicker than their thumb and did not leave permanent injury (Fagan, 1996). The shift in early common law views on wife abuse did not occur until the women's suffrage movement of the 1920s. Women fought for equal rights, and in addition to winning the right to vote, wife abuse was made illegal in all 50 states. Although this was a step in the right direction, the social culture of the time still viewed wife abuse as a stigmatized private matter that should not require a public or judicial response. From the 1920s through the 1960s, the criminal justice system response to wife abuse remained lax, and police departments did not want to intervene in these cases beyond providing conflict resolution (Houston, 2014). Although most police departments had specific policies to address wife abuse, these early polices actively discouraged arrest and promoted what was known as "counseling" or "crisis intervention" (Buzawa et al., 2017). For example, a common police response was to have the husband leave to cool down or see if the wife could go to a family or friend's house for the night while her husband cooled off. No further protective measures were employed, no resources were provided to the wife, and arrests were typically not made.

Domestic violence as police know it today was not formally recognized either socially or by the criminal justice system until the battered women's movement (BWM), which began in the 1970s. During the 1970s and 1980s, feminist advocates from the BWM called attention to the widespread abuse women continued to experience at the hands of their husbands. Feminist advocates argued that the justice system needed to intervene to protect women from spousal abuse and hold this type of perpetrator criminally accountable. Throughout the 1970s and 1980s, work done by advocates from the BWM led to a variety of social interventions and changes in many laws and criminal justice policies (Hall, 2014).

Although activists work for change across all spheres of the criminal justice system, there has always been a critical eye on law enforcement and how police respond to domestic violence. Throughout the 1970s and 1980s, police were regularly criticized for their dismissive response to domestic violence calls, treating perpetrators too leniently and failing to make arrests in cases with clear probable cause (Lee, Zhang, & Hoover, 2013). Police commonly replied to this criticism as being an issue with the law, limiting their ability to make a **warrantless arrest** with **probable cause** in misdemeanor cases. In felony cases, an officer can make a warrantless arrest with probable cause if there is an immediate threat of danger to the victim or public, or a likelihood evidence could be destroyed. However, in misdemeanor criminal cases an officer cannot make a warrantless arrest based on probable cause unless they actually witnessed the crime (Brandl, 2018). Most cases of domestic violence involve a misdemeanor assault and/or battery and typically happen behind closed doors, out of the view of the public and police. This legal restriction limited the ability for police to make arrests in most domestic violence cases throughout the 1970s and 1980s.

Advocates struggled to get police and lawmakers to make changes regarding arrest laws until the landmark Minneapolis Domestic Violence Experiment (MDVE) was published in 1984. The MDVE was a controlled experiment that showed making an arrest was more effective at reducing future repeats acts of domestic violence compared to simply "counseling" or temporarily separating the parties (Sherman & Berk, 1984). Although replication studies today have shown this initial finding may not be completely accurate (Buzawa et al., 2017), the MDVE findings during the mid-1980s provided activists the scientific evidence needed to pass legislation that allowed for warrantless arrests in misdemeanor domestic violence cases. By the end of the 1980s, most states had enacted some form of domestic violence legislation that required mandatory police training in domestic violence and allowed for the warrantless probable cause arrest in misdemeanor domestic violence cases. Advocates hoped this legal reform would lead to increased arrests and prosecution of domestic violence cases, but it did not have a significant impact on either.

Police officers continued to receive criticism and blame into the 1990s from advocates claiming that low arrest rates contributed to low prosecution rates, along with increased incidence rates for domestic violence and unnecessary injury to victims (Buzawa et al., 2017). Using the results from the MDVE study, along with several lawsuits that implicated police departments for violating domestic violence victim's equal protection and due process rights (for failure to arrest), advocates pushed for laws requiring police to make an arrest when they established probable cause (Barata & Senn, 2003). Today, these laws and policies are commonly known as **preferred arrest** and **mandatory arrest**. Throughout the 1990s, variations of preferred/mandatory arrest laws were passed across most states, and police departments enacted a variety of both preferred and mandatory arrest departmental policies (Hirschel, 2008).

As a result of the advocacy for and implementation of preferred/mandatory arrest policies, along with increased officer training, arrests were routinely being made in misdemeanor and felony domestic violence cases by the end of the 1990s (Buzawa et al., 2017). Initially feminist scholars and advocates from the BWM were proponents of these arrest polices, but as arrest rates increased, several unintended consequences emerged. Today, preferred/mandatory arrest policies are controversial due to the increase in **dual arrests** (when both the victim and offender are arrested) and the increase in female victims being arrested. Describing the research related to dual arrest and increased arrests of victims in detail is beyond the scope of this chapter (Harper & Gover, in press). However, these issues are important for two reasons: First, they highlight the difficulties and complexities that occur within domestic violence cases that polices officers are faced with trying to unravel, often with limited evidence. Second, they demonstrate how research increases our knowledge and the need to continually update policies and police training to incorporate evidence-based best practices grounded in theoretical research.

Theories of Domestic Violence and Police Interventions

It is important for law enforcement to have a basic understanding of the primary theoretical frameworks regularly applied to explain domestic violence for two key reasons: First, these theories underlie the current legal definitions, policies, interventions, and allocation of resources. Second, recognizing the different theories or explanations can help police officers better understand domestic violence, leading to more successful policies and practices. Similar to the changing legal and police responses, theoretical research in domestic violence also evolved with the BWM in the 1970s. A complete overview of theories used to explain domestic violence is beyond the scope of this chapter (Buzawa et al., 2017), but it is important to briefly review relevant domestic violence theories on which current police policies and practices are based.

Feminist theories have had and continue to have the greatest influence and impact on police polices for domestic violence (Wagers, 2012). From the feminist perspective, domestic violence is deeply embedded in the social structure of patriarchy and focuses on the historical power imbalances between men and women as a root cause of domestic violence and other forms of violence against women (Dobash & Dobash, 1979). In the 1980s several key theories on domestic violence emerged from feminist researchers that are still used in police training today. One of these theories was Lenore Walker's (1979) cycle of abuse theory. Based on a series of interviews with "battered women," Walker noted a consistent pattern with four phases (see Figure 10.1), which tended to replay. Walker also noted that as the cycle repeated, the length of time between phases decreased and in many cases phase 3 (reconciliation) and phase 4 (calm) would completely disappear as the violence tended to escalate.

Although the work done by Walker was significant, the most influential work came from the Duluth Domestic Abuse Intervention Project (DAIP). The DAIP originated in the

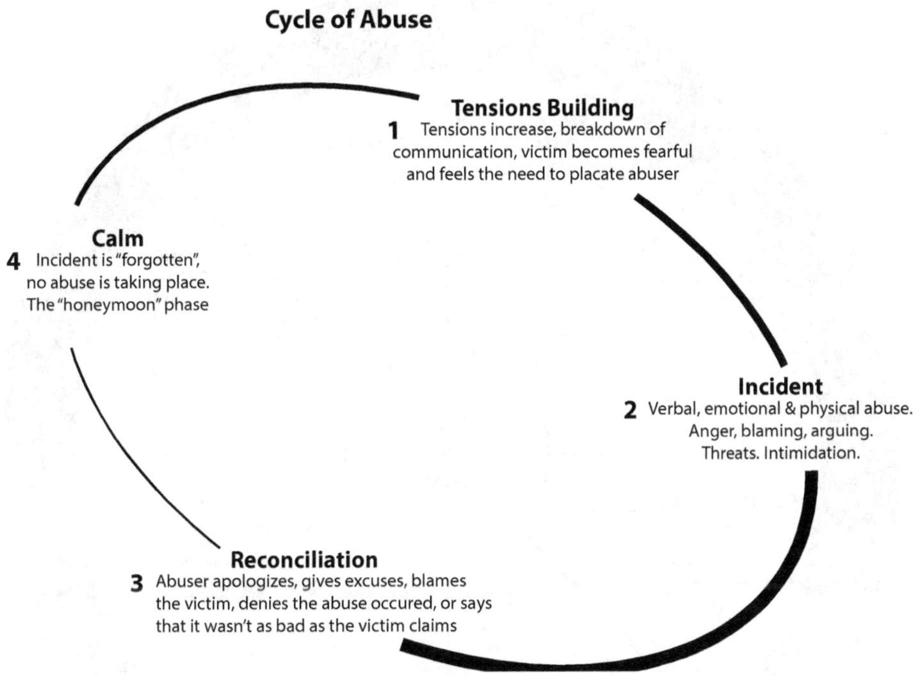

FIGURE 10.1: Cycle of abuse.

Source: https://commons.wikimedia.org/wiki/File:Cycle_of_Abuse.png.

city of Duluth, Minnesota, after a particularly brutal homicide occurred in 1980 (Pence & Paymar, 1993). In response to this event, a small group of feminist researchers and advocates got city, county, and private social service agencies in Duluth to adopt and commit to new policies and procedures designed to coordinate their interventions in domestic violence cases. From this work two significant distinct and important components emerged. The first component was the creation of a multi-disciplinary program designed to address the issue of domestic violence in a community, which is now commonly referred to as a "coordinated community response." The second component was an educational curriculum that theorized and conceptualized the dynamics of domestic violence.

The Duluth curriculum originated from interviews with battered women attending classes and support groups offered by the local battered women's shelter. From this research, Pence and Paymar (1993) conceptualized domestic violence as "a pattern of physical, psychological, and sexual abuse, coercion, and violence with the intent to dominate and control" (p. 2). They further stated, "[V]iolence is used to control people's behavior ... the intention of the batterer is to gain power and control over their intimate partner's actions, thoughts, and feelings" (Pence & Paymar, 1993, p. 2.). The research from Duluth established the concept that domestic violence involves "battering," which over time evolved into commonly used mantra "domestic violence is about power and control." (Wagers, 2015). Additionally, from this early research emerged the well-known power and control wheel (see Figure 10.2), which provides a pictorial representation of battering. By using the feminine pronouns "she" and "her," the power and control wheel only addresses the experience of women battered by men. By keeping the focus specifically on that demographic, it is able to address things such as using male privilege that are unique to that demographic.

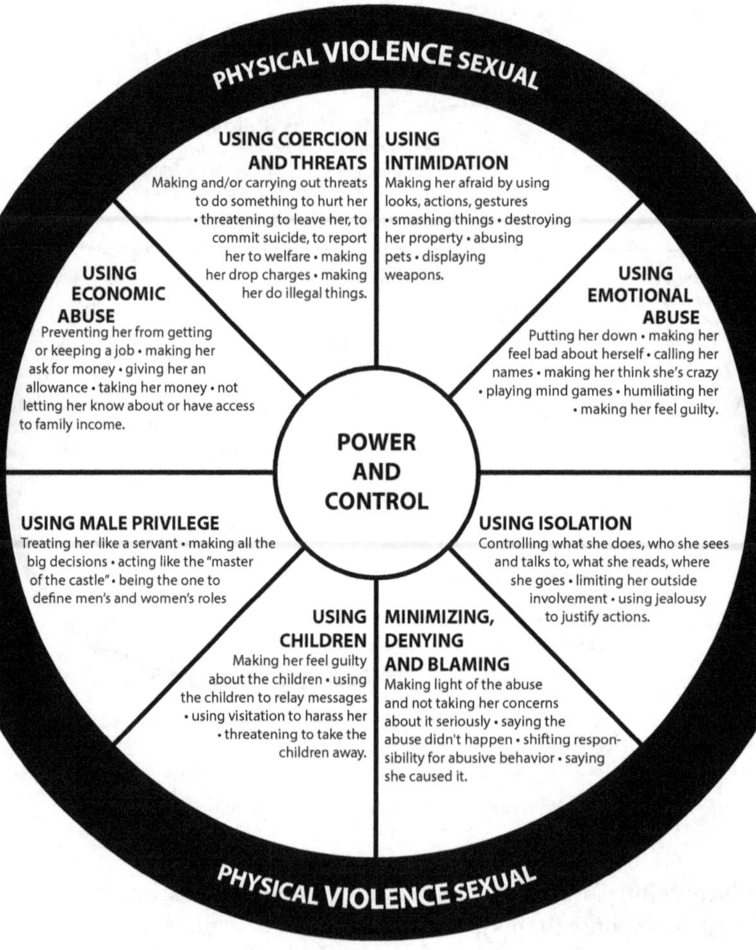

FIGURE 10.2: Power and control wheel.

The significant and widespread impact of Duluth's work is noted by the inclusion of battering—the use of patterned violence and the need for power and control—in the commonly used definitions of domestic violence across all social spheres. For example, the definitions used by the National Coalition of Domestic Violence, the Centers for Disease Control and Prevention, and the U.S. Department of Justice all include a reference to patterned behavior of abuse and violence to maintain power and control over the other person. The power and control wheel, along with Lenore Walker's cycle of abuse theory, are still commonly used together today in police trainings to help explain the dynamics of domestic violence.

Throughout the early 2000s, police departments were regularly receiving training in the dynamics of domestic violence (grounded in Duluth's power and control model and Walker's cycle of violence theory), but they were also becoming frustrated and cynical about domestic violence calls. Police frustrations were connected to several issues such as repeatedly returning to the same house, the lack of prosecution in many of these cases, and the lack of victim cooperation (Horwitz et al., 2011). However, police were also continually expressing that not all domestic violence cases fit the definition of battering, and it was difficult to determine who they should and should not arrest. Police officers noted that most incidents of domestic violence are "situationally ambiguous" and it is not uncommon for both parties to appear as both a potential victim and offender on a given day (Durfee, 2012). Additionally, battering involves an ongoing pattern of verbal, emotional, and physical abuse over a period of time, but criminal law directs police to investigate a specific incident, not a pattern (Stark, 2007). The law does not allow police officers to consider the history of calls or prior incidents of violence when determining if a new crime occurred on a specific day and if there is enough evidence to warrant an arrest (Stark, 2007). Police argued that these issues made it difficult to simultaneously follow preferred/mandatory arrest policies and avoid the unintended outcomes of dual arrests and occasionally arresting female victims of battering (Buzawa et al., 2017).

Recognition of these issues led to two significant shifts in police training and responses. The first shift was training police to understand, identify, and arrest only the **predominant aggressor** and the second was the use of **risk assessments** for future violence and domestic homicide. The predominant aggressor is the individual who is using verbal, emotional, sexual, and physical coercive abuse tactics on an ongoing basis to control and dominate the other person. Learning how to identify which person was the predominate aggressor helped to reduce dual arrests and decreased arrests of victims. In addition, the development of a lethality assessment checklist (Campbell, 2004; Campbell et al., 2003) provided police with a means to identify those cases with the highest likelihood of increased violence and repeat calls for service. The goal was for officers to use the lethality risk assessment checklist during their investigation to connect victims with a high risk of repeat violence and potential homicide with domestic violence victim services in their area.

Although learning to identify the predominant aggressor and use risk assessments helped police in domestic violence calls, police still noted some issues. Specifically, police continued to argue that not all domestic violence calls for service involved battering, and in some cases women were also violent, but their violence did not follow the pattern of battering. Researchers also noted these differences and began investigating the possibility that a variety of types of domestic violence might be present in these cases and that women's use of violence might be different from men's (Pence & Dasgupta, 2006).

In fact, throughout the 1990s and 2000s scholars have engaged in a plethora of research across multiple disciplines including but not limited to psychology, sociology, family studies, and criminology. This research has examined personality characteristics, psychopathology of perpetrators, typologies of batterers based on attachment theory, social learning theory, and conflict within the family (see Wagers, 2012). Much of this work led to a heated political debate regarding the **gender symmetry** versus **gender asymmetry** of domestic violence

(Johnson, 2008; Johnson & Ferraro, 2000) and arguments that some perpetrators need serious therapeutic treatment over simply attending an educational group based on power and control (Babcock, Green & Robie, 2004). Multiple studies scientifically supported both sides of the gender symmetry/asymmetry debate, along with various theoretical perspectives (Wagers, 2005), leaving police officers during that time confused and frustrated.

In the mid 2000s several researchers began examining ways to resolve or make sense of the gender symmetry versus asymmetry debate. For example, Michael Johnson (2008) identified battering as one type of domestic violence he called "intimate terrorism" but argued there were other types of violence he called "situational couple violence," which did not involve battering. Johnson's research, along with psychologists (Babcock, Green & Robie, 2004), has demonstrated that multiple types of violence can occur between intimate partners. This work combined with Evan Stark's (2007) work outlining **coercive control** has shown that domestic violence is very gendered in a variety of ways. Specifically, men and women use different types of violence with different motives and these variations are often connected to larger social cultural issues of patriarchy and inequality referenced by feminist scholars. Although the feminist argument of gender inequality should not be ignored as it explains and addresses battering very well, it fails to explain all types of violence. Therefore, many researchers today recognize the importance of continuing current responses based in Duluth's power and control model to address battering, while incorporating the emerging research regarding other types of violence (Wagers, 2012).

This emerging research is important for law enforcement because it supports their experiential claims that not all domestic violence is the same. It also demonstrates the need to develop different responses or interventions based on the type of violence occurring and the type of victim-offender relationship. Although battering accounts for a large portion of domestic violence calls and has more difficulties, challenges, and consequences compared to some other types of domestic violence calls (Police Executive Research Forum [PERF], 2015), it is inaccurate and ineffective to continue to consider and respond to all domestic violence calls as if they all involve battering. Although more research is needed into the different types of violence, understanding what has already been established and learning how to recognize the various types in a police call is important for developing best practices. Following is a list of the different types of domestic violence or violence between intimate partners with a brief explanation of each (the types and explanations are excerpted from Pence & Dasgupta, 2006).

- **Battering**: An ongoing patterned use of coercion, intimidation, and violence to establish and maintain a relationship of domination and control. It is characterized by one intimate partner systematically utilizing a series and variety of emotional, verbal, physical, and sexual abuse tactics that restricts his or her intimate partner's autonomy. However, physical violence is not always, nor does it have to be, present for the perpetrator to achieve his or her goal or be engaging in battering. The motivation or goal of this violence is to control and oppress the other person. This type of violence typically escalates over time and has a higher likelihood of severe injury and homicide. This is the same type of violence as Michael Johnson's (2008) intimate terrorism.
- **Resistive/reactive violence**: Typically, this type of violence is used by victims of battering and it may or may not meet, in a given instance, the legal requirements of self-defense. The goal of this violence is to escape and/or stop violence that is or is about to be perpetrated against them. It is used as an attempt to establish some type of parity in the relationship or as a means of protection for themselves or a child. This type of violence is present in relationships where battering is occurring but will typically be committed by either the victims of the battering or their

children to protect either the victim or themselves from being beaten. The target of this type of violence is the offender/abuser or who has been typically identified as the predominant aggressor. This is the same type of violence as Michael Johnson's (2008) violent resistance.

- **Situational violence**: This type of violence is distinct from battering and resistive violence because it does not have a pattern or use of a variety of coercive control tactics. The motive is not to dominate or oppress the other person, but resolve the conflict occurring in that moment. It is typically situational and results from an argument or other conflict. Typically, this violence is used in conflict because the individual lacks healthy coping skills or the ability to effectively communicate. It can be difficult to distinguish this type of violence from battering for law enforcement because they intervene in a specific incident of violence and are not always trained in how to identify if the incident is part of a pattern or only situational. A key difference in this type of violence compared to battering is the victim, here, may not be presenting with a generalized fear of his or her partner. This is the same type of violence as Michael Johnson's (2008) situational couple violence.
- **Pathological violence**: Individuals who suffer from mental illness, have physical disorders, neurological damage, or who abuse drugs and alcohol may use physical violence against their intimate partner, other members of their family, or in other areas of their life. Sometimes there is a causal connection between the pathology and the use of violence. Although these individuals may target a specific person such as their spouse, their violence is not typically focused on a particular individual. For example, an alcoholic or drug addict may become belligerent toward the investigating officer or other family members who attempt to intervene. Additionally, even though this type of individual may use violence repeatedly, it is not typically patterned and connected to other types of coercive control, but more in response to a specific situation or connected to their pathology. It can be difficult for police officers to distinguish this type of violence from battering because they may be called to the same residence multiple times for repeat acts of violence.
- **Antisocial violence**: This type of violence is not restricted to a specific partner. This type of violence may be connected to the development of antisocial personality or other antecedents, such as childhood abuse and lack of moral maturity. These individuals are typically violent and abusive in a variety of social settings such as at bars, home, work, sporting events, etc. These individuals typically have little to no understanding of the consequences of their behavior on others and no feelings of remorse or shame.

Although understanding these different types of violence is helpful, it does not mean the categories are mutually exclusive and may not satisfactorily explain all the types of domestic violence police officers encounter. It is important to note that regardless of the type of violence, it is harmful and traumatic to the victim, it is a crime, and police need to intervene and make arrests. Additionally, the intended goal is for police to use this knowledge to enhance investigations and develop better interventions.

Recommendations and Best Practices

There is a growing awareness that law enforcement policies and interventions need to evolve and incorporate the scientific knowledge gained over the past 40 years to become more effective at domestic violence response (PERF, 2015). This does not mean we should stop intervening, arresting, and using current domestic violence policies. It simply means that law enforcement domestic violence policies and programs need to become more differentiated and less one size fits all. To that end, police need to recognize that violence between intimate partners is different from other types of family violence and that within intimate partner violence there are variations. These variations affect the potential risk for future violence as well as officer safety and may require different interventions. For example, individuals who engage in battering need consequences but also need programs that address gendered belief systems, but individuals engaging in pathological violence need treatment programs that address their pathology. Additionally, those engaging in resistive violence need protection from the battering and supportive resources. However, in cases of situational violence, both parties need programs to learn new behavioral coping mechanisms and/or anger management counseling. Individuals using antisocial violence are the least responsive to any type of treatment and need harsher consequences (Pence & Dasgupta, 2006).

Today, there are several programs and best practice recommendations for law enforcement, which have demonstrated some effectiveness in reducing and preventing domestic violence. For example, research consistently shows that using a coordinated community response model is the most effective response (Buzawa et al., 2017). This model requires an interagency approach that brings social service interventions and the justice system together around the primary goal to protect victims from further abuse and to hold offenders accountable. It uses empirically tested intervention strategies that build safety and accountability into all elements of the infrastructure for processing domestic violence cases. It has well-defined methods of interagency cooperation guided by advocacy programs. Good examples of traditional and effective programs based on coordinated community response models are Duluth's DAIP model, the lethality assessment program (LAP) (2018), and family justice centers (Alliance for Hope International, 2018).

Additionally, a new model utilizing a focused deterrence strategy has demonstrated some effectiveness at reducing domestic violence incidents (Sechrist & Weil, 2018). This is a criminological approach based on deterrence theory, which requires punishment to be swift and fit the crime. Focused deterrence as a policing strategy is based on the premise that most serious crime is committed by repeat offenders, and it focuses on the actions and motives of the individual engaging in the criminal act. Focused deterrence was originally used to address issues of gang and drug offenders, but an argument has been made that domestic violence offenders share similar traits and can be used to reduce domestic violence (Saul & Wagers, 2017; Sechrist & Weil, 2018). Focused deterrence programs are similar to the DAIP, LAP, and family justice centers because they utilize a form of community coordinated response. However, they differ because the focus of the police department is primarily on the offender, and oversight of the offender is conducted by the police department, beginning with the initial call for service regardless of the court process. Therefore, punishment and connection to services is swift and victims are provided some additional safety because the police are monitoring the offender immediately (Saul & Wagers, 2017).

In addition to these program models, research shows that police need specific and continuous training on how to investigate domestic violence calls to gather more evidence and distinguish battering from other types of violence (Pence & Dasgupta, 2006). Responding officers need to look for and develop as much physical evidence as possible, even when the incident may at first appear to be isolated. For example, police today are trained to follow up with victims after several days to see if bruises are present and photograph the injuries as evidence. Another area requiring further training is how to investigate for strangulation, which is now a separate criminal statute in many states carrying a felony charge (Training Institute on Strangulation Prevention, 2018). In addition to using typical investigatory skills and training, police officers should consider a few broad questions: Who is doing what to whom? What is the motive? What is the impact? And, Is this an isolated incident or is there a pattern of coercive control (even if only verbal and emotional control)? Lastly, police should work collaboratively with domestic violence advocates and other agencies to connect both victims and offenders to services even in calls that do not reach the level of a crime but demonstrate the potential for battering or risk of future violence.

In addition to domestic violence programs and investigation tactics, police should always consider officer safety when developing domestic violence policies. Regardless of the type of violence occurring in a domestic violence call or the parties involved, these calls are dangerous and have the propensity for fatal escalation. Based on current empirical studies (Breul & Keith, 2016), it is recommended that all police departments enact policies with the following recommendations in mind for officer safety:

- DV calls need to be treated with the utmost caution.
- The responding officers need to be provided with full and accurate information. Dispatch personnel need to remain on the call until officers arrive on scene and need to collect and communicate important information.
- Officers must have adequate manpower. At any given time, enough officers need to be on shift to ensure at least two officers can be sent to DV calls and more can respond if needed.
- Information and knowledge are constantly changing. Officers need ongoing yearly training to include both safety and how to coordinate, communicate, and act in concert.
- Always send and have at least two officers on scene.

Conclusion

Police are the gatekeepers to the criminal justice system and part of the front line to prevent future acts of domestic violence and all forms of family violence. In many cases they are the first responders to these situations and play a key role in intervening and connecting perpetrators and victims to treatment and support systems. For police departments to develop and implement effective police responses to domestic violence, they need continuous training that includes updates on the latest research and best practices. The policies and intervention programs police departments develop, along with the decisions individual officers make to either arrest or refer perpetrators and victims, can have profound effects on the future prevention of domestic violence.

Key Terms

antisocial violence: A type of violence arising from a personality disorder that is typically used toward a variety of individuals across multiple social settings.

battering: An ongoing patterned use of coercion, intimidation, tactics of control, and violence for the purpose of maintaining a relationship of dominance over an intimate partner.

coercive control: A concept developed by Evan Stark that refers to abuse as a strategic course of oppressive behavior designed to expand gender-based privilege by using a regime of domination that includes a variety of verbal, emotional, sexual, and physical violence.

domestic violence: A pattern of violent or aggressive behaviors used by an individual to maintain power and control over his or her intimate partner. The behaviors can be minor or severe and include verbal, emotional, sexual, or physical abuse and aggression. The intimate relationship can include those who are married, dating, living together as if a family, and/or have a child in common. The term "intimate partner violence" is also used and has the same meaning.

dual arrest: Both the victim and offender in a domestic violence case are arrested during the same incident.

family violence: A term used to describe acts of verbal, emotional, sexual, and physical abuse and aggression that occur among various types of family relationships other than intimate partners, such as between siblings, cousins, and children toward their parents, etc.

gender asymmetry: A political argument that females are disproportionately victims of domestic violence and males are disproportionately perpetrators of domestic violence.

gender symmetry: A political argument that males and females both commit acts of violence and are victims of violence at the same rate.

intimate partner violence: A pattern of violent or aggressive behaviors used by an individual to maintain power and control over his or her intimate partner. The behaviors can be minor or severe and include verbal, emotional, sexual, or physical abuse and aggression. The intimate relationship can include those who are married, dating, living together as if a family, and/or have a child in common. The term "domestic violence" is also used and has the same meaning.

mandatory arrest: Either a state law or police department policy that instructs officers that they must make an arrest in cases of domestic violence when they have probable cause (also known as preferred arrest).

pathological violence: A type of violence that arises from substance abuse, mental illness, neurological damage, or a physical disorder. It can be directed toward a specific person or other individuals.

predominant aggressor: An individual who is using verbal, emotional, sexual, and physical coercive and abuse tactics on an ongoing basis to control and dominate the other person.

probable cause: A level of evidence present that leads a reasonable person to conclude that a crime was committed and that a specific person committed it. It is a legal standard of proof that allows officers to either obtain an arrest warrant or, in some cases allowed by law, make a warrantless arrest.

resistive/reactive violence: A type of violence that is used by a victim of battering to resist or retaliate from abuse to either protect themselves or to establish some equality in the relationship.

risk assessments: Checklist tools supported by scientific research used by police and advocates to determine the likelihood of repeat violence and the potential for homicide in domestic violence cases.

situational violence: A type of violence that typically arises from a situational conflict and is used to achieve a goal in that particular conflict. It has no pattern of control and does not typically escalate over time.

spouse abuse: Early term used in the 1970s to describe violence that occurred between a husband and a wife. Today the term "intimate partner violence" or "domestic violence" is used in its place.

warrantless arrest: A type of arrest that allows a police officer to make an arrest in a misdemeanor domestic violence case or felony case without obtaining a warrant from a judge.

wife abuse: Early term used in the 1970s to describe violence women were experiencing at the hands of their husbands. Today the term "intimate partner violence" or "domestic violence" is used in its place.

Discussion Questions

- What do you think about the policing challenges posed in domestic violence after reading the chapter?
- What does the term "warrantless arrest" mean and why is it so important to policing domestic violence?
- What are the pros and cons to using preferred/mandatory arrest policies in cases of domestic violence?
- Explain the similarities and differences in family violence, domestic violence, and wife abuse.
- Imagine you are a new police chief and your city has a higher rate of domestic violence compared to most other cities in your state. What would you do to address this problem?
- Imagine you are a new police captain and you were told to rewrite and update your department's domestic violence policy. Your department is in a mid-sized city and domestic violence calls account for about 40% of your department's calls for service. The current domestic violence policy in use was last revised in 1999. What are the best practices you think should be included in the updated domestic violence policy?
- Here is a common type of domestic violence case scenario. Read through the scenario and then answer the questions that follow.

Tim and Jane have been a couple for several years and have been living together for the past year. They are at Jane's parents' house for dinner. Tim hates going to Jane's parents' house because he cannot stand the way Jane's dad treats her mother and he can't stand how much Jane drinks. Shortly after they arrive at the house, Jane's mom is in the kitchen cooking their dinner. Jane's father walks into the kitchen and starts berating Jane's mother. He is calling her names, telling her how she can't cook and is using his body to push her into the oven and knock her off balance. Tim observes Jane's dad lift his hand and make several jerking movements to imitate he may backhand Jane's mom in the face. Jane's mom twitches away and appears scared. She tries to keep cooking, but Jane's dad intentionally knocks over the pot of sauce onto the kitchen floor. He yells at Jane's mom and calls her clumsy and says she is an idiot. She says she is sorry she is so incompetent but will have dinner ready soon. He orders her to clean it up, start over, and get it right this time. Jane's mom starts cleaning up the mess and then starts the sauce over. As Jane's dad walks out of the kitchen he says to Tim, "See you have to keep them in line and show them who is in charge."

As Jane's father sits on the couch, Jane starts drinking heavily, which she always does when she is at her parents' house. A couple hours go by and Tim notices Jane is getting drunk and starting to get loud. Then Jane's dad goes back into the kitchen and starts berating Jane's mom again about dinner. He is yelling at her, saying how incompetent she is and corners her against a wall. He makes a fist, pulls his hand back and tells her she knows what happens when she doesn't get dinner right. Tim watches Jane come running into the kitchen yelling at her Dad to stop. As Jane enters the kitchen she grabs a pan from the counter and hits her father over the head. He falls to the kitchen floor unconscious and Jane's mother slumps on the floor crying. Tim starts to call 911 and Jane forcefully grabs the phone from his hand. Jane is yelling at Tim not to call anyone when the police knock on the front door.

- If you were the investigating officer who would you arrest and why?
- Which of the five different types of violence (battering, resistive, situational, pathological, and antisocial) occurred in this scene and who engaged in which ones? Explain your response.
- Is there a predominate aggressor in this scenario? Explain your response.

References

Alliance for Hope International. (2018). *About family justice centers*. Retrieved from https://www.familyjusticecenter.org/affiliated-centers/family-justice-centers-2/

Babcock, J. C., Green, C. E., & Robie, C. (2004). Does batterer treatment work? A meta-analytic review of domestic violence treatment. *Clinical Psychology Review, 23*(8), 1023–1053.

Barata, P., & Senn. C. Y. (2003). When two fields collide: An examination of the assumptions of social science research and law within the domain of domestic violence. *Trauma, Violence, & Abuse, 4*(1), 3–21.

Brandl, S. G. (2018). *Police in America*. Thousand Oaks, CA: SAGE.

Breul, N., & Keith, M. (2016). Deadly calls and fatal encounters. Washington, DC: Department of Justice. Office of Community Oriented Policing Services.

Buzawa, E. S., Buzawa, C. G., & Stark, E. D. (2017). *Responding to domestic violence: The integration of criminal justice and human services*. Thousand Oaks, CA: SAGE.

Campbell, J. (2004). Helping women understand their risk in situation of intimate partner violence. *Journal of Interpersonal Violence, 19*(12), 1464–1477.

Campbell, J. C., Webster, D., Koziol-Mclain, J., Block, C. R., Campbell, D., Curry, M. A, … & Wilt, S. A. (2003). Assessing risk factors for intimate partner violence. *National Institute of Justice Journal, 250*, 14–19.

Dobash, R. E., & Dobash, R. P. (1979). *Violence against wives*. New York, NY: Free Press.

Durfee, A. (2012). Situational ambiguity and gendered patterns of arrest for intimate partner violence. *Violence Against Women, 18*(1), 64–84.

Fagan, J. (1996). The criminalization of domestic violence: Promises and limits (Report no. NCJ 157641). *National Institute of Justice.* Washington, DC: U.S. Department of Justice. Retrieved from https://www.ncjrs.gov/pdffiles/crimdom.pdf

Hall, R. J. (2014). Feminist strategies to end violence against women. In R. B. & W. Harcourt (Eds.), *The Oxford Handbook of Transnational Feminist Movements.* New York, NY: Oxford. Retrieved from http://www.oxfordhandbooks.com/view/10.1093/oxfordhb/9780199943494.001.0001/oxfordhb-9780199943494-e-005

Harper, S. & Gover, A. R. (in press). One step forward, two steps back: The criminal justice response to intimate partner violence. In *The Handbook on Interpersonal Violence Across the Lifespan* (Vol 2.). New York, NY: Springer.

Hirschel, D. (2008). Domestic violence cases: What research shows about arrest and dual arrest rates. *National Criminal Justice Reference Service.* Retrieved from https://www.ncjrs.gov/App/Publications/abstract.aspx?ID=244581

Horwitz, S. H., Mitchell, D., LaRussa-Trott, M., Santiago, L., Pearson, J., Skiff, D. M., & Cerulli, C. (2011). An inside view of police officers' experience with domestic violence. *Journal of Family Violence, 26,* 617–625.

Houston, C. (2014). How feminist theory became (criminal) law: Tracing the path to mandatory criminal intervention in domestic violence cases. *Michigan Journal of Gender and Law, 21*(2), 217–272.

International Association Chiefs of Police. (2018). *Need to know ... domestic violence.* Retrieved from http://www.theiacp.org/model-policy/wp-content/uploads/sites/6/2018/03/DomesticViolenceNeedtoKnow2018.pdf

Johnson, M. P. (2008). *A typology of domestic violence: Intimate terrorism, violent resistance, and situational couple violence.* Lebanon, NH: Northeastern University Press.

Johnson, M. P., & Ferraro, K. J. (2000). Research on domestic violence in the 1990s: Making distinctions. *Journal of Marriage and the Family, 62*(4), 948–963.

Kline, R. (2009). Practical implication of current domestic violence research: For law enforcement, prosecutors and judges. Retrieved from https://www.ncjrs.gov/pdffiles1/nij/225722.pdf

Lee, J., Zhang, Y., & Hoover, L. (2013). Police response to domestic violence: Multilever factors of arrest decision. *Policing and International Journal of Policing Strategies & Management, 36*(1), 157–174.

Lethality Assessment Program (LAP). (2018). *How LAP works.* Retrieved from https://lethalityassessmentprogram.org/about-lap/how-lap-works/

Pence, E., & Dasgupata, S. D. (2006). Re-examining battering': Are all acts of violence against intimate partners the same? *Praxis International.* Retrieved from http://www.ncdsv.org/images/Praxis_ReexaminingBattering_June2006.pdf

Pence, E., & Paymar, M. (1993). *Education groups for men who batter: The Duluth model.* New York, NY: Springer.

Police Executive Research Forum (PERF). (2015). Police improve response to domestic violence, but abuse often remains the "hidden crime.' *Subject to Debate, 29(1).* Retrieved from http://www.policeforum.org/assets/docs/Subject_to_Debate/Debate2015/debate_2015_janfeb.pdf

Saul, B. & Wagers, S. M. (2017). Focused deterrence: Looking to past success to determine future uses. *The Police Chief* (July 2017): 38–41.

Sechrist, S. M., & Weil, J. D. (2018). Assessing the impact of a focused deterrence strategy to combat domestic violence. *Violence Against Women, 24*(3), 243–265.

Sherman, L. W., & Berk, R. A. (1984). The specific deterrent effects of arrest for domestic assault. *American Sociological Review, 49*(2), 261–272.

Stark, E. (2007). *Coercive control: How men entrap women in personal life*: Oxford, NY: Oxford University Press.

Straus, M. A., & Gelles, R. J. (Eds.) (1990). *Physical violence in American families: Risk factors and adaptations to violence in families.* New Brunswick, NJ: Transaction.
Training Institute on Strangulation Prevention. (2018). *Investigating domestic violence strangulation*. Retrieved from https://www.strangulationtraininginstitute.com/investigating-domestic-violence-strangulation/
Wagers, S. M. (2005). *Differences in frequency and severity of intimate terrorism across genders: A test of Johnson's theory* (Master's thesis). Retrieved from Scholar Commons University of South Florida.
Wagers, S. M. (2012). *Deconstructing the "power and control motive": Developing and assessing the measurability of internal power* (Doctoral dissertation). Retrieved from https://scholarcommons.usf.edu/cgi/viewcontent.cgi?referer=&httpsredir=1&article=5444&context=etd
Wagers, S. M. (2015). Deconstructing the "power and control motive": Moving beyond a unidimensional view of power in domestic violence theory. *Partner Abuse, 6*(2), 230–242.
Wagers, S. M., Pate, M., & Brinkley, A. (2017). Evidence-based best practices for batterer intervention programs: A report from the field on the realities and challenges facing BIPs today. *Partner Abuse, 8*(4), 409–428.
Walker, L. (1979). *The battered woman*. New York, NY: Harper & Row.

CHAPTER 11

Beyond Community-Oriented Policing

Injecting Humanism Into Our Efforts to Improve Police Community Relations

By Patrick J. Solar

Opening Questions

Answer the following question before reading this chapter:

> What do you know about community-oriented policing prior to reading this chapter?

Answer the following question while reading the chapter:

> What are some concepts from the chapter that stand out to you? Why do you think they are important?

Introduction

Community-oriented policing has been the focus of efforts to reform law enforcement for over 30 years, yet one would be hard pressed to discover a consensus on exactly what it means or whether it is actually effective in reducing crime. The ambiguity of the term, like the policing function itself, begs for a more specific articulation of the attitudes, behaviors, and assumptions that make community-oriented policing such an attractive concept. The purpose of this chapter is to place community-oriented policing into its historical context and identify a more precise path forward.

A Brief History of American Policing

In the wake of the professional policing era championed by the likes of August Vollmer[1], O.W. Wilson[2], and William Parker[3] came a new philosophy of policing, one that was "community oriented." Whereas a professional police agency adheres to professional standards based on a continuously evolving body of knowledge and best practices, the community-oriented philosophy stresses the need to build and maintain community relationships.

A window of opportunity for change presented itself in the late 1980s as the United States wrestled with a growing and frightening violent crime problem. The professional policing model, pejoratively referred to as the "traditional" policing model, was thought inadequate for combatting the fear this drug abuse–driven crime problem was creating in the urban centers.

Understanding where we have been in policing philosophy offers insight into how the craft could advance to meet current demands.

The Past

The American police officer of the 19th century owed his allegiance to the local political power structure, in the urban centers that would be the ward-boss. New officers were handed a badge and sent out on patrol. They wore a standard uniform that they purchased themselves and were armed, depending on if they owned a firearm. They received little training beyond advice provided by veteran officers and perhaps a rule book, but the wise officer soon learned that his or her survival on the street depended greatly on his or her ability to integrate with the citizens with whom he or she interacted. There was no effective supervision, communication, or backup, so these officers, working alone, depended on the good will of community members to assist them should the need arise.

The absence of professional standards for selection and training, the lack of quality supervision, and the need to cultivate strong ties with certain members of the community to retain the job took its toll on the reputation of the American police in the late 19th century. Opportunities for graft and corruption were abundant in America, and the *dark side* of policing emerged as a dominant force. Subcultural pressures were strong. This was true not only for those new officers who simply wished to be accepted into the police subculture.

---

1 Widely recognized as the "father of modern law enforcement" Vollmer reformed the Berkley California police department in an effort to elevate policing beyond its amateurish, corrupt, and haphazard reputation. He required his officers to attain college degrees and persuaded the university to teach criminal justice in a successful effort to advance policing as a profession. Vollmer also established one of the first crime laboratories that sought to inject scientific methods into the investigation of crime.

2 Wilson was a protégé of Vollmer and went on to lead police agencies, including the city of Chicago where he developed and advanced modern administrative management theory, as applied to police organizations. He authored one of the first text books on police administration and advocated for the professionalization of law enforcement and police management.

3 William Parker served the Los Angeles police department beginning in 1927, rising to head that department. He is credited with transforming the LAPD into a world-renowned, professional law enforcement agency. He advocated for increased efficiency in police operations such as rapid response to calls for service, discipline, and strict adherence to standards of professionalism.

There was also pressure to conform with even unlawful behavioral norms under the threat of being ostracized from the group. These pressures were, and still are, powerful motivators in American policing. There were countless opportunities to extort money, protect unlawful enterprises, and peddle the power and authority of the police to the highest bidder. Not all officers were corrupt, but the freedom of the job and the lure of easy money provided them with powerful incentives for corruption. Police officers were part of the political machinery, reinforcing the will of the dominant political actors as opposed to impartial criminal justice officials (Cox, Marchinonna, & Fitch, 2017).

The Birth of Professional Policing

A reform effort emerged in the early 20th century, led by police chiefs, that was directed at "professionalizing" the police service in the United States. Because of the nature of police work, external reform efforts are usually ineffective; changing the police is most effectively accomplished when support for needed change is recognized and accepted by those who are actually engaged in the work (Bayley, 1994). The idea of professionalization was attractive to officers and police leaders due to the prestige the term implies, even though the commitment to such a concept was not likely to have been well understood at the time.[4]

Under the leadership of progressive police chiefs, most notably August Vollmer[5], the characteristics of the professional police agency began to take shape. These characteristics included first the recognition of police officers as experts in the detection, investigation, and prevention of crime; the ability to bring their knowledge and training to bear on crime problems was critical. Second, the agency was insulated from politics; political influence over the **discretion** of officers was minimized or eliminated. Chiefs were appointed based on merit and were given employment contracts that extended beyond the tenure of the elected chief executive of the municipality. Third, the rules that governed police operations were based on best practices and generally accepted norms for the function. They were not crafted with regard to the priorities and wishes of local elected officials. Fourth, efficiency of operation governed management practices. Officer deployment and work priorities were not based on arbitrary standards or past practices. Rather, data drove decisions on where to assign officers and what cases to work (Uchida, 2015).

Vollmer articulated a new vision for the police as a craft free of political influence committed to the betterment of society, not just the prevention of crime. The agenda included organizational reform to eliminate patronage, raising selection standards and adopting modern management technology. The modern *professional* police organization

---

4 A professional is characterized as someone who is engaged in the practice of conforming to the technical and ethical standards of a recognized "profession." This involves a commitment to education, lifelong learning, behaviors that are in compliance with commonly accepted standards, and the practice of contributing to the body of knowledge, among others. Police officers who view themselves as professionals are likely to put forth a more limited behavioral definition such as exhibiting a courteous, conscientious, and generally businesslike demeanor in the workplace and in interactions with the client(s) (Merriam-Webster, n.d.).

5 August Volmer was chief of the Berkley California police department in the 1920s. He stressed the need for professionalism based on credentials such as a college education. He was the first chief to institute intelligence, psychiatric and neurological testing for police applicants as well as vehicle patrol and forensic investigation.

is a centralized, authoritarian, bureaucracy focused on crime control as opposed to social service. (Walker, 1998)

The move toward policing professionalism in America also had an unexpected side effect. As more and more officers began to view themselves as "professionals," they drew back into themselves. Engaging with the community became an "unprofessional" endeavor as the trained police officers were viewed as the experts in crime control where the citizen had no role other than prompt crime reporting. The reformers' insistence on limiting the police function to crime and disorder gave officers the impression that calls for service that did not involve crime or a violation of the law were not their job.

At the same time, the public was expecting more from its police as the result of technical innovations, such as more efficient administrative practices, motorized patrol, and rapid response to calls for service, leading to more arrests and less crime. Conflict arose over the role of the police, with the police viewing themselves as crime fighters and the public demanding not only crime reduction but social services. This became an excuse for the police to hunker down in their crime-fighting image and to disengage from the communities that they served; even into the 1980s police chiefs could be heard to say "Stop trying to council those kids. Find something to arrest them for. We are not social workers!" (A statement made by the author's first chief).

Advancing the Idea of Community-Oriented Policing

The professional model of policing had limitations that undermined the trust and legitimacy of the police in the eyes of many groups. In the wake of the riots of the 1960s and 1970s, and the drastically increasing crime rates of the 1980s, another reform movement emerged with the goal to bring the police back to their roots in terms of community engagement. This was a philosophic idea that led to a new paradigm that put forth the idea the police cannot and should not be separate from the communities they serve.

The professional model allowed officers to drive into work from the suburbs, work their shift, and then leave, maintaining "professional" separation from their customers and clients. In contrast, the community-oriented philosophy promoted community linkages. If officers were not required to live where they worked, then they were to be assigned fixed geographical areas or beats where they worked every day in the hope that positive interaction and community relationships would develop. In general, it was thought that returning to an earlier era of community partnership and engagement would be effective in combating a growing crime problem.

Community-oriented policing also called for organizational reforms such as flattening the bureaucracy and allowing officers to engage in creative practices to combat crime problems (i.e., **problem-oriented policing**) (Goldstein, 1990). The idea that the police should be more proactive in response to potential crime problems was supported by the theory of **broken windows** whereby the police could head off serious crime problems by paying more attention to the little things such as nuisance violations, pan-handling, loitering, and indifference to quality-of-life issues that create the conditions that lead to more serious crime (Kelling & Wilson, 1982).

New and innovative ideas and programs developed as a result of this wave of reform. Putting officers back on foot walking beats in primarily downtown areas was thought to bring them closer to the community. Getting cops out of their cars was facilitated through programs such as walk and talk, cops in the schools, neighborhood substations, youth athletic programs, and a host of other innovations that were aimed at building better relationships with the community. Bayley (1994) outlined three primary dimensions of this effort:

- Engaging and interacting with the community
- Solving community problems
- Adapting internal elements of the organization to support these new strategies (i.e., organizational re-design)

The problem with this new philosophy is that it used the same professionally minded cops to employ it, most of whom signed up as crime fighters, not social workers with badges.

Many of the fundamental beliefs about how to combat crime such as rapid response and preventative patrol were cast in doubt by the community-oriented model due to their reactive nature. What was needed was a more proactive approach that targets potential crime problems and attacks them at their source.

Unknowingly, many of those intent on reforming the police today, under the banner of community-oriented policing, advocate for the same local control that led to some of the worst examples of governmental corruption, graft, and abuse during the political years. They attack the professional model of policing as the enemy of the kind of policing promoted by Sir Robert Peel, but the two policing models are not incompatible; they can be integrated and made complimentary if we consider what it takes to be truly community oriented.

Addressing the Ambiguities and Clarifying the Mission

In 1829, sir Robert Peel laid down his principles of policing. What many fail to grasp today is that these principles were crafted in an environment that was hostile to the policing function; people in London were highly resistive to a centralized police force. Peel's mission was to sell the idea of the police to a citizenry that had no interest in having their freedoms curtailed by a body of men reminiscent of an occupying military force, hence his first principle:

> The basic mission for which police exist is to prevent crime and disorder. (Dempsey & Forst, 2014, p. 7)

Under the ambiguity of community-oriented policing and the common rhetoric today, one can assume that the mission of the police is to build trust and relationships. What Peel put forth 190 years ago is still true today; the first mission is controlling crime and disorder, but as any experienced police officer knows, this is much easier to accomplish when the police, especially individual officers, enjoy a positive relationship with the people they serve. *Building trust and legitimacy is a means to the end of controlling crime, not an end in itself.*

Peel went on to outline other policing principles. As a testament to his mission of convincing a reluctant and suspicious population of the necessity of having police,[6] he put forth another principle that has proven particularly problematic today.

---

6 What exactly were the citizens of London suspicious of? The expanding power of government. This was even more of a concern in the United States. So much so that our Constitution struggled for ratification until the founders included the Bill of Rights to specifically *limit* the power of the federal government. Our Constitution is a *power-limiting* mechanism, not an enabling one.

> Police, at all times, should maintain a relationship with the public that gives reality to the historic tradition that the police are the public and the public are the police, the police being only members of the public who are paid to give full time attention to the duties which are incumbent on every citizen in the interests of community welfare and existence. (Dempsey & Forst, 2014, p. 7)

The idea that the police are the public and the public are the police may have been appropriate and useful in 1829 when people were more accepting of their societal duties. The alternative to an organized police force was the watch-and-ward system where every citizen had the responsibility for standing his or her watch to keep the community safe. Today, policing has evolved into a craft that is profoundly different than the amateurish practices of the 19th century watch-and-ward system. People have grown used to having a force of professionally trained men and women available to respond to all manner of situations and complaints ranging from mass shootings to teenage students refusing to surrender their cell phones in class.

The police are *absolutely not* the public. Law enforcement officers have been entrusted with authority no other citizens may exercise. As such, they are held to account for that authority in such a way as to alienate them, the police, from the citizens that they police through no fault of their own. To charge the police today with the responsibility to build trust and legitimacy in an environment in which the very nature of governmental authority is challenged on a daily basis is unwise.

The real meaning of community-oriented policing for the police is being responsive to the needs of the communities that they serve. For the individual police officer, the heart of any community-oriented effort is a willingness to be held accountable to that community under the law, demonstrating respect for each individual at all times, being sensitive to the needs of individuals, displaying empathy, and exercising compassion whenever possible.

The Real Meaning of Being "Community Oriented"

One of the primary driving forces of the early movement toward community-oriented policing was its promise of transforming the police from a purely reactive entity under the professional-traditional-policing model to a proactive force. The selling point was that the police were no longer going to wait for crime to occur; they were going to seek out and attack underlying crime problems before they could undermine community life. The mechanism that could be used to facilitate this transformation was knows as problem-solving or problem-oriented policing (Goldstein, 1990).

The concept of community-oriented policing included the implementation of problem-solving techniques such as scanning, analysis, response, and assessment, or **the SARA method**. However, given the ambiguous nature of the policing function, implementation of such a systematic and rational process for dealing with the everyday calls for service is problematic.

Police officers, by and large, are not analysts; they deal with calls for service as problems demanding solutions then and there. The broken windows approach was much easier to grasp and actually proved effective as one of the best crime-fighting strategies (Bratton, 2015; Kelling & Wilson, 1982). But like most good things, when taken to the extreme, new problems arise; in this case the downside is the impact of aggressive law enforcement tactics on minority communities (New York City Department of Investigation, 2016).

Being community oriented means that the police actively seek out input and feedback from the community, not just the vocal elite or activists, but the whole community, with the realization that there are many different and overlapping communities that make up the whole.

Individual officers must no longer view their role as crime-fighting warriors; they must view themselves as servants spending their free time seeking new and innovative ways to provide value in the neighborhoods that they police.

Leadership in the community-oriented agency actively seeks out mechanisms to reward the kinds of officer behavior that support the service mind-set. Recognition and reward can come in the form of officer performance appraisal systems that encourage the professional development of officers along these lines, promotional processes that support "wise"[7] policing, as well as less formal actions and rewards that are sometimes as simple as a sincere "well done."

Slowly the organizational culture will shift away from the much-maligned warrior mindset to something that more closely resembles what we collectively want from our police. All that is required from police leaders is consistency and gentle pressure relentlessly applied.

The skills that need to be sought after in police recruits and developed and rewarded within the police organization are known as human relations skills. The basis of wise, community-oriented policing are the same skills and abilities that have defined highly effective individuals and organizations in the private sector for years. The foundation of these skills is communication.

Communication and Rapport

The ability to communicate effectively relates to both the *choice* of words used and *how* the words are used. Choice of words not only facilitates understanding, but it also communicates to others how they are viewed, their relative importance, and individual self-concepts and attitudes. For example, the use of highly technical language when conversing with a college professor may be expected, but in a discussion with a significant other, one may use less technical language, as the goal is to help him or her understand what has been learned in college.

On the other hand, one may make the choice to use a certain kind of language because of a wish to communicate superiority or inferiority to others to facilitate rapport. The choice of communication strategy is always situational and dependent on location and surroundings and the relationship between the individuals. The goal of interpersonal communication is rapport, the linkage that develops between people that forms the basis of their relationship.

Rapport

Rapport can be described as a harmonious and reciprocal mini relationship between individuals or an individual and a group. It takes the form of a connection or link between parties who are in sync with each other. Most individuals are familiar with the phrase "it's not what you say; it's how you say it." Such a statement may be an indication of the lack of rapport or the lack of acceptance of the message, or it may be an indication that a specific message was made perfectly clear, depending on the situation.

---

7 "Wise" policing is smart policing. Wise officers do not shy away from the need to exert their authority when necessary, but they do so judiciously with the full realization that in America, exerting governmental authority inevitably generates citizen resentment.

Gaining rapport with another person can be hard work. It begins with the goal to establish commonality, to communicate likeness, and to minimize perceptions of dissimilarity. In a diverse society, this can mean a heightened level of awareness and complete control over one's bias, prejudice, and emotions. Since nonverbal communication is critical to interpersonal relations, one wrong move can destroy even the most skillful attempts to gain rapport. The goal for a police officer is to seek similarity. People like people who are like themselves, and police officers are automatically not like other people. *Anything that the officer can do to minimize this dis-similarity is a positive step toward rapport.*

Threats to a Community Orientation

The typical "cop on the beat" views him- or herself as a law enforcer; the reality, however, is that they exist to maintain order, sometimes by enforcing the law (Solar, 2015). "Police typically envision their role as enforcers[;] making arrests is paramount. They tend to view other activities as unimportant and a hindrance on their crime fighting ability. They avoid tasks perceived as non-essential" (Trojanowicz, Kappeler, & Gaines, 2002).

The way we view ourselves determines how we interact toward others. This can be determined simply by how we choose to dress. When given a choice, a police officer may select a range of dress and accouterments that can range from full battlefield dress uniforms (BDUs) to a suit and tie. What do these choices say about how officers view themselves and their role in the community? What choices should officers make if they are truly community oriented?

These choices are often influenced by the police subculture, as opposed to what may even be in the best interests of community-oriented officers. The police subculture presents other problems that can hinder an officer's ability to gain rapport. Law enforcement demands strict adherence to procedure over the needs of individuals. However, given that the majority of what the police do does not involve law enforcement and legal mandates, there is certainly room for compassion (Alexander, 2011).

Humanistic Policing as a Path Forward

The law enforcement function can have the impact of dehumanizing police officers. There are both subtle and not-so-subtle pressures within this function and within the police subculture that sometimes allows officers to step beyond what would be considered acceptable moral boundaries.

Reports involving officers justifiably killing unarmed individuals are accepted under the law as reasonable; the law provides the rationalization for such action. Through training and socialization into the law enforcement culture, police officers accept the law as the primary source of moral guidance. Society invests police officers, out of necessity, with the discretion to use deadly force, and it collectively expects them to do so when it is legally justified. When officers are not charged with crimes for their actions, it is not a failure of the legal system. The fact that these kinds of events occur in the first place is an indication of a failure elsewhere, perhaps in the very fabric of our society, because as a source of moral guidance, the law is woefully inadequate (Bittner, 1970).

Policing is a people business; finding clues to increasing the effectiveness of the modern police officer in terms of building better relationships and trust can be found in the field of human relations.

Human Relations

Human relations can be defined as the study of human behavior, including an examination of why self-image, beliefs, attitudes, prejudices, and bias sometimes cause problems in professional and personal contacts and relationships. For the police officer, competency rests in the understanding that all productive work is done through relationships. The very first relationship that needs to be cultivated is with the self, then the particular individuals one relates to, and then the groups with which individuals associate.

Police agencies hire individuals for particular competences that the agency feels are important to the organization. What many are realizing, however, is that effective policing depends on human relation skills; technical competency cannot be separated from the individual's particular characteristics or attributes. The total person concept relates to the understanding that an individual's characteristics, skills, attitudes, self-awareness, and values are interrelated and interdependent. When a department hires someone, it hires the total package or *total person.* Factors that influence an individual's human relation skills include communication (internally and externally), self-awareness, self-acceptance (worth), motivation, trust, self-disclosure, and conflict resolution (conflict management) (Reece, 2014).

Applying Humanism to the Police Organization

Accepting people with understanding and compassion begins within the police organization itself. Leadership need not give up its right to manage the enterprise to facilitate an organizational culture that is based on mutual respect. Once the agency internalizes this concept, it is natural to assume that it will filter down to the rank and file in terms of its interactions with community members.

The Tactic of Respect

Emotionally intelligent individuals who practice human relations skills understand that they have a choice in how to respond to others. They can choose to be rude, condescending, and abusive, or they can choose unconditional respect. Thinking individuals recognize that the former will likely result in dysfunctional outcomes, but the latter, choosing to display respect for themselves and others (even those acting rude, condescending, abusive, and even threatening), have the real power in any given situation (Colwell & Huth, 2010).

Expecting others to automatically respect the police today is unrealistic. Respect cannot be demanded; it has to be earned. Due to no fault of their own, individual police officers—thanks to the highly publicized actions of a few—should not expect deference or respect from many individuals they will encounter. Knowing this, police officers may question whether they should respect disrespectful people.

Do other people have to earn the respect of the police? Colwell and Huth (2010) put it this way:

> True respect is "earned" by virtue of our individual existence. In a very real sense, respect can be considered the realization of another's intrinsic value as a human being and the accompanying degree of unpredictability—and thus danger—that comes with being human; therefore, it is possible to respect someone without requiring any particular behavior on his part. It is a fundamental truth; one can choose to have regard for another, while still recognizing the presence of differing

value systems and memory schema that render the other person potentially unpredictable. (p. 25)

Even when faced with extreme disrespect the humanistic police officer has power when they demonstrate respect unconditionally. Colwell and Huth (2010) put it this way: "Unconditional respect provides an additional layer of 'body armor' for officers, protecting them not only from physical attack but from the other hazards endemic to police work" (p. 26).

Humanistic Policing: An Example

One of the greatest challenges police officers face today is how they interact with people of color. Tension between the police and African American citizens challenges the capabilities of even the most competent officers in trying to maintain law and order.

Understanding African American Communities

The law enforcement function is one that generates conflict, especially in those who have a negative impression of the police. The reasons for this negative impression on the part of African Americans relates to the history of how African Americans have been treated, the structural and cultural factors that divide White from Black, and the legacy of discrimination that persists in the form of residual discrimination (President's Task Force on 21st Century Policing, 2015).

The wise police officer knows how to mitigate conflict in the law enforcement role, but the policing role offers abundant opportunities to bridge the divide between the police—regardless of whether the officer is White or Black—and the African American community. It is in this role where the techniques of conflict management can be employed to fulfill the policing mission of order maintenance. However, there are unique characteristics of people of color that should also be considered in any genuine effort to support these individuals and build trust in these communities.

Building Better Relationships with African American Communities

In addition to the structural factors that have a devastating impact on African American communities, there are lesser cultural aspects of being an African American that should guide any efforts to support them (Wilson, 2009). Much of what is known about men of color comes from recent literature from the education field put forth by Wood and Harris (2017). Their work provides insight that police officers can use in their efforts to understand and support African American communities.

Specific Relationship-Building Techniques for Police Officers

Calls for service and emergency situations rarely allow the time to engage in relationship building, but when time allows or at their own initiative, the best officers recognize the value of getting to know their community or neighborhood better. This is done one individual at a time and has the dual propose of intelligence gathering for problem solving. The following suggestions can make these efforts more productive (Wood & Harris, 2017; President's Task Force on 21st Century Policing, 2015):

1. Get to know individuals by name and refer to them by name. This affirms their personhood and is a sign of respect. When engaged in law enforcement interactions, allow them to maintain their dignity whenever possible. Since men will fight to maintain their dignity, there is no benefit from causing them to lose it. Praise people publicly, allow them to save face, and be ready to assist them in making a fresh start.
2. Be "intrusive" but with a nonconfrontational tone. This means to engage proactively and seek out opportunities to engage in nonenforcement contacts. Avoid disengagement or creating the perception that individuals should approach you first or that the police have more important things to do. Don't erect walls; there are enough of those already.
3. Be fully present. This means focusing on the individual and treating each person as important. Ignore or set aside interruptions to demonstrate a commitment to the individual at that moment.
4. Make use of "appropriate" disclosure by revealing things about yourself. Tell a brief story to let individuals know that the police are human, too, and are sometimes vulnerable.
5. When there is an opportunity to provide more formal assistance, connect individuals to people directly. Perhaps there is a job available at a business down the street; walk or drive the individual to the location and personally introduce him or her to the owner.
6. Demonstrate a personal commitment to the individual's well-being. A business card with a phone number is a good start, but other symbols may become appropriate and available with time and experience.

Summary

What lies beyond the community-oriented policing era? Humanistic policing does, where the techniques of human relations can be brought to bear on the policing function. Policing is a people business, finding clues to increasing the effectiveness of the modern police officer in terms of building better relationships and trust can be found in the field of human relations.

Human relations is the study of human behavior—why self-image, beliefs, attitudes, prejudices, and bias sometimes cause problems, but also how they can create opportunities. For the police officer, competency rests in the understanding that all productive work is done through relationships. The very first relationship that needs to be cultivated is with the self, then the particular individual(s) one relates to, and then the group(s) that individual associates with.

Emotionally intelligent individuals who practice human relations skills understand they have a choice in how to respond to others. They can choose to be rude, condescending, and abusive, or they can choose *unconditional respect*. Wise individuals recognize that the former will likely result in dysfunctional outcomes, but the latter, choosing to display respect for themselves and others (even those acting rude, condescending, abusive, and even threatening), have the real power in any given situation.

Key Terms

broken windows theory: A theory in policing that minor problems lead to major problems, with the assumption that addressing minor problems will result in a decrease in major problems.

community-oriented policing: A theory of policing that states police will best serve their communities when they work together with their community partners.

discretion: Official decision-making capacity. The ability of officers to choose what they do at work and how they handle situations.

human relations: The study of human behavior, including an examination of why self-image, beliefs, attitudes, prejudices, and bias sometimes cause problems in professional and personal contacts and relationships.

humanistic policing: Utilizing the techniques of human relations in the policing function.

problem-oriented policing: A method of policing that involves police officers determining the underlying causes of crime and disorder and addressing them, rather than simply addressing the disorder.

SARA method: An acronym meaning scanning, analysis, response, and assessment. It is a problem-solving technique where the police scan their environment for problems, analyze what is causing those problems, implement a response, and the assess the effectiveness of that response.

Discussion Questions

- Why was it important for policing to be insulated from politics?
- Why is it important that reform efforts come from inside the policing profession?
- Around the turn of the century, broken windows policing was quite popular. Do you think it was a good strategy for community-oriented policing? Why or why not?
- What do you think is the real meaning of being "community oriented?"
- Can you think of other threats to a community orientation that were not noted in the chapter?
- Do you think police should have to earn respect, or should it be given to them based on their office?
- What do you think about community-oriented policing after reading the chapter?

References

Alexander, M. (2011). *The new Jim Crow: Mass incarceration in the age of colorblindness.* New York, NY: New Press.

Bayley, D. (1994). *Police for the future.* New York, NY: Oxford University Press.

Bittner, E. (1970). *The functions of the police in modern society.* Chevy Chase, MD: National Institute of Mental Health.
Bittner, E. (1991). Functions of police in modern society. In C. B. Klockars & S.D. Mastrofski (Ed.), *Thinking about Police: Contemporary Readings* (pp. 35–51). New York, NY: McGraw-Hill.
Bratton, W. J. (2015). *Broken windows and quality-of-life policing in New York City.* New York, NY: New York City Police Department.
Colwell, J. L., & Huth, C. (2010). *Unleashing the power of unconditional respect.* New York, NY: Taylor and Francis.
Cox, S. M., Marchinonna, S., & Fitch, B. D. (2017). *Introduction to policing.* Thousand Oaks CA: SAGE.
Dempsey, J. & Forst, L. S. (2014). *An introduction to policing* (7th ed.). New York, NY: Cengage.
Goldstein, H. (1977). *Policing a free society.* Cambridge, MA: Ballinger.
Goldstein, H. (1990). *Problem-oriented Policing.* New York, NY: McGraw-Hill.
Kelling, G., & Wilson, J. Q. (1982, March). Broken windows: The police and neighborhood safety. *Atlantic Monthly.* Retrieved from https://www.theatlantic.com/magazine/archive/1982/03/broken-windows/304465/
New York City Department of Investigation. (2016). *An analysis of quality-of-life summonses, quality-of-life arrests, and felony crime in New York City, 2010–2015.* New York: City of New York.
Presidents Task Force Report. (2015). President's Task Force on 21st Century Policing. Washington DC: Office of Community Oriented Policing Services.
Reece, B. L. (2014). *Effective human relations* (12th ed.). Mason, OH: South-Western Cengage Learning.
Solar, P. J. (2015). Police culture and use of force. *Police Forum, 26*(3), 9–19.
Trojanowicz, R. C., Kappeler, V. E. & Gaines, L. K., (2002). *Community policing: A contemporary perspective.* Cincinnati: Anderson.
Uchida, G. D. (2015). The development of the American police. In R. A. Dunham (Ed.), *Critical issues in policing* (7th ed.) (pp. 11–30). Long Grove, IL: Waveland.
Walker, S. (1998). *Popular justice.* New York, NY: Oxford University Press.
Wilson, W. J. (2009). *More than just race.* New York, NY: Norton.
Wood, L. J., & Harris, F. (2017). *Supporting men of color in the community college: A guidebook.* San Diego, CA: Montezuma.

CHAPTER 12

Thoughts on Improving Human Value in Policing

By Ronald Connolly

Opening Questions

Answer the following question before reading this chapter:

> What do you know about the place of human value in policing prior to reading this chapter?

Answer the following question while reading the chapter:

> What are some concepts from the chapter that stand out to you? Why do you think they are important?

Introduction

I turned on the television this morning, and as is the case all too often lately, I viewed another media report of excessive use of force by a police officer. This incident happened in Hallandale Beach, Florida (Guirola, 2018). The video footage revealed that, through the use of several baton strikes, a resistant suspect had been brought to the ground. As the arrestee was lying face down, without offering any further resistance, one of the two officers involved delivered a deliberate and final strike to his right leg. As the suspect was resisting, the baton strikes used to get him to the ground may have been explainable. However, once he offered no further resistance, there appeared to be no justification to deliver the additional blow. As I watched the footage, it reminded me of another report that I had viewed nearly a month earlier, in which a suspect in Miami, Florida, had been handcuffed behind his back and was also lying face down on the ground (Oquendo, 2018). As one officer had control of his arms, another officer ran toward the suspect and kicked him in the head. Prior to the approach of the second (kicking) officer, the man appeared to be offering no resistance.

As a caveat let me assert my firm belief that the majority of officers who serve the public each day are doing so respectfully and without the use of excessive force. However, in such previously described instances, where the video evidence seems irrefutable, it leads me to wonder, what could compel an officer to engage in such unprofessional and inhumane behavior toward another human being? There are many possible explanations ranging anywhere from poor officer vetting to training deficiencies, to personal, emotional, or psychological issues. There is another possibility that occurred to me after reading the book *On Killing: The Psychological Cost of Learning to Kill in War and Society* by retired Army Lieutenant Colonel Dave Grossman (1996). That possibility is the **dehumanization** of people by way of intentional **categorization**, social ranking, stereotyping, and objectification. Dehumanization, after all, is the gateway to abuse.

Factors of Dehumanization

Despite my first inclination, based on Grossman's title, I found that the book was not at all a how-to manual on the extermination of humans. Rather, it accentuated the phenomenon of human adversity to killing other human beings and how such adversity, manifested by many soldiers whose responsibility it was to kill enemy combatants, had become problematic during wartime engagements. Evidence of such unwillingness to kill other human beings has been chronicled throughout history, from the Napoleonic wars to Vietnam. Artifacts discovered on the Civil War battlefield were indicative of the aversion to killing, when, on the front lines of the battlefield, in target rich environments, despite going through the motions (as trained) of loading weapons, soldiers failed to fire them at anyone. Muskets were frequently found with multiple rounds loaded into their barrels, one on top of the other, having never been fired (Grossman, 1996). Grossman (1996) further cited the dismal firing rates of U.S. soldiers during World War II (15–20%) and the Korean War (50%). In fact, he points out that reluctance to fire on an enemy dates back nearly as far as the inception of the use of black powder in weaponry. According to Grossman (1996), the resistance of one human to killing another is the result of "a powerful combination of instinctive, rational, environmental, hereditary, cultural and social factors" (p. 39). Adversity to killing, in many instances, is derived from a recognition of the humanistic and existential commonalities that the would-be killer shares with the would-be killed, or the similarity of the enemy to ourselves. In other words, by killing another human, we are killing a part of ourselves.

To overcome this impediment to warfighting capability, a number of factors were identified to offset adversity to killing humans which included (a) social distance/social stratification (Hogg & Tindale, 2008), (b) moral advantage associated with defending the welfare of the community, (c) mechanical distance (Grossman, 1996), (d) group think, and (e) psychological enabling (desensitization, conditioning, denial defense mechanisms) (Grossman, 1996).

Through **social distance** and **social stratification**, people can become desensitized to others who are not perceived to be like themselves because they assign them a status that is inferior to their own. **Moral advantage** is associated with defending the welfare of the community and offers justification of actions because the protection of the safety and security of home, community, country and way of life is perceived as a noble endeavor. **Mechanical distance** involves the application of the adage "out of sight, out of mind." In other words, if you cannot actually see the people involved in a situation, it is easier not to identify them as people at all. **Group think** employs a mentality that enables people to justify, in mass, what individuals might find to be objectionable, inappropriate, immoral, or inhumane. Finally, **psychological enabling** incorporates techniques such as desensitization, in which an enemy is regarded as being something other than human. For example, during wartime, enemies have been intentionally referred to in racist or other bigoted terms in an effort to portray them more as subhuman organisms or as objects rather than people, thereby diminishing the moral imperative to treat them with human regard. Conditioning can be accomplished through repetitive and reinforced inhumane action toward a perceived inferior, whether a person of lesser status or a population deemed to be subhuman. Therefore, when the time comes to actually engage a human being in combat, there will be less inhibition in carrying out an assault. Furthermore, denial defense mechanisms are used to reinforce the idea that what is being eradicated is not a human being but rather something that is undesirable or evil.

Application to Policing

So far, what has been referenced from Grossman's (1996) book was written in the context of killing, which begs the question, "What application could this possibly have to policing?" Even when an officer must resort to the use of deadly force, the intent is not to kill, but rather to stop a threat. Consider the Hallandale Beach and Miami incidents that I mentioned in the first paragraph. Add to those the event that occurred in an Evansville, Indiana, motel room where the officer, after arresting a cooperative suspect on a warrant, handcuffed the arrestee, shoved him onto a bed and intentionally struck him in the groin (Fater, 2017). Further, consider the Baltimore officer who verbally abused and physically assaulted a teenage skateboarder for making an unsolicited remark and calling the officer "Dude" (Associated Press, 2012). In McKinney, Texas, a police sergeant was caught on video being disrespectful to teens scattered throughout a neighborhood who had attended a pool party (Campo-Flores, 2015). At one point, the sergeant drew his firearm, despite the lack of an apparent deadly force threat, and used what appeared to be an excessive amount of force on a teenage female onlooker who did not leave the area quickly enough. In New York City, an off-duty detective approached an immigrant Uber driver and became verbally abusive and demeaning to him, berating him for his misspoken English and his lack of understanding of the way things operate in America (Schiavocampo, 2015). These are all instances of officers operating with diminished regard for the inherent value of others.

Despite the professional and responsible performance of the majority of officers throughout the United States, in this day of ubiquitous technology, surveillance, and communication capabilities, there seem to be abundant examples of officers who are engaging in unwarranted disregard for the respect of others. It makes one question what could compel an officer to engage in such unprofessional and inhumane behavior toward another human being, especially given that his or her career might be on the line. Perhaps one possible answer lies in the lessons learned from Grossman (1996). Outside the parameters of war, is it possible to treat people with lesser degrees of human value through factors similar to those that offset adversity to killing humans? In answer to that question, let us examine each of the five factors that offset adversity to killing human beings in an attempt to identify whether they could also account for diminished levels of respect for others and disregard for human value.

Social Distance/Social Stratification

People are attracted to developing social categories and categorizing others for a number of reasons (Hogg & Tindale, 2008). First, categorization is less work intensive. Assessing individuals on each of their respective merits is not expeditious. It requires that we take the time to consider someone else's background, motivations, and perspective. Categorization, on the other hand, only requires the grouping of people with a perceived commonality and, when undertaken outside the purview of scientific research, can be done rather quickly. One effect of lumping people into categories is that instead of regarding individuals as unique and thus unpredictable, placing them in a preexisting category creates a greater probability of being able to easily predict what will happen (Hogg & Tindale, 2008). For example, if one is included in a group categorized as peak performers, then there is a perception that anyone selected from that group will excel at an assigned responsibility. Conversely, with regard to a so-called substandard or incompetent group, perceptions of inadequacy or a lack of capability may be assumed of its members, regardless of the individual attributes of those included in the group. Another effect of categorization is that as perceived similarities of people in a single category become exaggerated, individuality disappears and it becomes easier to stereotype those within the category (Hogg & Tindale, 2008). Consequently, if people of a particular race, ethnicity, socioeconomic status, or criminal background are lumped together in categories that carry a negative social connotation, regardless of their personal life situations, individual motivations, or characteristics, they will lose their individual identity. They may be labelled as criminal, indigent, socially dependent, homeless, untrustworthy, lazy, or as having any number of traits that would render them socially undesirable. Their behavior then would be expected to be reflective of the negative stereotype. Once they have been characterized as undesirable because of their predicted behavior, they are likely to be treated with greater degrees of disrespect and lesser degrees of human value (Hogg & Tindale, 2008).

Just as categorization can affect police interaction with individuals outside of the department, it can also affect relations inside the department. Categorization can also serve as a catalyst for behavior modification, particularly in situations where individuals seek acceptance of a particular group. Aspiring members may change their behavior to more closely match the category prototype (typical group member) in an attempt to gain approval or acceptance (Hogg & Tindale, 2008). Although not unique to policing, consider the informal vetting that takes place for new officers. They are not fully accepted by the group of their peers until they have proven, through attitude and action, that they fit the police subculture. They must demonstrate as many of the characteristics of the category prototype as necessary for inclusion. To a certain extent, within the behavioral modification to gain acceptance, the prospective member of the group undergoes a degree of depersonalization to be more like everyone else. This effect is itself akin to stereotyping. The officer must fit the established subculture stereotype to be accepted by the group. The new officer is willing and often eager to do this because it leads to both positive social identity and a higher level of self-esteem.

The professional mandate placed on police to keep the community safe demands that they must prevail in situations that threaten to compromise public safety. When it comes to ensuring the safety and welfare of the community, the expectation is that they must win. In the process, they are also required to be respectful of each individual's civil rights. It is the regard for individual rights that must temper how officers respond to the demand to win. If the category prototype for the subculture of a particular police agency is unevenly weighted toward an aggressive response to crime with lesser emphasis on the regard for each individual's rights, officers, in an attempt to live up to the category prototype, might take a more verbally and physically aggressive tact (i.e., "kicking ass and taking names") toward a group categorized as criminal. In addition, if crime is occurring in an area known to be prevalently occupied by people of lower economic status and people of color, then to more easily predict behavior, everyone in that area, regardless of criminal propensity, is at risk of being categorized as criminal. Such a stereotype assaults the individuality of those living in that area. Furthermore, with the assumption that everyone in the high crime area is criminal, a situation develops that is highly susceptible to abuses of authority such as verbal disrespect or excessive force. This situation could be exacerbated by officers who are willing to compromise their ethical integrity to gain the acceptance or praise of their peers.

Moral Advantage Associated with Defending the Welfare of the Community

As previously indicated, when it comes to ensuring the safety and welfare of the community from crime or disruption of the peace, the police must win. Consequently, the police exert significant effort to preventing crime and disorder, as well as responding to such situations as they occur and when they are reported. Imagine our society without the protection of the police. Crime would be rampant and personal safety of citizens and the security of their homes and possessions would be in constant jeopardy. Civil relationships would deteriorate and vigilantism would be one of the few tools available with which to attempt to maintain order. With that in mind, policing in America continues to be a critical element in ensuring public order and, overall, it performs well in that regard. The problem comes when the police feel that they are superior to those they serve, owing to their place as the defender of the community. In an instance where the community or the police have categorized an area as crime ridden, it is easy to establish a negative stereotype of the people living there. All at once they may be perceived as being criminal, undesirable, or the worst that society has to offer. Consequently, abuses similar to those articulated in the social distance/social stratification section could develop. It is possible for an officer to attempt to moralize acts such as verbal assault or excessive force as necessary to maintain the quality of the good portions of the community and to ensure that the undesirable element is eliminated or minimally controlled, all of this being done from a position of moral authority. I have personally encountered officers who have defended their use of profanity toward members of a stereotyped community by claiming that "It's the only language these people understand."

Mechanical Distance

Mechanical distance is the dehumanization caused by viewing people through some sort of device (Grossman, 1996). Considering the close personal proximity within which police and the public interact, it may be surprising that it is possible for mechanical distance to play a part in officer abuse of authority that results in harm to individuals. Consider one of the main features of categorization: disappearance of individual identity. It is difficult to make a case that police could lose sight of the public as being comprised of individuals since most personal encounters between citizens and the police occur within a zone that ranges anywhere from 3 feet to 25 yards in distance. Most commonly, as reflected in law enforcement training, police encounters take place within distances of 3 to 20 feet. At such short distances, it is nearly impossible *not* to identify people as individuals, even when they are embedded in a crowd.

There is an exception though. Visualize that you are driving on an interstate highway. You are heading up a gentle incline and as you crest the top of a hill you suddenly see a state patrol car ahead in the median. Perhaps in your mind that's no reason for concern, but if you are anything like me, the surprise reaction usually involves the utterance of an expletive, followed by an immediate brake check. Then, after passing the cruiser, a rapid succession of glances into the rearview mirror take place to see if it is coming for you.

If this strikes a familiar chord, consider this: At the moment that you saw the state patrol car, did you identify it as representing an individual trooper or a predatory vehicle? In my case, without exception, it is the latter. The personal identity of the officer was lost to the image of the predatory vehicle.

By its very nature, vehicular traffic generates mechanical distance. Our ability to interact on a personal level is diminished and, to a great extent, individuality is diminished. Think about the things you say about other motorists when you are behind the wheel. Most of them are not the same things you would say if you were pushing a cart behind those same people at a grocery store. Now, flip this around to the perspective of the officer responding to an emergency call. As the officer operates an emergency vehicle through traffic at elevated rates of speed, does that officer perceive the vehicles to be individual people or obstacles through which to navigate?

On July 8, 1998, in the state of Maine, Cumberland County Sheriff's Deputy Debra Hall was responding to the call of an "out of control 6-year old child." She was travelling westbound on a two-lane, undivided highway with her emergency lights activated and her siren intermittently on. Her speed was approximately 86 mph as she attempted to pass other westbound vehicles and crashed into a vehicle turning southbound from the westbound lane. The driver of the stricken vehicle was 18-year-old John Norton. His mother, Michelle Norton was the right, front passenger, and his 15-year old brother, Matthew, was riding in the back seat. All were wearing their seatbelts. As a result of the collision, both John and Matthew were killed (Charette, 2012). It is possible that Deputy Hall did not see the Norton vehicle prior to the collision, or, if she did, perhaps she did not have time to take evasive action. Just prior to the collision, she was advised by dispatch that the situation had calmed down. Deputy Hall's attention to traffic then became distracted by her attempt to use the microphone and turn off her siren.

It is impossible to know what was going through Deputy Hall's mind as she was responding to this call. When en route to an emergency, officers must frequently divide attention between emergency vehicle operation and approach considerations such as response route, resources that may be needed at the scene, necessity for back-up officers, or other emergency response or support personnel. I cannot speak for Deputy Hall, or any other officer for that matter. I can say, as a former police officer with nearly 2 decades of experience, in my own response to emergencies, I do not recall thinking, in the moment, about vehicles in traffic representing individual people. The cars, trucks, and busses that I passed represented obstacles that required safe avoidance to proceed to the location of the call. As police officers, we are never relieved of our responsibility to drive with due regard for others. The Norton story serves as an example to help officers look beyond traffic as being a series of obstacles. Each vehicle represents an individual or a number of individuals. If officers allow mechanical distance to dull their sensitivity to that fact it enables a lapse in the regard for human value and creates opportunities for abuse of power and authority.

Group Think

People think differently in groups than they do as individuals. Although I am not a big basketball fan (unless my son happens to be playing in his community league), one of the most memorable examples of the dangerous capabilities of group think came in 2010 when the Los Angeles Lakers defeated the Boston Celtics to win the NBA championship. Immediately after the last game of the seven-game series, a mob of fans gathered outside of the Staples Center. According to the *Los Angeles Times*, "Crowds hurled bottles and other objects at police, smashed marquees, jumped on vehicles, broke windows, and set rubbish dumpsters and vehicles on fire" (Allen & Linthicum, 2010). What was so remarkable was that this was the reaction of a group of fans when their team won. In contrast, imagine a family in their living room, watching the same game on the television: the final seconds of that final game tick away and the home team Lakers win. It would be absurd to imagine the father jumping to his feet and smashing the TV screen with a potted plant while the mother throws a chair through the picture window and the kids set fire to the curtains. So why do people in crowds act differently than individuals? First, people derive tacit approval of their own inappropriate behavior from the misbehavior of others. In other words, if another person is doing something questionable or even taboo but is getting away with it, then it must be okay for others to do it as well. The same justification of bad behavior takes place when victims of a disaster, such as Hurricane Katrina, loot storefronts. Second, there is anonymity in groups, particularly in large groups comprised of many people wearing the same type of clothing. In such an environment, it is much easier for someone, acting inappropriately, to simply blend into the crowd and remain unidentified.

Anonymity contributes greatly to the final characteristic of group think: lack of accountability. Certainly it is difficult to hold someone accountable for an action that they cannot be identified as contributing to. Further, even if they are identified, they can deny any responsibility by simply claiming to be a follower of someone else in the crowd or by blaming the entire group itself. Sadly, extreme evidence of the danger of group think is abundant throughout history. Atrocities such as the Holocaust or ethnic cleansing in Bosnia or Rwanda all demonstrate the dark capabilities of humans when caught up in the whirlwind of group think.

Earlier, I mentioned that categorization can also serve as a catalyst for behavior modification, particularly in situations where individuals seek acceptance by a particular group. Such situations demand that the individual adopt the same mind-set as the other members of the group. In spring of 2008, Katie Couric, then a correspondent for the CBS news magazine *60 Minutes*, interviewed former Chicago police officer Keith Herrera who had been a member of the Special Operations Section (SOS). The SOS was tasked with reducing violence that once made Chicago the "murder capital of the country." According to Herrera, the mandate from his supervisors was clear: "Get the guns and drugs off the streets, no matter what, at any cost, just get 'em off" (Couric & Herrera, 2008). As a result, Herrera and other members of the SOS were accused of entering homes without search warrants, detaining people illegally until they surrendered guns and drugs, and making illegal arrests. When Couric asked what Herrera's supervisors thought of his tactics, he replied, "Keep it up. Long as you got the guns, long as you got the drugs, long as you're getting the bad guys, keep it up.' And if they tell you 'Keep it up,' you keep it up" (Couric & Herrera, 2008). When asked about falsification of police reports to justify illegal actions taken by members of the SOS, Herrera stated, "'Creative writing' was a certain term that bosses used to make sure that the job got done" (Couric & Herrera, 2008). Within his special unit, Herrera's unethical and illegal behavior was not only ignored, but often encouraged and praised. This is a clear example of gaining the approval of the group by fitting the categorical prototype of an SOS officer as a "hard charger" who is tough on gun and drug crime. As a result of compromising his integrity and getting caught up in the dynamics of the SOS group think, he abused his authority, violated the rights of others, and became a criminal perpetrator.

Psychological Enabling

The final factor in treating people with lesser degrees of human value is psychological enabling, which includes the elements of **desensitization**, **conditioning**, and **denial defense mechanisms**. In the context of motivation to kill the enemy with less inhibition, Grossman pointed out that it was necessary to desensitize soldiers to the humanity of their adversaries (Grossman, 1996). This was accomplished by referring to them in subhuman and often racist terms. Likewise, I believe it is possible to enable abuses of authority (such as disrespect, verbal assault, excessive force, falsification of official reports, and other unethical, immoral and even illegal behavior) through similar means.

Desensitization

A degree of desensitization has been evident within the ranks of numerous police agencies representing every law enforcement level (local, state, and federal). I have heard officers refer to people as dirt bags, dirtballs, mopes, scumbags, scum balls, trailer trash, sleaze bags, and by a variety of other terms. Repeated use of such descriptors in reference to a group of people who have been categorized and stereotyped is dehumanizing. As previously mentioned, categorization helps make the actions of the categorized more predictable (Hogg & Tindale, 2008). Officers may intentionally seek out instances of, or even attempt to induce, behavior they expect of the categorized. Additionally, if people are continuously described as something undesirable, disgusting, or even criminal, they may begin to behave in accordance with the stereotype. In other words, a dynamic of self-fulfilling prophecy could occur.

Conditioning

Conditioning is the result of an individual's appearance being continuously associated with undesirable or criminal behavior. For example, if people of color are stereotyped as lazy, socially dependent, unemployed, or criminal and such stereotypes are supported by a police subculture, that enables officers to become conditioned to believe that such characteristics are inherent of all people of color. Such conditioning then paves the way for a ritual of unfair and abusive treatment of the people stereotyped.

Denial Defense Mechanisms

Denial defense mechanisms are tools used to ease the conscience of those inflicting harm on others. According to Grossman (1996), denial defense mechanisms include **manufactured denial** and **manufactured contempt**. Manufactured denial involves the contrived reality of inflicting harm on an object rather than a human, which allows the subject to continue such action with less inhibition. For example, scumbags or a dirtballs are not human. Therefore, if you have labeled human beings as such and you have devalued them to have less worth than other human beings, it makes it easier to treat them oppressively. Manufactured contempt involves convincing oneself that someone is undesirable (such as an outlaw), thereby making it easier to inflict harm on that person.

The Fallout

Desensitization, conditioning, and denial defense mechanisms are all means by which to objectify people. Once people are regarded as objects rather than human beings, it is much easier to mistreat them without feelings of guilt (Grossman, 1996). After all, the only thing being mistreated is an object, undeserving of the same respect as a peer, an equal, or another human being. Effectively, the objectified have been reduced to the rank of nobodies, while at the same time the objectifiers are somebodies with the power to determine who is a somebody and who is a nobody. In his book, *Somebodies and Nobodies: Overcoming the Abuse of Rank,* author Robert Fuller (2003) explains, "Regardless of surface distinctions such as ethnicity, religion, color, or gender, persistent abuse and discrimination is predicated on power differences inherent in rank" (p. 3). Categorization is a convenient way to identify rank. For example, a group classified as criminal is likely to be perceived as lower in rank than those given the authority to enforce the law and restrict an individual's liberty. The reason for the difference in rank, according to Fuller (2003) is that one category of people do not have the same authority and power as the other. That does not mean that everyone with power and authority will abuse it. However, from the perspective of those without power, it is difficult to abuse something you do not have. "Nobodies are insulted, disrespected, exploited, and ignored. In contrast, somebodies are sought after, given preference, and lionized ... the indignity suffered by those who have been 'nobodies' festers. It builds to indignation and sometimes erupts in violence" (Fuller, 2003, pp. 5–6) The last part of that quote could provide insight into the development of social movements including Black Lives Matter, the Me Too movement, and the March for Our Lives initiative. Fuller (2003) goes on to say that "people will become apologists for crimes they would otherwise condemn to get even with those they believe have 'nobodied' them" (p. 7). This could be an explanation, albeit grossly unjustifiable, for the recent surge in violence and deadly ambushes against police officers.

The Search for Solutions

> *"Overcoming **Rankism** would therefore undermine racism, sexism and other-isms that have been fought under those names, but ultimately derive their force from power differences woven into the social fabric."*
>
> —Fuller, 2003, p. 2

The question to be answered is: How do we begin to overcome categorization, objectification, and rankism to head off abuse of power and authority and to ensure that all who are served by the police are valued?

Perhaps the first step involves education and training of prospective, new, and veteran police officers to recognize the characteristics of categorization, objectification, and rankism. Next, collective effort must be made to ensure that the factors that enable abuse of power and authority are not allowed to gain a foothold. Further, police administrators and leaders cannot afford to be complacent, apathetic, or tolerant of engagement in these harmful practices.

If rankism deprives those classified as nobodies of power and authority to influence their community in positive ways and improve their quality of life, then **coproduction policing** may be key in ensuring that the disenfranchised are represented, heard, and take an active role in promoting mindful policing strategies. In a report written for the enterprise security risk management consulting firm Hillard Heintz, Kenneth Bouche (2017) explained,

> In order for police to build this [trust], communities must be afforded the opportunity to have an equal, meaningful, and constructive voice in key aspects of the way their neighborhoods are policed. In other words—and this is absolutely vital—the community must assume co-responsibility for public safety in their respective neighborhoods. (para. 4)

Through this cooperative effort, communities are empowered rather than being marginalized.

Finally, adherence to procedural justice will diminish efforts to improvise and exercise street justice, as in the case of the Special Operations Section of the Chicago Police Department. "Procedural justice (sometimes called procedural fairness) describes the idea that how individuals regard the justice system is tied more to the perceived fairness of the process and how they were treated rather than to the perceived fairness of the outcome" (Gold, 2013, para. 2). The four pillars of procedural justice include fairness in processes, transparency in actions, opportunities to have a voice, and decision making that relies on impartiality (Office of Community Oriented Policing Services, 2016). There is no place for the institutional or cultural support of a Machiavellian, ends-justify- the-means approach to policing, particularly when the means lack regard for human value (Office of Community Oriented Policing Services, 2016).

Conclusion

It is clear that we are navigating a number of tumultuous currents in America socially, politically, economically, and in our relationships with others. Such a challenge is nothing new to this nation. We have weathered many a storm, but the contemporary demand is for action beyond simply holding out until the present controversies have passed. Now is the time for us to listen to each other with common regard for human value and to act mindfully in response to what we hear. That process will not always be a comfortable one, but it is a necessary one if we wish to flourish as a society. For all its perceived shortcomings, America remains a great nation. A preoccupation with returning to greatness may not be our most fruitful endeavor. Rather, facing the issues that detract from our values, acknowledging that there is work to be done, and problem solving together reflects the spirit that distinguishes this nation as great. If we are to maintain our integrity, we have to be clinical and analytical about arriving at the root of the problems we face so that we may solve them effectively. My hope is that in reading this, it has prompted you to engage in a deeper examination of what is happening to produce the challenges that we face and to help create effective solutions. Rather than a focus on sweeping change, our most productive effort may come in the form of seemingly small but incremental strides, which, when made on a number of fronts, will collectively contribute to significant improvement for the welfare of all. I embrace this philosophy and I look forward to working with many kindred spirits in pursuit of that end.

Key Terms

conditioning: A form of learning where a stimulus and a response are linked. In this case the result of an individual's appearance is continuously associated with undesirable or criminal behavior

coproduction policing: A model that gives the community an equal voice to defining the community's strategy on policing (Bouche, 2017)

categorization: the grouping of people with perceived commonalities by placing them in preexisting categories in order to create a greater probability of being able to easily predict how they will act

dehumanization: Diminished regard for the inherent value of others

denial defense mechanisms: Tools used to ease the conscience of those inflicting harm on others

desensitization: A reduced emotional reaction to a stimulus, created by recurring exposure to that stimulus

group think: A psychological phenomenon where members of a group make decisions to minimize in-group conflict and promote harmony rather in the interest of making a good decision. To do this, group members may either self-edit their opinions or stifle those in the group who are expressing contrary views

manufactured contempt: Convincing oneself that someone is undesirable (such as an outlaw), thereby making it easier to inflict harm on that person

manufactured denial: The contrived reality of inflicting harm on an object rather than a human, which allows the subject to continue such action with less inhibition

mechanical distance: The dehumanization caused by viewing people through some sort of device. This device could be binoculars, a monitor screen, or a car window

moral advantage: A utilitarian perspective that can lead police to do unethical acts because they are doing so to protect the community

procedural justice: The concept the criminal justice process itself should be fair. It includes not only the concept of due process, but also transparency of the system

psychological enabling: Using psychological means to empower or rationalize dysfunctional behavior. Psychological enablers include desensitization, conditioning, and denial defense mechanisms

rankism: Abusive, discriminatory, or exploitative behavior toward people because of their rank in a particular hierarchy (Fuller, 2003)

social distance: The difference between individuals on the social stratification hierarchy

social stratification: The differentiation of people into a hierarchy of groups based qualities such as wealth, race, power, and so on

Discussion Questions

- Explain how elements of enablement of killing in wartime (as explained in Grossman, 1996) relate to police interactions with the community. What are the similarities? What is the result?
- Define what is meant by the term "categorization." Discuss both the productive value and harmful nature of categorization as it relates to police practice.

- Discuss objectification and the impact it has on relationships between the police and the community. Offer examples of your own observation of objectification in daily encounters.
- Consider labeling and the consequences of designation as either a "somebody" or a "nobody." What challenges does such practice present for policing in general? What impact does it have on local communities and on the nation as a whole?
- What is coproduction policing and how may it be helpful in improving police professionalism?
- Briefly explain procedural justice and discuss the bearing it may have on relationships within the community. Expound on how it may be beneficial to both policing and the community.
- What do you think about the place of human value in policing after reading the chapter?

References

Allen, S., & Linthicum, K. (2010, June 18). Despite heavy LAPD presence, violence breaks out after Laker's cictory. *LA Times.* Retrieved from http://articles.latimes.com/2010/jun/18/local/la-me-0618-lakers-20100618

Associated Press. (2012, April 28). Baltimore cops vs. skateboarder. *CBS.* Retrieved from http://baltimore.cbslocal.com/2012/04/28/firing-upheld-of-md-officer-in-skateboard-video/

Bouche, K. (2017, April 25). The future of law enforcement: Co-produced policing—Returning authority to communities. *Hillard Heintze.* Retrieved from https://www.hillardheintze.com/law-enforcement-consulting/co-produced-policing-2/

Campo-Flores, A. (2015, June 7). Texas officer placed on leave after video shows teenage girl wrestled to ground. *Wall Street Journal.* https://www.wsj.com/articles/texas-officer-placed-on-leave-after- video-shows-altercation-1433724054?mod=trending_now_1&mod=videorelated

Charette, W. (Producer). (2012, May, 9). Alert international: Association of professional law enforcement emergency vehicle response trainers [Video file]. *The Michelle Norton story.* Retrieved from https://vimeo.com/41825567

Couric, K. (Interviewer) & Herrera, K. (Interviewee). (2008). Officer Herrera goes public: Indicted Chicago police officer Tells *60 Minutes* his "bosses" knew of and encouraged lies. *CBS.* Retrieved from http://www.lawreport.org/ViewStory.aspx?StoryID=97

Fater, T. (2017, August 6). Bodycam shows cop striking suspect in groin area. *Courier & Press.* Retrieved from https://www.courierpress.com/story/news/local/2017/09/11/epd-officer-hit-handcuffed-suspect-groin-area/654515001/

Fuller, R. W. (2003). *Somebodies and nobodies: Overcoming the abuse of rank.* Gabriola Island, BC, Canada: New Society.

Gold, E. (2013). The case for procedural justice: Fairness as a crime prevention tool. *E-Newsletter of the COPS Office, 6*(9). Retrieved from https://cops.usdoj.gov/html/dispatch/092013/fairness_as_a_crime_prevention_tool.asp

Grossman, D. A. (1996). *On killing: The psychological cost of learning to kill in war and society.* New York, NY: Back Bay Books.

Guirola, J. (2018, May 31). Hallandale Beach Police investigating video of officers hitting suspect with batons. *NBC.* Retrieved from https://www.nbcmiami.com/news/local/Hallandale-Beach-Police-Investigating-Video-of-Officers-Hitting-Suspect-With-Batons-484220971.html

Hogg, M. A., & Tindale, R. S. (Eds.). (2008). *Blackwell handbook of social psychology: Group processes.* Hoboken, NJ: Wiley.

Office of Community Oriented Policing Services. (2016). *Community policing topics: Procedural justice*. Retrieved from https://cops.usdoj.gov/Default.asp?Item=2866
Oquendo, V. (2018, May 4). *Cop caught on video kicking suspect in head* [Video file]. Retrieved from https://www.youtube.com/watch?v=FWNjI-RXXz4
Schiavocampo, M. (2015, April 1). *NYPD officer who berated driver placed on desk duty* [Video file]. Retrieved from https://www.youtube.com/watch?v=6dntko6DZ5E

CHAPTER 13

Body Cameras in 21st-Century Policing

The Essentials

By Cory Kelly

Opening Questions

Answer the following question before reading this chapter:

> What do you know about police body cameras prior to reading this chapter?

Answer the following question while reading the chapter:

> What are some concepts from the chapter that stand out to you? Why do you think they are important?

Introduction

Implementing a **body-worn camera** program in a police organization can be challenging. Yet, with careful planning and execution the program will restore community trust and officers will support the efforts of the profession and its increased need for **accountability**. This chapter will examine an organization's journey from the days prior to body-worn cameras to the organization being the first in the world to deploy a body-worn camera that integrates with the portable radio equipment to *every* officer.

Understanding Waukegan, Illinois

Waukegan, Illinois (pronounced "walk" and "eegan"), is a unique city that is situated along the shores of Lake Michigan, midway between Chicago, Illinois and Milwaukee, Wisconsin. Waukegan's rich history is comprised of industrial fortune and a diverse population to industrial failure and diversity. The city of Waukegan is the ninth largest in the state of Illinois. By any measure, the size and location of Waukegan make it a destination.

For avid boaters, Waukegan has a magnificent harbor with boat docking. There are many boat sizes and some that are classified as yachts. For those into entertainment, there is a historic theatre that hosts many acts a year, bringing in fans from all over the region. In Waukegan, there is an award-winning Park District and an entire downtown district dedicated to art. The citizens of Waukegan are diverse and Lake County, Illinois, has designated Waukegan as the county seat. Home to Jack Benny's birthplace, Waukegan boasts one of the largest consolidated school districts within Illinois. During the day, the transient population is increased through the different people representing spokes in the criminal justice wheel.

Waukegan has been described as a melting pot. According to the 2000 U.S. Census (n.d.), Waukegan was 20% White (not Hispanic or Latino), 55% Hispanic or Latino, 16% Black or African American, and 5% Asian. Much like neighborhoods in many large cities, Waukegan can informally be categorized by several of the areas with populations of people that have settled into one area. The citizens of Waukegan are predominately blue collar and experience crime rates similar to other cities across the United States that are comparable in size.

The Waukegan Police Department is housed in a building built in 1963. Although the building has undergone some upgrades, the 161 sworn officers and 49 support staff can often be heard discussing the lack of curb appeal the "station" provides to citizens. Nonetheless, the Waukegan Police Department handles approximately 85,000 calls for service annually. Those calls range from loud noise complaints to murder. Regardless of the interior and exterior of the building, technology in Waukegan has certainly kept in step with other law enforcement agencies throughout the country.

Evolution of Policing

The arena of law enforcement equipment has evolved since its inception some 150 years ago. There have been strides in automobiles, radar, cameras, communications, handguns, and many other categories. A patrol vehicle of the 1990s was equipped with a large, bulky computer and a radio for communication. Today's police patrol squad car carries items such as: a computer laptop, cameras, rifle rack, multiple radios, stationary radars, automated external defibrillator (AED), Naloxone (reversal for opioid overdose), and global positioning systems (GPS).

Items carried in the police patrol squad car have evolved, just as have items an officer carries in a patrol uniform. An officer 2 decades ago would carry a revolver, handcuffs, radio, nightstick, flashlight, oleoresin capsicum (commonly referred to as pepper spray), and extra magazines and bulletproof vests were often optional. Tools carried by today's law enforcement officer may include a cell phone, a semi-automatic handgun, extra magazines, a conducted electrical weapon (commonly referred to as a taser), an expandable baton, pepper spray, a tourniquet, a pressure bandage, handcuffs, flex cuffs, rifle magazines, a knife, flashlight, radio, and a body-worn camera. An officer in 2018 may have his or her duty belt supported by suspenders and his or her equipment affixed to his or her bulletproof vest carrier. Officers' hip and back problems were addressed by lightening the load on the belt and putting police equipment on the body, much like in the military.

Several items officers now carry came through by way of trials and tribulations of law enforcement. When citizens and officers perished due to loss of blood, officers were encouraged to carry medical equipment (Hewlett, 2014). Even if an officer uses deadly force on a suspect, the goal is to save the individual's life once the threat has stopped. An instance may be an officer shoots an offender who is pointing a gun; the offender drops the gun and is wounded. The officer can safely approach the offender and apply medical equipment (tourniquet/pressure bandage) while waiting first responder medical staff to further care for the offender.

Twenty-one years ago a bank robbery in Los Angeles, California, changed the course of the way police agencies armed themselves. Two bank robbers, Larry Phillips and Emil Matasareanu, out powered the police with high-powered rifles (Smith & Mather, 2017). That incident is most commonly referred to as the LA Bank Robbery. Most agencies either carried a shotgun or nothing for power beyond their handguns. Special Weapons and Tactics (SWAT) teams were trained and outfitted with long guns. Yet, the LA Bank Robbery proved it was too long to wait for a SWAT team to arrive, as patrol officers needed better equipment. It was imperative to change law enforcement after that incident injured 11 officers. Law enforcement needed to train and outfit patrol officers with rifles and allow them to carry higher caliber handguns.

A more recent and notable tribulation resulted in a public outcry for body-worn cameras. By the close of 2014, agencies throughout the United States were feeling the **Ferguson effect** (Byers, 2014). St. Louis, Missouri Police Chief Sam Dotson coined that phrase as the area prepared for the grand jury announcement in the Michael Brown case. The idea behind the Ferguson effect suggests that officers are less inclined to partake in marginal police work to avoid liability, and offenders feel empowered by the lack of police aggressiveness.

With the Ferguson effect creeping into organizations, it was time to embark on the reality that body-worn cameras were going to be a part of the police workplace. Given this reality, and the Waukegan Police Department' desire to stay on the forefront of public accountability and technology, the Waukegan Police decided in 2014 that all police officers employed would use a body-worn camera.

Making the Decision

The Waukegan Police Department does not have an exceptionally diverse staff. There are approximately 75%, White males employed as police officers. Yet, the police department experienced only a limited number of complaints that involved race or improprieties on behalf of the police. Despite the low complaints, the movement in policing and a demand by the public for police accountability was not something the Waukegan Police Department was going to ignore. Body-worn cameras were a mechanism to bridge the gap between the police and the public and to address the **transparency** issue that many law enforcement agencies were experiencing, specifically through extensive media coverage.

Since anyone with a cellphone can record a video, the police have been under the watchful eye of the citizens they serve for many years. It only made sense to carry a piece of equipment that can document the encounters the police have with citizens and preserve those encounters for evidence. A piece of equipment that can relay a series of events through the perspective of the officer can not only be helpful with citizens but also for officers, as footage can be utilized for training purposes.

Like any agency making high volume arrests, there were negative social media posts about police, community activists calling for more accountability, and minor protests about singular incidents, but situations that arose were far and few between. Complaints against officers were not on the rise, with about 50 complaints taken per year. This number held steady year after year. When the Waukegan Police Department decided to outfit officers with body-worn cameras, it was not a decision that happened in a moment. The decision had to be calculated and all decision makers needed to be committed. Collectively, the mayor and police chief realized that striking while all issues were being addressed was best. The community wanted accountability from the police department. The police department wanted to provide accountability, and thus, body-worn cameras were the answer.

When making decisions that large it is advisable to consider the most amount of buy-in from stakeholders. Citizens, politicians, officers, and anyone with a vested interest should be consulted. There are major repercussions (both positive and negative) with taking on a body-worn camera program, which will be discussed later, in more detail. Financial and public access are two great hurdles that should be discussed prior to making the decision to outfit an agency with body-worn cameras. Otherwise, the support garnered by the agency from the community may be lost if videos are not made available or if the cost exceeds budgets and the program fails.

Following the Law

Illinois made it clear, via a law, to agencies using body-worn cameras that a policy must be in place. It was welcomed direction, and the mandatory law left few questions as to when, where, and how the body-worn camera would be worn. Here is an excerpt from the Illinois Compiled Statues:

1. Cameras must be equipped with pre-even recording, capable of recording at least the 30 seconds prior to camera activation, unless the officer-worn body camera was purchased and acquired by the law enforcement agency prior to July 1, 2015.
2. Cameras must be capable of recording for a period of 10 hours or more, unless the officer-worn body camera was purchased and acquired by the law enforcement agency prior to July 1, 2015.
3. Cameras must be turned on at all times when the officer is in uniform and is responding to calls for service or engaged in any law enforcement-related encounter or activity, that occurs while the officer is on duty.
    a. If exigent circumstances exist which prevent the camera from being turned on, the camera must be turned on as soon as practicable.
    b. Officer-worn body cameras may be turned off when the officer is inside of a patrol car which is equipped with a functioning in-car camera; however, the officer must turn on the camera upon exiting the patrol vehicle for law enforcement-related encounters.
4. Cameras must be turned off when:
    a. the victim of a crime requests that the camera be turned off, and unless impractical or impossible, that request is made on the recording;
    b. a witness of a crime or a community member who wishes to report a crime requests that the camera be turned off, and unless impractical or impossible that request is made on the recording; or:
    c. the officer is interacting with a confidential informant used by the law enforcement agency (50 ILCS 706/10-20).

Since it is irresponsible to make such a large commitment, purchase, and organizational decision about a product, test wears were sought from several body-worn camera companies. Also, in governmental bodies a bid process needs to be sought. Bids limit the illegal issues of bribery and pay-to-play politics. Companies are not shown preferential treatment, and the best product with lowest price most often wins the bid. A decision that will impact each and every officer is better digested when those that it will most impact are part of the input in selecting a product that has been tested by the end user. Not all decisions within police organizations can be democratic, but a change in police and public culture this large should include officers from each rank. The companies chosen had to provide equipment that was capable of adhering to the guidelines set forth in the Illinois law.

The Policy

Prior to the test wear launch (called a pilot program within the Waukegan Police Department), a policy needed to be put into place. The complete policy was developed from the **International Associations of Chiefs of Police** (IACP) template, curtailed departmental needs, and included the Illinois law mandates. It was distributed with the understanding it would be a work in progress and would be tweaked during the pilot program. The understanding was between the police officers and administration. Specifically, the collective bargaining unit of patrol officers and the chief of police had a memorandum of understanding, discussing the implementation of the body-worn cameras.

The patrol officers were concerned about quite a few important aspects of the new technology. There was not unease in the way the officers performed their jobs but about issues such as turning the camera off for personal conversations, having the camera in the restroom, not being able to hear conversations in the pre-record mode, and disciplinary issues stemming from the video footage and how the camera footage would be reviewed. Addressing those concerns with a collective bargaining unit were critically important to put the bulk of officers at ease about the new technology. The following is an excerpt from the final Waukegan Police Department policy. This is included so the reader can observe the detail as to an officer's obligations with respect to proper use of the body-worn camera.

Officers assigned a Body-Worn Camera will activate the system to record the entire incident for all:

1. Routine calls for service
2. Investigatory stops
3. Traffic stops
4. Foot and vehicle pursuits
5. Emergency driving situations (unless MAV is activated) or vehicles may be captured on video leaving the crime scene (unless Mobile Audio Visual is activated)
6. High-risk situations, including search warrants
7. Situations that may enhance the probability of evidence-based prosecution
8. Transportation of any prisoner or citizen
9. Situations that the officer, through training and experience, believes to serve a proper police purpose, for example, recording the processing of an uncooperative arrestee.

NOTE: Officers will not unreasonably endanger themselves or another person to conform with the provisions of this order. If exigent circumstances exist which prevent the camera from being turned on, the camera must be turned on as soon as practicable (Waukegan Police Department, 2016, p. 3)

Selecting Officers

E-mails were sent to all officers, looking for volunteers, letting them know a pilot program was forthcoming and those interested in testing and evaluating different products should respond with their interest. There was enough interest because the officers knew the department was going to transition to body-worn cameras and it was suggested they have a part in the decision-making process on brands. Announcements were made via roll call and again on e-mail when the products were available for testing. The ideal test group would be two officers on each of the patrol shifts. With four patrol shifts, eight officers was a good sample size to test and evaluate. The chatter in the ever-present rumor mill of all police agencies about transitioning to a body-worn camera agency gained momentum with the e-mail looking for volunteers. Officers who wanted to have a say so in their equipment, policy, and technology stepped forward. Others who were merely curious wanted to be part of the pilot program. Officers who were motivated, able to articulate opinions, and in good standing were selected to test the body-worn cameras.

When officers experience change of any type, it can have an adverse effect. Typically police officers are regimented people, with consistency being their comfort. However, if agencies never change, change too quickly, do not have buy-in from the officers, or change too much there could be morale issues. Morale issues come in many forms but most often are officers complaining about not being a part of a process, not being consulted for their input, or otherwise general disdain toward administration. The Waukegan Police Department made a slow and deliberate effort with the body-worn camera program launch to alleviate potential issues. Ensuring there is adequate dialogue among supervisors and the rank and file is a best practice for police organizations. Specifically that dialogue is important when launching a program that touches every citizen the police will have contact with, along with every officer.

Selecting the Right Product

All companies promised many of the same the components. Most were recording capacity, prerecording features, and storage of data. The plan began to be tested in practice when the administration was asked and agreed to be the test site for Motorola Solutions' si500 body-worn camera. The equipment was state of the art and paired with the police portable radios.

The Waukegan Police Department had just purchased new radios for every officer, manufactured by Motorola. The new radios brought new technology to the officers, too. Each officer was assigned a radio. There was no sharing of radios, changing of radio numbers daily, or shortage of portable radios. The new portable radio and communications upgrade used the more efficient digital signals as opposed to analog. Although the Federal Communications Commission forced the change with a mandate, Waukegan planned and implemented the upgrade before many surrounding jurisdictions (Bercovici, 2006; Ruck, 2014).

Waukegan was to be the first police department in the world to have the equipment and body-worn camera, which Motorola designed. Once the agreement was set that Waukegan would beta test the Motorola body-worn camera that paired with the Motorola portable radio, the pilot program was nearly ready to start.

The features of the si500 were as follows: A screen that could view incidents after they were captured, the ability to place a report number with the incident captured instantly, a microphone to the portable radio, Bluetooth, stand-alone mode, and a wide rotational lens (to view incidents at different angles). The device itself is no larger than a cellular phone, with a large screen on one side, much like today's cellular phones. Those features seemed to be a step above of competitors. Also, when discussing the advancement in technology with law enforcement, it should be noted the more tools an officer carries, the more cumbersome the load is to manage. With the si500, there was immediate reprieve to lighten the load for officers. Instead of an officer carrying a portable radio, a microphone, and a body-worn camera with other products that were tested, the officer would carry a portable radio and a si500. The si500 had a dual function of being a microphone to the portable radio and a body-worn camera. This was an obvious first-of-its-kind technology and the premier body-worn camera technology.

Beta Test and Pilot Program

The beta test was countless hours on behalf of Motorola Solutions developers and the officers using the product. Motorola Solutions was on site at the Waukegan Police Department for months. There was data that needed to be uploaded and feedback needed from officers on the likes, dislikes, wants, and needs with respect to the product. Waukegan Police Officers were the face of the si500 as it made its way out of beta testing and into the market.

The pilot program for the police department wound up testing several companies, and Motorola was still the best suited for the department. Officers at the Waukegan Police Department had direct input on some of functionality of the si500, and feedback was considered and implemented. The police department selected Motorola as the body-worn camera that would lead the agency well into the 21st century. The Waukegan Police Department is credited with being the first police agency in the world to outfit all officers with the Motorola si500.

Launching the Product

The body-worn camera was launched to the entire police department in the summer of 2016. There were training sessions for each officer to ensure there was ease in use. Motorola Solutions provided the training, and several officers who were familiar with the product assisted in training and helped fellow officers when operational questions arose from time to time. The official body-worn camera policy was released and all officers were expected to follow it. There were quizzes given to officers to make sure they understood the fundamentals of the new policy.

With any new product, there were growing pains. Simply forgetting to turn on the camera was the most common problem. Within 3 months, it was routine to accept a call for service and turn the body-worn camera on. Officers caught on quickly and the department officially was a body-worn camera department by August of 2016.

Benefits of Body-Worn Cameras

Body-worn cameras reduced the number of sustained complaints against officers. In years past, when an officer was accused of racial profiling or rudeness, it too often became an issue of "he said, she said." Hours of interviewing and writing statements out had to be completed. With the body-worn camera footage, the reduced time it takes to investigate a complaint of rudeness or simple policy violation is only a fraction of the previous hours of legwork. The video is prima facie evidence for the complaint. The Waukegan Police

Department office of professional standards commander, Joe Florip, when asked about the body-worn camera program as it specifically relates to complaints, indicated officers are helped far more than hurt by footage on the body-worn cameras. Florip added that if an officer is rude or violates a policy, it is extremely helpful to show the officer the footage and have punishment administered to move on and try to be better.

All data on the body-worn camera is stored for a minimum of 90 days unless there is a special hold placed on the footage to be held longer for an arrest, complaint, training, or lawsuit. There is not the capability for an officer or anyone, other than the body-worn camera administration, to purge a video. Even when video is purged, there is still a document that a video existed and was purged.

The body-worn camera has the function to be a camera and take still images. This function proves invaluable when evidentiary photographs are needed and can be documented with a chain of custody. There is an audio recorder, too. If a citizen wants to make a verbal statement only, the body-worn camera can behave in the mode of a voice recorder only.

Being able to release footage that is redacted in specific incidents allows the public to see the perspective of the officer. In December of 2017, there was a police-involved shooting of a man armed with a BB gun. The officer was justified in the shooting, but body-worn camera footage along with the state attorney's decision went a long way in showing the public the point of view the officer had. There was not one protest with respect to that incident.

The copious amounts of footage retrieved proves to be valuable for training fellow officers. When there is an incident that officers can learn from (good tactics and bad), the footage can be used to train other officers. A large criticism of the police profession has been training. When officers can see relevant and real incidents, they will be able to use the skills learned from training to better perform their job. All video can be retrieved in a Web-based program. Officers are able to upload their body-worn camera content via Wi-Fi.

All incidents are on the body-worn camera and there is protection for the community and the police officers. There can be no disagreement about what occurred, what was said, or the manner in which a call for service was disposed. When the police and the public have that added layer of protection, there is a trust that is built but that is unable to be fully measured.

Drawbacks of Body-Worn Cameras

With all technology there can be errors that occur. During the beta test, there were flaws that were worked out, such as a battery issue that was discovered. The body-worn camera needed two batteries to last an entire shift of 12 hours. The officers would need to have access to batteries for the cameras. Chargers were installed in vehicles and around the police station and officers carried spare batteries on their person. The battery for the body-worn camera was small in comparison to the portable radio battery, but they were not interchangeable. The cameras do not have an internal battery that allows recording to continue after the rechargeable battery is dead. Therefore, if an officer is recording an incident and the battery dies, the incident will not be captured in its entirety.

Also, the redaction software process to exclude people who have expectations of privacy is time consuming. The ability to release video to the public takes too many staffing hours. Therefore, most Freedom of Information Act requests for body-worn camera footage are not released. A more ideal system would be to make body-worn camera footage readily available for all of the public to see via a website.

Expenses are the concern of all governmental bodies, especially with such an extensive program and commitment. The expenses include the hardware, high-speed Internet, training, and storage, but also having one person with a dedicated position to deal with all body-worn camera issues. When the state's attorney requests body-worn camera footage, that interaction and log must be completed and documented. One may argue that there is absolutely no price one can put on improving community relations and transparency of an organization.

Only a handful of officers have turned the camera off prematurely, turned it on too late, or not turned it on at all. Each and every officer was disciplined, pursuant to collective bargaining agreements and progressive discipline. Yet, those instances are types that lend the other 84,995 calls to be ignored when being critiqued. When some citizens want to judge a law enforcement agency or profession negatively, they can use the five instances in which there was a policy violation for swift discipline and still have doubts with respect to the body-worn cameras.

Conclusion

When Waukegan decided to move toward having body-worn camera policies, it was the perfect time to implement a program for the officers and community. The use of body-worn cameras can only improve public trust. The idea to include end users in the pilot program and slowly introduce the concept helped the change process, which could have backfired if done too quickly. Having technologically advanced radios assisted in making the decision to choose the Motorola si500 as the sole body-worn camera for the Waukegan Police Department. The launch of the product to all officers went smoothly because of a robust policy and dialogue between all ranks of the organization.

Although there have been a few incidents of technological issues and officers not having their camera on, the program is a success. A measure for success is that officers don their body-worn cameras with their uniform, just as routinely as they have with their handguns and handcuffs. When an incident comes into question, the public can be held accountable for inflammatory false accusations made against officers with body-worn camera footage. Or, the onus of the police officers' professionalism is available for critique and used for appropriate discipline to restore integrity to the department.

The successful implementation of a body-worn camera program in Waukegan, Illinois, did not happen by accident. A decision to provide officers with technology needed to perform their duties is guided by each incoming administration. Technology evolves and that technology can make police officers' jobs more difficult when criminals have it. Yet, it can also be utilized for police officers to keep them safer and restore public trust. That public trust is lost on a national level when significant events occur in law enforcement that paint all officers with the same brush.

This is not to say that Waukegan police will not face adversaries in the community who doubt the integrity and pride the officers swore to uphold. However, it is saying that this technological advancement was implemented successfully and the body-worn program is here to stay.

Key Terms

accountability: The quality of being responsible for one's actions.

body-worn camera: A wearable audio-video recording system worn by law enforcement officers to document their encounters with the public. Also known as a body camera.

Ferguson effect: A phenomenon observed in policing nationwide after the shooting of Michael Brown in Ferguson, Missouri, in August 2014. Characterized by officers who are less inclined to partake in marginal police work to avoid liability, and offenders feel empowered by the lack of police aggressiveness.

International Association of Chiefs of Police: An organization of law enforcement professionals dedicated to improving the profession of policing through research and program development.

transparency: A quality of organizational decision making characterized by openness to the public and clarity of the decision-making process.

Discussion Questions

- What do you think about police body cameras after reading the chapter?
- Why was it important for the Waukegan police to adopt body cameras?
- What were some of the important considerations for the Waukegan police when adopting body cameras?
- How did Waukegan police develop their policy about body cameras? Why do you think it is important to involve or rely on organizations such as the International Association of Chiefs of Police to develop these sorts of policies?
- Why is it important to involve the members at all levels of the organization when selecting and beta testing the equipment?
- What are some of the benefits of using body cameras? What are some drawbacks?
- Why do you think Waukegan met such success in the body camera program?

References

Byers, C. (2014, 15 November). Crime up after Ferguson and more police needed, top St. Louis area chiefs say. *St. Louis Post-Dispatch*. Retrieved from https://www.stltoday.com/news/local/crime-and-courts/crime-up-after-ferguson-and-more-police-needed-top-st/article_04d9f99f-9a9a-51be-a231-1707a57b50d6.html

Bercovici, M. (2006). *Federal Communications Commission narrowbanding mandate: A public safety guide for compliance*. Retrieved from https://transition.fcc.gov/pshs/docs/clearing-house/guidelines/Narrowbanding_Booklet.pdf

Hewlett, M. (27 May 2014). Man shot by officer died from blood loss, police say. *Winston Salem Journal*. Retrieved from https://www.journalnow.com/news/local/man-shot-by-officer-died-from-blood-loss-police-say/article_32532c8a-9438-55a7-bfea-17c36825fe01.html

Illinois Compiled Statutes, 50 ILCS 706/10-201 (2018). Retrieved from http://www.ilga.gov/legislation/ilcs/documents/005007060K10-20.htm

Ruck, W. (2010). Narrowband conversion and digital modulation [White paper]. CSI Telecommunications. Retrieved from http://www.csitele.com/wp-content/uploads/2014/06/Narrowbanding.pdf

Smith, D & Mather, K. (2017. February 28), 20 years ago, a dramatic North Hollywood shootout changed the course of the LAPD and policing at large. *Los Angeles Times*. Retrieved from http://www.latimes.com/local/lanow/la-me-ln-north-hollywood-shootout-revisited-20170223-htmlstory.html

U.S. Census Bureau. (n.d). *Waukegan city, Illinois quick facts.* Retrieved from https://www.census.gov/quickfacts/fact/table/waukegancityillinois/PST045216

Waukegan Police Department. (2016). General Order—Oper. 11. Retrieved from http://www.waukeganweb.net/DocumentCenter/View/1362

CHAPTER 14

Beyond the Supply Side

Crime, Policing, and the Fourth Industrial Revolution

By Mark A. Tallman

> *"Border Patrol erects this fence, only to go out a few days later and discover that these guys have a catapult. And they're flinging hundred-pound bales of marijuana over to the other side. A catapult. We've got the best fence money can buy, and they counter us with a 2,500 year old technology."*
>
> —Michael Braun, former DEA chief of operations (Anderson, 2012)

Opening Questions

Answer the following question before reading this chapter:

> What do you know about modern criminal manufacturing and its effect on policing prior to reading this chapter?

Answer the following question while reading the chapter:

> What are some concepts from the chapter that stand out to you? Why do you think they are important?

In June 2013, a psychologically disturbed man named John Zawahri went on a carjacking and shooting spree across Santa Monica, California. The incident resulted in six deaths, ending in a brief firefight with police at the Santa Monica College Library (Office of Emergency Management, 2014). It seemed to fit the mold of what has become a *perfectly routine shooting spree*, but investigators later discovered an unusual detail. Two years earlier, the Department of Justice denied Zawahri the right to possess firearms due to his psychiatric records. This made him unable to *legally* possess firearms, and he failed the background checks at any licensed retailer. Instead, he carried out his attack with a fully functional semiautomatic rifle cobbled together from **precursor parts**. He legally purchased the rifle's barrel, stock, fire-control components, and other unregulated secondary parts. The primary component of the weapon was the lower receiver, and a background check was required to purchase one in functional condition. Zawahri circumvented this requirement by purchasing a nonfunctional receiver blank. This is the central part of a firearm, except that the fire-control cavity area is completely solid and un-machined (i.e., it cannot shoot). However, he was able to complete it in his own workshop with inexpensive tools. Zawahri made himself a **ghost gun**. Until the morning of his killing spree, he was the only person who knew his gun existed.

Fifteen hundred miles to the south in September 2016, the U.S. Coast Guard and Joint Interagency Task Force South intercepted a **narco-submersible** off the Central American coast. Narco-sub crews frequently scuttle their craft when intercepted (Bunker & Ramirez, 2015). This minimizes evidence recovery and forces pursuers to divert resources toward rescue. In this case the submariners failed to scuttle in time. The Coast Guard arrested five smugglers and seized the submarine's 2.6-ton cocaine payload (Woody, 2016). The seizure represented more than $73 million in street value. Yet, this may only reflect a modest loss for the well-resourced trafficking organizations that build and crew these boats. Payloads on larger narco-submersibles can reach values in excess of $200 million per shipment (Bunker & Ramirez, 2015), and a majority of these clandestine craft are believed to elude interdiction.

Besides their obvious criminality, what do these seemingly disparate incidents have in common? Both were facilitated by **clandestine illicit manufacturing**. In the cases of so-called ghost guns and narco-submarines, the ability to clandestinely produce functional analogs of industrial items is critical to criminal success. Ghost guns and narco-submersibles have received media attention in recent years, but there are many manifestations of illicit manufacturing to be found in 21st-century crime.

Criminal manufacturing is diverse and oftentimes imaginative: Police have encountered precision-manufactured **card skimmers** that steal user data while appearing to be legitimate components of automated teller machines (Krebs, 2011). Counterfeiting of consumer goods has grown by as much as 10,000% in the last 20 years (Chaudhry & Zimmerman, 2013). Precision forgeries of art and artifacts have led major auction houses to develop sophisticated forensic units (Gates, 2018). In many countries, counterfeit cigarettes and pharmaceutical drugs are significant substitutes for the real thing. Drug traffickers maintain sophisticated supply chains to manufacture and deliver their illegal wares. Militias, traffickers, and extremist groups manufacture their own weapons. Nowadays, these include not only small arms but aerial drones, improvised explosives, mines, light infantry weapons, and armored vehicles. ISIS terrorists use commercial parts to build aerial drones and weaponize them with small explosive payloads.

Media attention gravitates toward high-tech criminal manufacturing phenomena such as 3D-printed firearms, weaponized drones, or new trends in illegal synthetic drugs. In truth, illicit manufacturing is not a new phenomenon. Governments from ancient times to the present have struggled to control illicit production of contraband and the counterfeiting of currency and goods. Many longstanding criminal phenomena involve some form of production. What differs today is the emergence of technologies that are revolutionizing how physical objects are made, used, and controlled.

What Is the Fourth Industrial Revolution?

Illicit production is a longstanding phenomenon, but there is concern about a widening scope of security challenges brought by ongoing advancements in manufacturing and information systems. Often referred to as the **fourth industrial revolution**, these advancements reflect an accelerating **democratization of capability**, which has been developing incrementally since the earliest days of industrialization. Smaller, more independent, and more widely dispersed parties are becoming capable of activities that were previously possible only for mainstream institutions.

The fourth industrial revolution is actually several technologic revolutions in one. These reflect major advances in electronics, robotics, digital fabrication and **distributed manufacturing** (DM), the **Internet of things** (IoT), artificial intelligence, nanotechnology, and biotechnology. The groundwork was laid by the digital revolution. Starting in the 1950s, the digital revolution supplanted mechanical and electrical devices with increasingly powerful and miniaturized digital electronics. Among a multitude of effects, the digital revolution enabled massive strides in generating, storing, transferring, and analyzing information through the use of digital devices. The digital revolution is completely embedded in modern life, and its impacts are so undeniable that it is often referred to as the third industrial revolution. The digital revolution enabled the fourth industrial revolution because the fourth revolution is based on digital electronics and information systems. Robotics, digital fabrication, the Internet of things, nanotechnology, artificial intelligence, and biotechnology are all advancing rapidly. These subfields are also integrating with each other as part of a wider cyber-physical revolution.

As the digital revolution democratized the capacity to generate, transfer, and leverage information through virtual space, the fourth industrial revolution promises to decentralize the design, manufacture, and operation of an ever-widening array of material goods in physical space (Schwab, 2016). Through a combination of old and new technologies, the barriers to manufacturing are falling. Digital fabrication tools can precisely fabricate objects based on digital instructions. Lower-tech shop tools have also become better, cheaper, and more accessible around the world. With skill, software, materials, and a workshop full of digital and analog tools, independent actors can increasingly emulate the products found in mainstream industries.

Digital manufacturing can be *additive* or *subtractive*. Three-dimensional printers are the most recognized additive tools. Through a series of innovative methods, 3D printers precisely build objects by repeatedly adding material until the desired object is formed (Lipson & Kurman, 2013). Digital fabrication can also be subtractive: Instead of adding material, subtractive tools cut away material to form the desired object. Historically, subtractive manufacturing is how most physical items have been made. Simpler hand tools, shop tools, and analog machine tools have been used for subtractive manufacturing since the earliest days of artisanal production. However, recent decades have seen major advances and cost decreases in digital tools. Digital subtractive tools are often referred to as computer numeric controlled (CNC). Similar to a 3D printer, the CNC mill can fabricate complex objects with outstanding precision based on digital instructions.

Digital fabrication can be undertaken using existing digital design files, or an operator can use computer-aided design and manufacturing (CAD/CAM) software to design and produce virtually any physical object the tool can accommodate. Image-capture technologies make some digital fabrication tasks accessible to users with less need for design and programming skill. When combined with high-resolution digital imagery, software can precisely measure an object's physical dimensions and automatically generate the code to replicate it.

Home printers are usually fed with prepackaged filaments of household plastics such as polylactic acid (PLA) or acrylonitrile butadiene styrene (ABS), while CNC mills can precisely carve objects from most metals, woods, or plastics. As digital fabrication advances, a wider range of materials will become available for home and small business applications. Printers capable of fabricating in metal alloys, carbon fiber, Kevlar, silicone, and plastic-metal hybrid materials have entered the market. Additionally, mixed-material printers enable fabrication using multiple materials in the same object, improving many products.

Along with these advances in digital fabrication, there are other advances in **open source** or do-it-yourself (DIY) production. With open source hardware projects such as Arduino, users design and build electronic hardware. More than 1.4 million users have used Arduino or other open-source DIY hardware and software kits to build digital fabrication machines, home computing devices, robots, thermostats, motion detectors, laser cutters, telecom devices, audio-visual electronics, network and wireless devices, cameras, laboratory equipment, lighting, automotive parts, unmanned aerial vehicles, and a variety of other creative items (Medea, 2013). With open-source hardware and designs, it is possible for users to build plastic and metal 3D printers. The RepRap project is focused on building 3D printers using open-source designs and materials, with the eventual goal of making printers that are fully self-replicating.

Digital tools and various forms of DIY production are moving into the chemical and biomedical fields as well. Three-dimensional printable medical devices, surgical instruments, and implants are already in use. With bioprinting, the ink is composed of biological material. Bio-printable cartilage, bone, stem cells, skin grafts, and entire organs are in development (Lipson & Kurman, 2013). Chemical compounds can be digitally fabricated, and in 2015 the first 3D-printable pharmaceutical drug won FDA approval (Hicks, 2016). Custom-printable chemicals and drugs will revolutionize medicine and other industries. Even without digital fabrication or access to institutional resources, DIY capabilities continue to expand. DIY biohackers and medical **hacktivists** use portable kits and equipment to produce drugs and medical devices and to engage in home genetic engineering projects (Baumgartner, 2018; Biggs, 2016; Garcia & Monticello, 2017; Greenfield Boyce, 2018; Ledford, 2015).

The fourth industrial revolution encompasses rapid developments and increasing integration between all these subfields. Some of the developments are quite straightforward, but their results become more complex when advancements in multiple fields combine. For example, robots have been used as a labor-saving tool in industrial assembly lines for decades. However, industrial robots currently remain limited to specialized manufacturing and assembly tasks and must be designed, configured, maintained, operated, and supervised by humans. Complex products still cannot be designed, manufactured, and delivered without substantial inputs of skilled and semiskilled human labor.

This will change. Artificial intelligence will assist in designing and testing products and will even design the tools and materials needed to make products. Digital fabrication tools such as 3D printers and CNC machines will enable a wide range of physical objects, drugs, chemicals, foods, medical devices, textiles, and electronics to be manufactured with outstanding precision from more locations. Robots will be networked with digital fabrication tools to build, assemble, and package physical products with minimal need for human labor. If a product is medical, agricultural, or even textile, it may include customized biotechnologies, nanotechnologies, or both. Networked autonomous vehicles will transport raw materials to the manufacturing line, then deliver finished products by air, land, and sea.

All these technologies are increasingly integrated into **cyber-physical** systems. Cyber-physical systems are configurations of technology that enable physical actions based on virtual commands. These systems already play an essential role in critical infrastructure, industries, and services. Examples can be found in complex industrial infrastructures such as natural gas pipelines, robotic assembly lines, or electrical grids. The systems are often controlled remotely by supervisory control and data acquisition (SCADA) software. The software monitors data it receives from sensors and other components. Users remotely control these systems by sending commands to components such as programmable logic controllers (PLCs). PLCs are miniaturized computers that can control the physical actions of other components.

Cyber-physical systems were initially developed to control industrial processes in real time. These types of cyber-physical industrial systems have been developing since the 1970s, but within the last decade an increasing number of consumer products have come to qualify as cyber-physical as well. The Internet of things refers to the rapidly growing number of networked devices. Through the networking of industrial tools, transportation systems, critical infrastructure, and consumer products, cyber-physical capabilities are becoming embedded in modern society. Products as varied as automobiles, home appliances, smart home systems, surgical equipment, medical devices and implants, consumer electronics, agricultural tools, electric meters, and toys now involve some element of cyber-physical connectivity. Up to 30 billion devices are expected to be connected by 2020 (Statista, 2018).

The practical result of these technologies is that more parties will be able to produce wider selections of physical, chemical, electronic, and biotech products, and the products will be increasingly sophisticated. This transformation is already bringing many concrete benefits for industry and consumers, and the fourth industrial revolution's positive potential cannot be overstated. Nevertheless, recent trends suggest that we will soon encounter many interesting expansions in illicit manufacturing and other criminal tactics enabled by it. Historically, many crimes have been defined in terms of *taking stuff*. Today, technology is providing more options for crimes that involve *making stuff*.

How Will the Fourth Industrial Revolution Impact Crime, Policing, and Security?

The advances of the fourth industrial revolution are extraordinary, and their security implications are numerous. Modern policing and regulatory systems arose during industrialization, and they are premised on industrial-era assumptions about how things are made. As the fourth industrial revolution proceeds, some of these assumptions will be challenged by new criminal uses of manufacturing technology. World Economic Forum Chairman Klaus Schwab forecasts that the fourth industrial revolution will "profoundly impact the nature of national and international security" (Schwab, 2016, para. 24). Arizmendi, Pronk, and Choi (2014) identified impacts to crime control, regulatory regimes, state security, legitimacy, and monopoly of force. Writing for the RAND Corporation, Trevor Johnston, Troy Smith, and Luke Irwin (2018) find that additive manufacturing alone has "the potential to dramatically disrupt the prevailing state system and international order" (p. 2), with potential for "dramatic effects on international conflict, violent extremism, and even everyday crime" (p. 13).

While we can only speculate as to the full scope of long-term impacts, there are several important dimensions in which the fourth industrial revolution can be expected to impact crime and policing. First, the fourth industrial revolution will undermine orthodox **supply-side** regulations and enforcement tactics. Second, it will expand the capabilities of criminals, extremists, police, and intelligence organizations. Third, it will produce wider socioeconomic impacts that may undermine security and safety. Last, high-tech illicit manufacturing will likely result in security cost attrition.

Undermining Supply-Side Enforcement Strategies

Historically, most governments have adopted regulatory systems to govern the manufacture and distribution of certain goods. Supply-side strategies involve disrupting and reducing the supply of contraband goods or reducing **diversion** of regulated goods to illicit markets or users. Supply-side strategies are ostensibly intended to reduce social harms by making it more difficult to access contraband. Narcotics interdiction provides one of the clearest examples of a supply-side approach. Narcotics interdiction attempts to reduce the use of illegal drugs by reducing consumer access to them. Attacking the complex supply chains behind illicit drugs has been a primary approach of narcotics interdiction since its inception. Reducing the illicit supply is assumed to reduce illicit access, and reducing illicit access is assumed to reduce the aggregate social burdens of illegal drug use.

While the supply-side approach is obvious in many drug enforcement initiatives, law enforcers adopt supply-side tactics for many other offenses. Anti-counterfeiting, anti-fraud, weapons-trafficking interdiction, counter-proliferation, counter-narcotics, and counterterrorism, each make some use of supply-side tactics. This may involve regulating the supply and distribution of certain legal products or attacking the supply chains that enable illicit manufacturing. Supply chain regulations can be powerful tools of social control because they impose material boundaries over what can be made, who can make it, who can buy or possess it, how the product will be monitored and tracked, and penalties for being caught in noncompliance.

However, the results of supply-side controls have been mixed. Controlling the supply of a product is easier for products legally manufactured by cooperating commercial businesses than for products that are manufactured clandestinely by illicit suppliers. Likewise, strong consumer demand for a product virtually guarantees that criminals will attempt to supply it at profit. The first and second industrial revolutions massively increased productivity by consolidating production of many goods to centralized factories and economies of scale. Centralization of manufacturing in licensed industrial facilities made it possible to monitor, track, and control the distribution of many legally made products. As a result, supply-side controls are often applied to narcotics and pharmaceutical drugs, explosives, firearms, military technologies, vehicles, and other items that are legally manufactured but potentially hazardous in the wrong hands.

However, it can be much more difficult to control a product that is illicitly produced. Legitimate manufacturers are accessible to state authorities and generally respond to regulatory requirements. In contrast, illicit production is clandestine and adversarial toward legal authorities. As technology expands the portfolio of products that can be illegally produced, supply-side tactics will be increasingly challenged. Some high-risk products may become more accessible outside of regulated supply chains. The security implications are clearest with regard to weapons. Despite media attention on much-hyped 3D-printed guns, printable weapons remain in their infancy, and the greatest strides in digitally fabricated weapons will not come from hobbyists or criminals but the defense industries. Nevertheless, criminals and independent hobbyists have produced innovative designs, and independent gun making appears to be popularizing.

High-quality firearms and accessories are legally produced by independent hobbyists and small businesses in the United States, and a range of firearms of varying quality are produced by illicit makers around the world. Most are metal firearms built with hand tools, electrified shop tools, or digital CNC. Some innovative DIYers have been experimenting with printable synthetic firearms. Around the world, organized crime, militias, and lone wolves build many styles of small firearms. Illegal gun making and customization certainly occurs in the United States, but the availability of high-quality industry-made firearms may reduce criminal incentives for homemade guns in the United States and in other nations where conventional guns are relatively easy to illegally acquire.

Some criminal organizations, terrorists, and street gangs have gravitated toward expedient homemade pistols and submachine guns or decommissioned firearms reactivated with workshop tools. Many of these weapons are knockoffs of simple industry products or are based on guerilla gunsmithing designs that circulate in print publications and the Internet. While firearms are an example of a consumer product that is tracked and controlled from the supply side, the reality is that firearms are already accessible to many illicit users around the world. Supply-side gun controls may be undermined by independent gun making, but DIY production is only one more source of illegal guns among many. Independent production of less common weapons may prove more disruptive for policing and national security.

Explosives are regulated and tracked similarly to small arms but are controlled more restrictively. Explosives are also produced in smaller volumes, and fewer explosive products are marketed to the public. Consequently, supply-side controls on explosives have been comparatively effective. For decades, terrorists and other **violent non-state actors** (VNSAs) have used available tools and materials to improvise explosives and light weapons such as mortars, grenades, mines, and recoilless rifles. However, digitally fabricated munitions and delivery platforms may further undermine the control of explosive weapons over time. Some analysts believe this would be a much more significant security development than homemade firearms, and the FBI has purchased digital fabrication tools to evaluate their viability for illegal bomb making (Tirone & Gilley, 2015; J. Wachtel, personal communication, 2016).

International efforts to prevent weapons proliferation to conflict zones have generally failed. However, increased manufacturing of weapons within conflict zones, or by the belligerents, may change the dynamics of terrorism, insurgency, and conflict resolution. Sustainable disarmament is difficult to guarantee when new weapons can be easily manufactured. Likewise, it could become more difficult to negotiate with violent groups, as hardliners may no longer depend on mainstream organizational support to procure weapons and equipment.

As criminal uses of digital fabricators increase, governments may seek to control information that can be used for illicit manufacturing. This introduces issues for privacy, civil liberties, intellectual property, and freedom of information. Censorship is also problematic since **data mules** already smuggle information into even the most repressive countries using current technology (Fenton, 2016; Greenberg, 2015b; News Desk, 2016). With continued development in open-source hardware, software, digital fabrication, and nanotechnology, options for spying, hacking, and data smuggling will increase. Chemical printing and bioprinting will challenge supply-side drug controls, and an increasing range of synthetic drugs and counterfeit pharmaceuticals may be manufactured. Counterfeiters already make convincing knockoffs of luxury watches, handbags, textiles, consumer electronics, art, and other products. These counterfeits will further improve, and their production will further decentralize. Supply-side strategies attempt to control social outcomes by controlling the physical distribution of goods. Yet, when more products can be manufactured outside of regulated supply chains, the longstanding supply-side approach to security and public safety may be fundamentally challenged.

Expanding Illicit Capabilities and Tactics

Expanded technical capabilities translate to expanded tactics. For example, digital fabrication of weapons or synthetic drugs doesn't only undermine controls on manufacturing these items, it also provides new criminal tactics to circumvent interdiction. Border security and trafficking interdiction tactics will be challenged as drugs, guns, and other contraband are manufactured closer to their illicit purchasers and require smaller criminal networks to make and distribute. Contraband products such as drugs, weapons, and weapon components may be custom manufactured to pass through screening systems.

Printable synthetic firearms are currently limited in capability, and their reliance on metal-cased ammunition makes them comparatively difficult to conceal from screening devices. Nevertheless, it is already possible to smuggle plastic and even metal weapons through screening portals undetected. Synthetic materials and custom designs will eventually create additional challenges for detecting weapons, drugs, and other contraband.

Further, though most printable firearms currently compare unfavorably to conventional products, the ability to rapidly destroy synthetic firearms may be appealing for offenders wishing to minimize exposure to law enforcement.

Building objects that can pass through security screening is a straightforward tactic, but cyber-physical technologies will introduce other methods to attack secure areas. Using software applications such as KeysForge, users can precisely replicate keys based on high-resolution photos taken from 200 feet away (Greenberg, 2015a). Hackers have already compromised cyber-physical systems such as electrical grids and industrial assembly lines. When digital fabrication becomes integrated with robotic assembly and autonomous vehicle delivery, it may be possible for hackers to remotely sabotage facilities, smuggle bombs or weapons by building them within secure areas, or cause weapons to be built remotely and delivered to targets elsewhere.

The ability to build increasingly sophisticated armored vehicles, aerial vehicles, submersibles, and remotely piloted and autonomous vehicles, will surely impact counter-terrorism and smuggling interdiction tactics. As self-driving vehicles involve fewer human drivers with fewer moving violations, the current legal bases behind traffic enforcement and highway interdiction may be undermined (Washington, 2016). Hackers can already monitor and control vehicles from afar (Federal Bureau of Investigation, Department of Transportation, & National Highway Traffic Safety Administration, 2016). As self-driving vehicles popularize, malicious actors may realize they can manipulate automated systems to create traffic jams, cause accidents, force-halt vehicles to attack passengers, or even kidnap victims remotely.

Consumer-grade aerial drones have been encountered smuggling contraband into prisons and across the U.S.-Mexico border (Carroll, 2016; S. Horowitz, 2018). Terrorists and home hobbyists have constructed and weaponized aerial drones (Bailey, 2016; Gettinger, 2016). Drug traffickers construct narco-submarines to smuggle large payloads undetected and use sophisticated industrial boring vehicles to dig underground smuggling tunnels (Anderson, 2014). Cartels, militias, and terrorists manufacture improvised armored vehicles (Axe & Dozier, 2017; Bender, 2015). Open-source software kits are enabling users to retrofit automobiles with self-driving systems (Dwoskin, 2016). Extremists have demonstrated the lethality of vehicle attacks in recent years, but defense may become more challenging when multiple self-driving vehicles can attack while the operator avoids capture. Narco-submarines appear to be a successful innovation, but they are dangerous to operate and their human crews require valuable payload space. Self-guiding narco-submersibles may solve this problem: Autonomous narco-submarines could devote more space to payload, travel longer ranges with lower risk of interception, can be refueled by a receiving crew, and be sent back for reuse.

Military, telecom, and intelligence capabilities will circulate more widely as it becomes easier to construct electronic devices. With the ability to make custom electronics comes the ability to make electronic warfare, eavesdropping, imaging, hacking, communications, and data smuggling equipment. Weinbaum, Berner, and McClintock (2017) observe that signals intelligence (SIGINT) technologies are becoming more accessible to non-state actors. Mexican drug traffickers have even built their own encrypted telecom infrastructures to avoid state surveillance (Beaubien, 2011). Regulated military technologies such as night vision optics, advanced sensors, avionics, electronic warfare, and navigational systems may become harder to control as they become easier to build. Digital manufacturing, chemical printing, bioprinting, and DIY biohacking may make it easier for terrorists or rogue states to develop poisons and weapons of mass destruction (WMD) (Greenfield Boyce, 2018). Trade controls on sensitive technologies are longstanding methods of containing WMD proliferation, but the fourth industrial revolution may provide rogue actors with added options to circumvent trade sanctions.

Social Effects

The disruptive impacts of the fourth industrial revolution will range far beyond crime or extremism. Mainstream economies, politics, and social life will be affected. Some forecasters believe additive manufacturing alone will constitute 50% of all manufacturing within 2 decades, and increasingly localized production could reduce global trade by up to 25% within 40 years (Leering, 2017). Such a significant reorganization of production could prove destabilizing for political systems, economies, and international trade. As the fourth industrial revolution proceeds, mainstream manufacturing will require fewer human workers. The remaining workforce would be high skill, but many lower-skill manufacturing and service jobs would disappear. The World Economic Forum finds that the fourth industrial revolution will eliminate over 5 million jobs in 15 countries over the next 5 years alone (Schwab & Samans, 2016). Johnston, Smith, and Irwin (2018) write that "[u]nemployment, isolation, and alienation of middle- and low-skilled laborers could be exacerbated by additive manufacturing, potentially leading to societal unrest in both developed and developing countries" (p. 16).

If technologic change leaves large populations economically or politically disenfranchised, the pool of individuals susceptible to criminal activity or violent radicalization may grow. Technical knowledge is an advantage for criminals and terrorists, and engineers may be overrepresented among terrorism offenders (Berrett, 2016). Economic displacements will eventually become significant, but they will not happen overnight. In the interim, education and workforce training for digital fabrication is expanding. More workers will have the skills to build more things, but many of the same workers could later find themselves unemployed as technology advances. Maintaining economic opportunity, political rights, and social dignity among those whose livelihoods are disrupted by the fourth industrial revolution may prove a necessary inoculation against criminality and extremism.

Economic disruptions could also impact criminal organizations. Transnational drug trafficking organizations generate massive revenues through large-scale supply chains. However, when drugs can be made closer to their consumers, local producers and distributors may become less dependent on cartel suppliers. Transnational traffickers will explore every opportunity to use new technologies but may lose much of their advantage as it becomes possible to supply synthetic drugs without centralized production or transnational smuggling. Violence may occur as local parties compete for dominance within markets previously claimed by comparatively stable cartel leadership. Local criminal groups will become less dependent on cross-border smuggling or on illegal diversion of legal products like firearms. This decentralization of illicit supply chains and organizational structures may prove more difficult to combat.

Security Cost Attrition

Technology has incrementally expanded the capabilities of criminals and violent groups since the early days of industrialization. Conventionally weak actors have increasingly prevailed against conventionally strong actors in armed conflicts (Arreguin-Toft, 2005), and criminal organizations have used technology to improve resilience, increase capabilities, and expand their supply chains (Albanese, 2011). Police and security organizations can gain great benefits from adopting new technologies. Yet, as illicit capabilities increase, the scope and costs of countermeasures do too. Attackers frequently enjoy the initiative: They choose when and where to attack, they can target many different vulnerabilities, and they typically have multiple attack methods to choose from. Smaller and more flexible organizations are better able to adopt new tactics (M. Horowitz, 2010), and bureaucratic policing institutions often struggle to keep pace with criminal innovations. Yet, the speed of criminal innovation is not the only reason the fourth industrial revolution could dramatically increase security costs. The costs of security also rise because new criminal capabilities do not eliminate the old ones.

Illicit actors gain cumulative benefits from accessing new technologies and tactics, while defenders must often pay cumulative costs to develop an ever-widening scope of countermeasures. Ghost guns and narco-submarines illustrate the dynamic. Ghost guns are an increasingly accessible option for illegal firearm procurement. Yet, even when authorities deem ghost guns worthy of new regulatory initiatives, conventional methods of procuring illicit firearms (such as theft, diversion, and smuggling) are already successful and will continue. Combating preexisting methods requires continued enforcement costs, while countering emerging methods entails new costs. Similarly, narco-submarines were a significant innovation in maritime smuggling. Due in part to the longtime monopoly on submersible technology held by state-approved military and research organizations, maritime interdiction has focused on detection of surface craft. Interdiction resources were reoriented to detect stealthy submersibles only after it became apparent that narco-subs were completing sorties undetected.

Narco-submarines cost only a small fraction of a single shipment's value. In contrast, reorienting interdiction forces toward combating narco-subs will require costly investments in anti-submarine equipment, training, and deployments. Even as defenders pay new costs to combat narco-subs, traffickers can combine submarines with preexisting methods. *Fast boats* are still used for short-range high-speed runs, bigger payloads are smuggled on large *slow boats*, and swarms of small and slow-moving *Panga* boats overwhelm Coast Guard abilities to intercept and search them all (Bunker & Ramirez, 2015). Each of these methods requires different countermeasures, and each new countermeasure tends to increase cumulative security costs. If a criminal method stops working, traffickers can stop investing in it. However, even when enforcement countermeasures are effective against a troublesome criminal technique, the countermeasures must be maintained indefinitely or criminals will start using the technique again. Malicious actors can adopt new methods as technology makes them available, but they can also use simpler methods simultaneously. As the fourth industrial revolution expands the scope of criminal capabilities, it is likely to expand the scope, costs, and invasiveness of the policing measures proposed to manage it.

Conclusion: Printing Pandora's Box: Challenges and Opportunities for Post-Industrial Policing

> *"Ultimately, the ability of government systems and public authorities to adapt will determine their survival. If they prove capable of embracing a world of disruptive change, subjecting their structures to the levels of transparency and efficiency that will enable them to maintain their competitive edge, they will endure. If they cannot evolve, they will face increasing trouble."*
>
> —Klaus Schwab, Chairman, World Economic Forum (Schwab, 2016)

"Police agencies should be looking five or ten years down the track. You've got technology as it is, but then you've got where it will be in five or ten years' time. You've got to start looking at that early or you'll be way behind the game."

—Nick O'Brien, Professor of Counterterrorism/International Terrorism Liaison Officer, New Scotland Yard Special Branch (Ret.) (Tallman, 2017, p. 735)

The fourth industrial revolution will bring new challenges for policing and security. Societies will increasingly reflect post-industrial conditions in which almost all material goods can be supplied cheaply and conveniently. As it becomes easier to make contraband, it will become harder to impose supply-side controls on some products. Malicious actors will gain new options for spying, smuggling, fraud, hacking, counterfeiting, and physical attacks. Socioeconomic changes may create challenges for politics, security, and social stability. The scope and costs of policing are likely to expand as authorities try to defend against a widening array of criminal capabilities.

However, the fourth industrial revolution will also bring incredible advances for mainstream manufacturing, medicine, transportation, construction, aerospace, mining, agriculture, defense, policing, and many other fields. Drones are increasingly deployed for tactical operations, surveillance, search and rescue, combat medicine, natural hazard mapping, and wildland firefighting. Digital fabrication will improve forensic sciences and crime scene reconstruction, while making it easier to customize and maintain weapons, fleet vehicles, electronics, and other equipment. Improved materials will make equipment lighter, more durable, and more protective. Improved drones, scanning tools, and miniaturized electronics will increase access to incident scenes, strengthen situational awareness, and provide better opportunities for less-lethal and nonlethal resolutions. Surveillance technology will improve investigation of many offenses, yet unrestrained deployment of surveillance technologies could fundamentally alter free society. Balance between security and civil liberties will be hotly debated while criminals, terrorists, researchers, courts, legislators, and law enforcers each try to adapt to the new realities of post-industrial crime.

Key Terms

card skimmers: Devices that steal user data while appearing to be legitimate components of legitimate financial transaction decives, such as automated teller machines or a merchant's credit card scanners.

clandestine illicit manufacturing: Covert industrial operations, usually at the individual level, intent on making functional equivalents or counterfeits of industrial items.

cyber-physical: Configurations of technology that enable physical actions based on virtual commands.

data mules: Computers that are transported from place to place, used to synchronize information on computers that are not connected to one another, to replicate the function of a physical network.

democratization of capability: The effect modern technology has had on the capability of individuals to engage in activities that were previously possible only for mainstream manufacturing institutions.

distributed manufacturing: Local manufacturing of goods.

diversion: The illicit rerouting of regulated goods (such as firearm parts of prescription drugs) from legal suppliers to the black market.

fourth industrial revolution: The current era of industry. Characterized by democratization of capability.

ghost gun: A homemade firearm that is a functional equivalent to an industry-produced firearm.

hacktivists: A portmanteau of "hacker" and "activist." Politically motivated computer hackers.

Internet of things: A term used to describe how the rapid proliferation of connectivity, availability of cloud computing, along with the miniaturization of sensors and communications chips have made it possible for physical devices such as homes, phones, automobiles, and so on to connect and exchange data (Harvard Business Review, 2014).

precursor parts: The constituent parts of a manufactured good. In the case of regulated goods, such as firearms, these parts are largely unregulated in and of themselves.

narco-submersible: A covertly manufactured submarine designed to smuggle illegal drugs by water.

open source: Cooperatively developed software licensed in such a way that allows for free distribution and allows users to modify the software as they like.

supply side: A regulatory system designed to govern the manufacture and distribution of certain goods, ostensibly intended to reduce social harms by making it more difficult to access contraband.

violent non-state actors: Individuals or organizations willing and capable to use violence for pursuing their objectives and not integrated into formalized state institutions such as regular armies, presidential guards, police, or special forces (Hofmann & Schneckener, 2011).

Discussion Questions

- What do you think about modern criminal manufacturing and its effect on policing after reading the chapter?
- What is the fourth industrial revolution and how will it affect policing both today and moving forward?
- How will the fourth industrial revolution affect current law enforcement strategies?
- What effect will the fourth industrial revolution have on the potential for criminality?
- What are the social effects of the fourth industrial revolution?

- What is your biggest concern about the democratization of capability that characterizes the fourth industrial revolution?

References

Albanese, J. S. (2011). *Transnational crime and the 21st century: Criminal enterprise, corruption, and opportunity.* Oxford, UK: Oxford University Press.

Anderson, B. (2012, June 18). Catapults and jalapeños: The ingenious smuggling tech of the world's top drug kingpin [Blog post]. *Motherboard.* Retrieved from https://motherboard.vice.com/en_us/article/qkkmzd/the-ingenious-smuggling-tech-of-the-worlds-top-drug-kingpin

Anderson, B. (2014, January 6). Mexican cartels are using firetruck-sized drillers to make drug pipelines [Blog post]. *Motherboard.* Retrieved from https://motherboard.vice.com/en_us/article/8qxax5/mexican-cartels-are-using-firetruck-sized-drillers-to-make-drug-pipelines

Arizmendi, C., Pronk, B., & Choi, J. (2014). Services no longer required? Challenges to the state as primary security provider in the age of digital fabrication. *Small Wars Journal, 22*(11). Retrieved from http://smallwarsjournal.com/print/15839

Arreguin-Toft, I. M. (2005). *How the weak win wars: A theory of asymmetric conflict.* New York, NY: Cambridge University Press.

Axe, D., & Dozier, K. (2017, March 18). Monster machines: ISIS's armored war Jeeps are professional grade. *Daily Beast.* Retrieved from https://www.thedailybeast.com/articles/2017/03/18/monster-machines-isis-s-armored-war-jeeps-are-professional-grade

Bailey, R. (2016, December 28). Weaponized drones and the Second Amendment [Blog post]. *Reason.* Retrieved from https://reason.com/blog/2016/12/28/weaponized-drones-and-the-second-amendme

Baumgartner, E. (2018, May 14). As D.I.Y gene editing gains popularity, 'someone is going to get hurt.' *New York Times.* Retrieved from https://www.nytimes.com/2018/05/14/science/biohackers-gene-editing-virus.html

Beaubien, J. (2011, December 9). Mexico busts drug cartels' private phone networks. *NPR.* Retrieved from https://www.npr.org/2011/12/09/143442365/mexico-busts-drug-cartels-private-phone-networks

Bender, J. (2015, February 19). 7 incredible narco tanks built by Mexican cartels. *Business Insider.* Retrieved from http://www.businessinsider.com/most-amazing-narco-tanks-2015-2

Berrett, D. (2016, March 23). Does engineering education breed terrorists? *Chronicle of Higher Education.* Retrieved from https://www.chronicle.com/article/Does-Engineering-Education/235800

Biggs, J. (2016, September 21). Pharma hackers create a DIY EpiPen, the EpiPencil. *TechCrunch.* Retrieved from http://social.techcrunch.com/2016/09/21/pharma-hackers-create-a-diy-epipen-the-epipencil/

Bunker, R., & Ramirez, B. (2015). *Narco-submarines. Specially fabricated vessels used for drug smuggling purposes.* Leavenworth, KS: Foreign Military Studies Office. Retrieved from http://scholarship.claremont.edu/cgu_fac_pub/931

Carroll, J. (2016, March 30). Narco-drones: The cartels' newest, tech savvy smuggling SOP spooks security experts. *Daily Caller.* Retrieved from http://dailycaller.com/2016/03/30/narco-drones-the-cartels-newest-tech-savvy-smuggling-sop-spooks-security-experts/

Chaudhry, P. E., & Zimmerman, A. (2013). *Protecting your intellectual property rights: Understanding the role of management, governments, consumers and pirates* [e-book]. New York, NY: Springer. Retrieved from https://www.springer.com/us/book/9781461455677

Dwoskin, E. (2016, November 20). Why a hacker is giving away a special code that turns cars into self-driving machines. *Washington Post*. Retrieved from https://www.washingtonpost.com/news/the-switch/wp/2016/11/30/why-a-hacker-is-giving-away-a-special-code-that-turns-cars-into-self-driving-machines/?utm_term=.9c5224469529

Federal Bureau of Investigation, Department of Transportation, & National Highway Traffic Safety Administration. (2016, March 17). Motor vehicles increasingly vulnerable to remote exploits. Retrieved from https://www.ic3.gov/media/2016/160317.aspx

Fenton, W. (2016, March 21). Black markets and secret thumb drives: How Cubans get online. *PC Magazine*. Retrieved from https://www.pcmag.com/article2/0,2817,2499712,00.asp

Garcia, A., & Monticello, J. (2017, October 19). DIY biohackers are editing genes in garages and kitchens. *Reason*. Retrieved from https://reason.com/reasontv/2017/10/18/diy-biohackers-editing-genes-garages

Gates, A. (2018, May 3). Where art forgeries meet their match. *New York Times*. Retrieved from https://www.nytimes.com/2018/05/02/arts/art-forgeries-sothebys.html

Gettinger, D. (2016). Drones operating in Syria and Iraq. *Bard College Center for the Study of the Drone*. Retrieved from https://docs.google.com/viewerng/viewer?url=http://dronecenter.bard.edu/files/2016/12/Drones-in-Iraq-and-Syria-CSD.pdf&hl=en_US

Greenberg, A. (2015a, August 4). This app lets anyone 3D print "do-not-duplicate" keys. *Wired*. Retrieved from https://www.wired.com/2015/08/this-app-lets-anyone-3-d-print-do-not-duplicate-keys/

Greenberg, A. (2015b, March 1). The plot to free North Korea with smuggled episodes of '*Friends*.' *Wired*. Retrieved from https://www.wired.com/2015/03/north-korea/

Greenfield Boyce, N. (2018, June 19). Report for Defense department ranks top threats from "synthetic biology." *NPR*. Retrieved from https://www.npr.org/sections/health-shots/2018/06/19/621350272/report-for-defense-department-ranks-top-threats-from-synthetic-biology

Harvard Business Review. (2014). Internet of things: Science fiction or business fact?. Watertown, MA: Harvard Business School Publishing.

Hicks, J. (2016, March 22). FDA approved 3D printed drug available in the US. *Forbes*. Retrieved from https://www.forbes.com/sites/jenniferhicks/2016/03/22/fda-approved-3d-printed-drug-available-in-the-us/#2d7879ad666b

Hofmann, C., & Schneckener, U. (2011). Engaging non-state armed actors in state- and peace-building: Options and strategies. *International Review of the Red Cross*, *93*(883), 603–621.

Horowitz, M. (2010). *The diffusion of military power: Causes and consequences for international politics*. Princeton, NJ: Princeton University Press.

Horowitz, S. (2018, January 8). Justice Dept. scrambles to jam prison cellphones, stop drone deliveries to inmates. *Washington Post*. Retrieved from https://www.washingtonpost.com/world/national-security/justice-dept-scrambles-to-jam-prison-cellphones-stop-drone-deliveries-to-inmates/2018/01/08/42492896-f4a0-11e7-b34a-b85626af34ef_story.html?noredirect=on&utm_term=.f2787a81cf5d

Johnston, T., Smith, T. D., & Irwin, J. L. (2018). Additive manufacturing in 2040. *Rand Corporation*. Retrieved from https://www.rand.org/pubs/perspectives/PE283.html

Krebs, B. (2011, September). Gang used 3D printers for ATM skimmers [Blog post]. *Krebs on Security*. Retrieved from https://krebsonsecurity.com/2011/09/gang-used-3d-printers-for-atm-skimmers/

Ledford, H. (2015). Biohackers gear up for genome editing. *Nature*, *524*(7566), 398. doi:10.1038/524398a

Leering, R. (2017). 3D printing: A threat to global trade. *ING*. Retrieved from https://think.ing.com/uploads/reports/3D_printing_DEF_270917.pdf

Lipson, H., & Kurman, M. (2013). *Fabricated: The new world of 3D printing*. Hoboken, NJ: Wiley.
Medea. (2013, April 5). *Arduino FAQ–With David Cuartielles* [Blog post]. Retrieved from http://medea.mah.se/2013/04/arduino-faq/
News Desk. (2016, December 18). How media smuggling took hold in North Korea. *PBS NewsHour.* Retrieved from https://www.pbs.org/newshour/world/media-smuggling-north-korea
Office of Emergency Management. (2014, March). *City of Santa Monica June 7th, 2013 shooting incident*. Retrieved from http://www.smgov.net/uploadedFiles/Departments/OEM/Video_Archive/Santa%20Monica%20Shooting%20Experience%20overFeb%202014.pdf
Schwab, K. (2016, December 12). The fourth industrial revolution. *Foreign Affairs*. Retrieved from https://www.foreignaffairs.com/articles/2015-12-12/fourth-industrial-revolution
Schwab, K., & Samans, R. (2016). Preface. *The future of jobs.* Retrieved from http://wef.ch/1PqcasD
Statista. (2018). *Internet of things–Statistics and facts*. Retrieved from http://www.statista.com/topics/2637/internet-of-things/
Tallman, M. (2017). Making crimes: Technology, law, and DIY firearms (Doctoral dissertation). Retrieved from Electronic Theses and Dissertations. (Accession No. 1246).
Tirone, D., & Gilley, J., (2015). Printing power: 3-D printing and threats to state security. *Journal of Policing, Intelligence, and Counterterrorism*, *10*(2), 102–119.
Washington, R. (2016, September 29). Driverless cars are coming. What does that mean for policing? *The Marshall Project*. Retrieved from https://www.themarshallproject.org/2016/09/29/driverless-cars-are-coming-what-does-that-mean-for-policing
Weinbaum, C., Berner, S., & McClintock, B. (2017). SIGINT for anyone: The growing availability of signals intelligence in the public domain. *Rand Corporation*. Retrieved from https://www.rand.org/pubs/perspectives/PE273.html
Woody, C. (2016, October 31). Watch the US Coast Guard seize narco submarine with cocaine in Pacific Ocean. *Business Insider.* Retrieved from http://www.businessinsider.com/us-coast-guard-seize-narco-submarine-cocaine-pacific-ocean-2016-10

CHAPTER 15

The Role of Technology in Hot Spots Policing

By Rachel B. Santos and Roberto G. Santos

Opening Questions

Answer the following question before reading this chapter:

> What do you know about the influence of technology on policing prior to reading this chapter?

Answer the following question while reading the chapter:

> What are some concepts from the chapter that stand out to you? Why do you think they are important?

Introduction

In this chapter, we provide a succinct discussion of the role of technology in proactive policing, specifically as it relates to the implementation of hot spots policing. Hot spots policing is a place-based proactive crime-reduction approach in which police strategies, such as **directed patrol**, subject and vehicle stops, offender checks, and crime prevention, are implemented in areas or **hot spots** that have disproportionately more crime than other areas within a jurisdiction (Braga, Papachristos, & Hureau, 2014). Importantly, the National Academy of Science's panel on proactive policing strategies finds that hot spots policing is one of the most effective ways that police, particularly the patrol function, can reduce crime (Weisburd & Majimundar, 2017).

A common component in all effective proactive policing crime-reduction strategies (e.g., hot spots policing) is the use of systematic crime analysis to help guide and prioritize crime-reduction efforts (Santos, 2014). Research finds that police are most effective when they focus on places, people, and problems (Weisburd & Majimundar, 2017). **Crime analysis** is a fundamental requirement for determining what, where, how, and on whom to focus

(Santos, 2016). Crime analysis is a process that can maximize the use of agency resources available for understanding and addressing crime, provide the basis for proactive initiatives to prevent crime, monitor police performance, and take advantage of the volumes of data collected by police and other agencies (Santos, 2016). Crime analysis involves the use of large amounts of data along with a set of systematic methods and techniques that identify patterns and relationships between crime data and other relevant information to assist police in criminal apprehension, crime and disorder reduction, crime prevention, and evaluation (International Association of Crime Analysts, 2014). Importantly, crime analysis requires modern technology to accomplish these tasks.

In addition to crime analysis, effective proactive policing strategies also require systematic ways of deploying resources, tracking responses, and holding people accountable; this is called **stratified policing** (Boba & Santos, 2011; Santos & Santos, 2015a). Historically, police managers and commanders have relied on official records from computer-aided dispatch and records management systems to determine the level of proactive activity by officers, such as officer-generated calls for service, traffic stop data, field interview cards, and arrests. In addition, hand-written or electronic officer log sheets as well as in-person discussion and observations have been used to verify whether proactive policing responses are implemented by patrol officers. However, in recent years new technology has been developed to assist with the operationalization of crime-reduction responses by facilitating officer deployment, and real-time communication, reporting, and accountability.

While these technologies can and are being used for a variety of proactive crime-reduction strategies, such as problem-oriented policing, disorder policing, focused deterrence, and intelligence-led policing, this chapter focuses on their application to hot spots policing specifically. The discussion covers how technology is used for the identification and analysis of hot spots of crime, for the deployment and management of responses within hot spots, and for the accountability of hot spots policing strategies.

We begin by contrasting the underlying rational, research, and implementation of the standard model of policing and the hot spots policing approach to illustrate how hot spots policing is different. Then, we discuss how technology is used for crime analysis to examine long-term, micro-time, and immediate hot spots and for operational purposes to support deployment and accountability of hot spots policing responses. The chapter ends with our conclusions and considerations for the future of technology in hot spots policing.

Overview of Standard Model of Policing

The underlying philosophy and use of technology for hot spots policing is different than that of the standard model of policing, so it is important to start by contrasting the two. The standard model of policing involves enforcing the law in a broad and reactive way by (a) increasing the number of police officers to increase the ability to detect crime and arrest offenders; (b) conducting unfocused, random motorized patrols to create a perception of a police omnipresence to deter crime in public places; (c) rapidly responding to calls for service to increase the likelihood of catching offenders; (d) conducting follow-up investigations by detectives to increase the solvability of the crimes; and (e) using general reactive arrest policies to deter and punish specific offenders as well as deter the general public from committing crimes (Sherman et al., 1997; Weisburd & Eck, 2004).

The purpose of most of the technology used within any police department today is to support these central tenets of the standard model. Technology at the officer level, such as their weapons (e.g., hand guns, rifles, and stun guns), cars, radios, body cameras, phones, and laptops, help them patrol, answer calls for service, and make arrests quickly, efficiently, and safely. Agency-wide technology facilitates these processes for officers and includes computer-aided dispatch systems, records management systems (RMS), case management systems, as well as fingerprint, evidence, and DNA systems. In addition, administrative technology facilitates recording and managing human resources data, tracking citizen complaints and use-of-force incidents, policy review and training for staff, and communication through e-mail and the department's intranet.

Notably, the technology necessary to support the standard model of policing does not include hardware or software that facilitates crime analysis. While some technology vendors claim that their CAD and RMS systems do include analytical functionality, most of the time the systems merely provide the ability to access individual records, generate lists, and count them (International Association of Crime Analysts, 2013). Some analysis is conducted within the standard model. However, this analysis focuses on administrative and operational functions occurring in the police agency, not on the analysis of crime and disorder for crime-reduction purposes. For example, to ensure rapid response to calls for service, analysis of calls for service data, specifically the date, call type, time spent on the call, and call location, inform how many officers are needed in patrol as well as where (geographic deployment) and when (shifts) they should be assigned (Gallager, Wartell, Gwinn, Jones, & Stewart, 2017).

Furthermore, within the standard model UCR Part I crime counts and aggregate statistics of arrests, traffic citations, and other activity are produced for administrators to determine staffing levels and long-term trends in crime (Santos, 2014). Crime statistics identify whether crime has increased or decreased from a broad view (i.e., year to year) and are primarily used for situational awareness so that sworn personnel, from patrol officers to the chief, have an idea of how crime has changed over time (Santos, 2016). However, this information is not used to inform proactive crime-reduction strategies because the standard model is primarily reactive and its proactivity is extremely limited (Weisburd & Eck, 2004). Consequently, data and technology are primarily used to identify individual offenders and provide investigative support (O'Shea & Nicholls, 2003).

Overview of Hot Spots Policing

Even though hot spots policing requires and utilizes all the technology implemented within a police department for answering calls for service and investigating crimes, some of these tools are used in a different way and additional technology is required to conduct crime analysis, manage deployment, and hold officers and commanders accountable for specific proactive hot spots policing responses. Before breaking down the various ways technology supports hot spots policing, however, first it is important to understand the theoretical foundation and goals of hot spots policing as well as how it is practiced.

Criminology of Place

Research has consistently shown that crime concentrates in both time and space at every level of geographic aggregation. This branch of criminology is referred to as "**criminology of place**" (Weisburd, Groff, & Yang, 2012). In 2015, Professor David Weisburd established a new criminological law called the "law of crime concentration." He defines it as follows: "For a defined measure of crime at a specific microgeographic unit, the concentration of crime will fall within a narrow bandwidth of percentages for a defined cumulative proportion of crime" (Weisburd, 2015, p. 138). This means that not only do we know that crime clusters by place but also that these clusters can be narrowly defined and are stable and predictable over time. Simply put, in any given city or town, crime analysis will show that a large percentage of crime and/or disorder happens in a small number of locations or small areas and that these locations are consistently higher.

The law of crime concentration and the results of research in criminology of place have guided police in implementing crime-prevention strategies with a geographic focus. Hot spots policing is one of these approaches in which crime-prevention strategies are based on the identification of specific places or areas that have disproportionate levels of crime. The primary crime-reduction strategy of hot spots policing is to increase police presence in hot spots to deter offenders and reduce opportunities for crime to occur (Braga et al., 2014; Weisburd & Majimundar, 2017).

The research on the effectiveness of hot spots policing in reducing crime is rigorous and plentiful. The results of many experiments over the last 30 years show that police response to hot spots, whether the hot spots are individual or clusters of addresses, street segments, or blocks, is effective in reducing crime (Braga et al., 2014; Telep & Weisburd, 2012). Even further, the National Academy of Science's committee on proactive policing recommends that hot spots policing be coupled with in-depth problem solving, that is, not just identifying the hot spots but also understanding why they are "hot." The committee concludes that a combined approach can be more effective, since problem-focused crime-reduction approaches, such as problem-oriented policing, have also been shown by research to reduce crime.

To understand the role of technology in hot spots policing, then, the practice of hot spots policing is best broken down into three areas: (a) crime analysis, (b) deployment of responses, and (c) accountability. The following sections detail how each of these is practiced and how technology facilitates the processes within each area.

Technology for Crime Analysis

Crime analysis is integral to hot spots policing, and the role of technology in the approach is centered on how the technology supports the identification, analysis, and evaluation of crime and disorder hot spots (Santos, 2014). In the early to mid-1990s, significant improvements in computer technology for police data systems made it possible for police to access the large amounts of data they collect on a daily basis. Data for crimes, arrests, traffic crashes, and calls for service became available electronically through computer-aided dispatch systems as well as through electronic records management systems. Geographic data, such as street maps, as well as census information aggregated by geographic area, became widely available in electronic format as well (Weisburd & McEwen, 1997).

At the same time, **geographic information system** (GIS) software moved from being facilitated through large costly mainframe computers to inexpensive desktop computers. A GIS is a set of computer-based tools that allow the user to modify, visualize, query, and analyze geographic and tabular data (Santos, 2016). A GIS is software that provides a framework and templates for data collection, collation, as well as spatial and tabular analysis. It is up to the user to decide what data to use, what functions of the software to use, and how to use them. A GIS does more than enable users to produce paper maps, as it also allows them to view the data behind geographic features, combine various features, manipulate the data and maps, and perform statistical functions (Chainey & Ratcliffe, 2005). The ability to access to large amounts of electronic data and analyze them in desktop spatial analysis software created the capacity for police to be more systematic and analytical about identifying where crime and disorder continually occur to direct their proactive crime-reduction responses.

Crime analysis, particularly the use of crime mapping and spatial analysis, has an important role in identifying the hot spots where the policing strategies are best implemented. Crime analysis is an important facet of hot spots identification because researchers have found that police do not accurately identify hot spots or regularly agree on what a hot spot is in their respective areas of responsibility (Bichler & Gaines, 2005; McLaughlin, Johnson, Bowers, Birks, & Pease, 2006; Ratcliffe & McCullagh, 2001). To more fully understand the use of technology for crime analysis within hot spots policing, the units of analysis can be broken down into three types that correspond to their temporal nature, that is, how long they occur. The following sections provide more discussion of each type of hot spot as well as how technology supports their analysis.

Long-Term Hot Spots: Problem Locations and Areas

There are two distinct types of long-term hot spots. The first is the problem location, which is also called a **risky place** (Clarke & Eck, 2005; Eck, Clarke, & Guerette, 2007). These are individual locations (e.g., one convenience store, one apartment complex, a bus stop) at which there is a concentration of crime or problematic activity. The second type of long-term hot spot is the problem area, which is typically what people think of when the term "hot spot" is used (Chainey & Ratcliffe, 2005; Eck, Chainey, Cameron, Leitner, & Wilson, 2005). It is a relatively small geographic area with a disproportionate amount of crime and/or disorder activity. The area typically contains more than one address and can be a single block face, a square block area, or one or a cluster of street segments. It can also be a designated police geographic area such as a reporting district, zone, or beat. Problem areas are typically defined small enough so that the opportunities for crime are similar across the entire area (i.e., distinguishing residential and commercial areas).

The technology used to identify a problem location is typically a standard GIS. Crime analysts create maps in which points on the map are graduated (i.e., larger) when more crime or disorder occurs at those individual locations (Santos, 2016). Crime analysts can also use statistical or spreadsheet software to conduct a straightforward analysis to determine which locations within a jurisdiction have disproportionate amount of crime. For example, there have been 250 fight calls for service at 50 bars in one city over the last year. The bar with the most fight calls had 40, the next bar had only 10, and the remaining 48 bars had less than 10 calls each. The bar with 40 fights calls would arise to the attention of the analyst and be identified as a problem location (i.e., hot spot) because it had so many more calls than the others.

Similarly, GIS software is primarily used to identify problem areas; however, some methods require advanced statistical extensions within the GIS. Most crime analysts use either crime, calls for service, arrest, or traffic data to create the graduated-color polygon maps, ellipses maps, and/or density maps (Santos, 2016). Crime analysts also use specific software that has been tailored to conduct these types of analysis and has been linked to the police department's data system to make the process simpler. Because new software is being developed each year and other software becomes outdated, specific programs are not discussed here.

What is important is the difference between crime analysts' use of a general GIS platform and their use of specially programmed crime mapping software that is tailored to conduct specific types of spatial analyses of crime. The tailored software is much easier to use because it is linked directly to the agency's data and has drop-down menus and streamlined functions that allow crime analysts and others to create maps in a few clicks. However, these programs do not provide as much functionality as the full GIS software that allows the analyst to use the entire capability of the software (Santos, 2016).

When hot spots policing is coupled with in-depth problem solving, crime analysis also plays a central role in identifying and understanding the nature of the hot spot to implement appropriate responses (Santos, 2014). In terms of technological support for this type of analysis, academics have worked with analysts to implement specific GIS programs that analyze more than just crime data to identify and more fully understand long-term problem areas. Software for risk terrain analysis is one example in which multiple datasets in addition to crime (e.g., liquor stores, bus stops, fast-food restaurants) are examined by the software to identify risk factors for crime and illustrate the results on a map (Caplan & Kennedy, 2016; Drawve, Belongie, & Steinman, 2018).

Micro-Time Hot Spots: Crime Patterns

The second type of hot spot that is addressed by police is the **micro-time hot spot**, which is considered one type of short-term crime pattern (Santos, 2016). The micro-time hot spot is rooted in the research on near-repeat victimization that has established that crimes occur near other crimes within a short time period, especially property crimes such as theft from vehicles and residential burglary (Bowers & Johnson, 2005). Consequently, a micro-time hot spot is the emergence of several closely related crimes within a few minutes' travel distance from one another that occurs within a relatively short period of time (i.e., several days to weeks)—a crime "flare-up" (Santos & Santos, 2015b).

Micro-time hot spots are different than long-term hot spots because although they may occur within stable long-term problem areas, micro-time hot spots also occur in other areas that are not accustomed to high levels of crime or that have an ongoing crime problem. Thus, it is important that police distinguish these two different types of hot spots to ensure they are addressing all types of crime clustering. Importantly, since micro-time hot spots are linked geographically, the GIS is integral technology for identification, particularly for crimes such as residential burglary, theft from vehicles, and street robberies.

Typically, to identify a micro-time hot spot, a crime analyst will map crime of a certain type (e.g., residential burglaries) for the last few weeks and then look for clusters. Statistical analysis or more complex spatial analysis, such as density mapping, is not required since the time frame is short and there are not large numbers of incidents. Once a cluster is found, the analyst looks more closely at each crime to determine whether they seem related (see Santos, 2016, chapters 10–12 for crime pattern analysis methodology). Crime analysts do this in a variety of ways. They use a combination of GIS and spreadsheet and database software together. Crime analysts also use software programs that have been created to provide techniques specific to short-term, tactical crime analysis because these functions were not available previously in one comprehensive program.

Once a micro-time hot spot is identified, crime analysts create a one-page professionally formatted bulletin using a variety of technology to include the GIS, spreadsheet, word processing, and publishing software (Santos, 2016). The information on the bulletin includes date, time, location, modus operandi, known offenders living in the micro-time hot spot, field interview information, and whether evidence was collected at the scene, such as finger prints and DNA (Santos, 2016). The GIS is used to create a map to illustrate the locations of the crimes in the hot spots, as well as any field contacts in the immediate area and residential addresses of the known offenders.

Specific software has been developed to assist crime analysts and other police personnel in creating standardized micro-time hot spots and pattern bulletins. One study found that the tailored software cut the time it takes for an analyst to create the finished bulletin in half (Santos & Santos, 2017). This is an example of how technology is used to streamline the analysis process for hot spots policing. Finally, e-mail, intranet portals, and agency management systems are used by crime analysts to disseminate the bulletins to the police and to communicate with them about new crimes occurring in the micro-time hot spot (discussed later in the chapter).

Immediate Hot Spots: Predictive Policing Boxes

The third type of hot spot is the **immediate hot spot**, which has been defined as a small area in which a single crime is predicted to occur in an immediate time period (Perry, McInnis, Price, Smith, & Hollywood, 2013). This type of hot spot is the unit of response of the **predictive policing** approach and is considered a derivative of hot spots policing (Weisburd & Majimundar, 2017). The primary method for identifying immediate hot spots is through specifically developed software that uses date, time, and location of a particular type of crime (e.g., robbery, property crime) to identify 500-by-500-foot areas called boxes that have a higher risk of an individual crime occurring within a particular 8-, 10-, or 12-hour patrol shift. The predictions are based on advanced analytical techniques known as algorithms that are dictated by the software (Mohler et al., 2015; Perry et al., 2013; Ratcliffe, Taylor, & Askey, 2017). Importantly, the exact method is often not known and cannot be changed by the police because it is proprietary to the software company that developed it (Perry et al., 2013).

This newer approach has been operationalized into several different software programs that are marketed, sold, and used by many police agencies in the United States and internationally (Benbouzid, 2016; Bond-Graham & Winston, 2013). To implement, a police department purchases a subscription to the software that is housed on a private server of the software company and allows the company to access the police data directly (Bond-Graham & Winston, 2013; Jackson, 2015; PredPol, 2017). The software company or police agency personnel print maps with the 500-by-500-foot boxes for each shift, which are distributed to managers or directly to officers in patrol briefings.

Importantly, the role of technology for the identification of immediate hot spots is much different than for the identification of long-term and micro-time hot spots. Immediate hot spot identification relies exclusively on the software program. Typically, in practice, there is no review or interpretation by a crime analyst and no attempt to understand the underlying problems that may be contributing to that specific location. In contrast, both long-term and micro-time hot spots are identified and analyzed by crime analysts.

Technology for Deployment, Responses, and Accountability

Over the last 20 years, most of the technology that is used to support hot spots policing has been for crime analysis, specifically crime mapping (Santos, 2016). More recently, current police technology is being used for deploying officers, and newer technology is being used to support crime-reduction responses as well as activities required to carry out hot spots policing effectively and efficiently. These activities include the dissemination of crime analysis, real-time communication, tracking response activity, and accountability. The following section discusses how current computer-aided dispatch (CAD) systems and automated vehicle locators (AVL) are used to deploy officers and track their activity; how license plate readers (LPR), facial recognition, gunshot detection, and surveillance cameras are used to support responses in hot spots; and how agency management systems support communication and accountability of an entire hot spots policing agency-wide approach.

Computer-Aided Dispatch

Police departments have begun using their existing computer-aided dispatch (CAD) systems to proactively dispatch officers to hot spot locations. We have worked with agencies whose first-line supervisors dispatch hot spots policing calls to officers directly. These are not officer-generated or citizen-generated calls but are calls created by the patrol supervisor in which the officers respond and conduct directed patrol, make contacts with suspicious persons and vehicles, and contact citizens in a specific hot spot. These calls are not optional assignments, but because they are managed through the CAD system, officers respond immediately, just as they would a citizen-generated call; dispatchers communicate with the officers while they are responding; and the time spent and outcome of each call is captured. Dispatching through the CAD system ensures a formal system of response in which officers are deployed and monitored and their responses are tracked.

Another way CAD has been used for hot spots policing is by assigning a specific call type for hot spots responses. In one department, officers were instructed to patrol designated hot spots during their uncommitted time while on patrol (Telep, Mitchell, & Weisburd, 2014). Officers were not dispatched individually, as in the previous example, but were required to generate the activity themselves when they were not answering citizen-generated calls for service (i.e., when they were uncommitted). Each time officers responded in a hot spot, they used the special call code (e.g., D1HOT) that signified that they were patrolling inside a hot spot. When they were done patrolling, they closed the call. This process allows the tracking of both the location (i.e., hot spot) and the amount of time officers spend responding each time as well as gives the ability to summarize all the time spent in the hot spot over a period of time.

Automated Vehicle Locator

To ensure that patrol officers are implementing hot spots policing responses in the field as directed, some police departments are using automated vehicle locator (AVL) technology. The general purpose of the AVL technology is to observe where the patrol cars are in real time as well as to examine historical data. AVL technology is used for standard models of policing to locate officers while on patrol for safety, accountability, and quicker response to emergency calls, as well as to make sure the jurisdiction is covered by adequate amount of patrol time. It is also used to examine data for administrative purposes (i.e., scheduling and gas used and mileage on cars).

For hot spots policing, AVL technology assists first-line patrol supervisors in the field. Because hot spots policing responses are supposed to take place when officers are not answering calls for service from citizens, before AVL technology first-line patrol supervisors either had to rely on the radio or drive out and see where individual officers were in person. With AVL technology, supervisors can monitor multiple officers at a time on their desktop or in car computers to ensure officers are implementing hot spots policing responses in the right places at the right times. For example, researchers worked with the Sacramento Police Department in California to study hot spots policing. They used its AVL system to ensure that officers were following the proper protocol for response (Telep et al., 2014).

Historical AVL data is also important in hot spots policing. The data can be aggregated over days, weeks, or months to measure the amount of response to determine whether adequate resources are being deployed and whether every unit and shift in the agency is pulling its weight in responding. A study in Montevideo, Uruguay, used what they called "traceability" information from the AVL system on their cars to measure dosage of police response within designated hot spot areas (Galiani & Jaitman, 2017).

Even further, an experimental study conducted in Dallas, Texas, showed that by providing AVL information to patrol commanders who oversee policing in specific hot spots, the commanders could more effectively monitor and ensure that officers were patrolling the hot spots as directed in their uncommitted time. The researchers conclude that "information generated from AVL can be used to increase directed patrol time at crime hot spots, and that these increased levels of patrol will lead to reductions in crime" (Weisburd et al., 2015, p. 367).

Technology Supporting Responses

As noted earlier, new technology is constantly being developed and implemented for policing in general, and most of that technology can be used to support hot spots policing as well. The following are some examples of newer technology that has begun being used for responses in hot spots of crime.

License plate reader (LPR) technology is a system in which high-speed cameras automatically capture license plate numbers, along with the location, date, and time. The photos capture the plate but can also capture the driver and passenger(s). LPRs can be attached to street lights, highway overpasses, and other fixed structures. For hot spots policing, LPRs can be placed on mobile trailers to be deployed temporarily into a micro-time hot spot and/or on police cars that are used for directed patrol in any type of hot spot. In both cases, the LPR can help to identify potential suspects and to find wanted offenders who are in the hot spot. A study in Mesa, Arizona, found that officers' use of LPR for checks of suspicious vehicles in hot spots was more efficient and possibly more effective than officers doing manual plate checks (Koper, Taylor, & Woods, 2013).

Gunshot detection systems can also support police responses in hot spots. This technology uses a variety of sensors to detect and locate the location of gunfire or other weapon fire. It can be deployed in hot spots areas with disproportionately higher amounts of gun violence to verify gunshot events, increase response times, identify suspects, and potentially reduce crime in the hot spot (Irvin-Erickson, La Vigne, Levine, Tiry, & Bieler, 2017).

Surveillance cameras have become a common technology used in public and commercial places around the world (Ratcliffe, 2006). Similar to LPR technology, mobile surveillance cameras can be temporarily placed in micro-time hot spots to detect crimes and suspicious activity as well as identify suspects and wanted offenders. Research shows that the implementation of surveillance cameras is more effective when they are monitored in real time (Ratcliffe, 2006), so placing and monitoring them in specific areas or locations determined to have a crime problem is an efficient use of the technology. In addition, their use might also be coupled with facial recognition software to more effectively identify suspects (Schuck, 2017). Finally, even though hot spots policing strategies have not been found to negatively affect citizens' perceptions of the police or their fear of crime (Weisburd & Majimundar, 2017), body-worn camera technology implemented for officers making proactive stops of citizens in hot spots can potentially help to mitigate any concerns that citizens may have about an increase presence of officers in a particular hot spot. (Ariel, Southerland, Henstock, Young, & Sosinski, 2018; White, Gaub, & Todak, 2018).

Agency Management System

An agency management system (AMS) is an intranet Web-based hardware and software system that facilitates communication and transparency within police agencies and streamlines internal police business (Santos, 2016). An AMS securely manages official communications, administration, and business functions in a police department. It can include modules that allow employees to review policies and general orders, track internal investigations and use-of-force incidents, disseminate crime analysis products, and facilitate communication about crime reduction and other operational activities. It allows for archiving and searching documents and information contained within the system (Santos, 2016).

There are different versions of AMS being used in police departments, and some of the platforms include modules that support the operational implementation of hot spots policing. Monitoring ongoing crime and response activity and communicating in real time about responses in the field are imperative for successful hot spots policing implementation (Santos, 2017). CAD systems are only able to facilitate and record real-time communication between officers and dispatchers in the field during a call for service. An AMS facilitates real-time communication among all levels and units of the police department including but not limited to patrol officers, detectives, supervisors, managers, commanders, and crime analysts. This communication can last days and weeks. The technology improves on e-mail and in-person communication since it links a group of individuals and allows them to communicate through a single "thread" or conversation about a particular topic (i.e., a hot spot) (Santos, 2016).

An AMS that supports hot spots policing facilitates dissemination of crime analysis results, real-time discussions about responses as they are implemented, and mechanisms for accountability. The following is an example of how an AMS would be used for responses to micro-time hot spots (Santos & Santos, 2015c):

- The crime analyst posts a micro-time hot spot bulletin to the system where all police personnel can access it through the intranet instead of e-mailing individuals or providing paper copies in a roll call briefing.
- Patrol officers who are assigned to respond to the micro-time hot spot post their responses into the system as they occur in the field. Other personnel responding (i.e., detectives, supervisors, and managers) can see the responses and post information themselves instead of having to talk to one another in person, on the phone, or through e-mail.
- When the micro-time hot spot is resolved, the managers can close the response and summarize the response activity (i.e., count the number of arrests, citizens contacted, field information cards, and direct patrol hours) within the thread for accountability purposes. The information is saved on the server indefinitely and can be accessed and/or aggregated for multiple threads.

Conclusions and Considerations

Based on the discussion in this chapter, it is apparent that technology is invaluable for the successful implementation of hot spots policing. However, there are still challenges in its implementation. Some police departments have relied solely on the acquisition of new and/or advanced technology to signify that they have implemented hot spots policing. National-level research shows that police leaders place a high priority on and claim that they are implementing hot spots policing, when in reality they have only created a capability for crime analysis by purchasing software for hot spots mapping and/or hiring a crime analyst (Smith, Santos, & Santos, 2017). At a broader level, we have seen police leaders struggle to implement the systematic use of agency management systems for hot spots policing. Those leaders who overcame the challenge and were finally successful at implementation did not simply rely on the technology but also developed a system of policies for use of the technology and accountability to ensure the technology was being used correctly (Santos, 2017; Santos & Santos, 2012).

Consequently, is it important that police leaders and policy makers do not underestimate the importance of the human factor in the role of technology in hot spots policing. Simply acquiring technology does not indicate the implementation or success of its use for hot spots policing. Looking to the future, much as it is today, the hot spots policing approach will likely take any new technology developed for policing and adapt its use for carrying out crime-reduction responses in hot spots.

However, most of the discussion in this chapter has been about what is being done in practice, because there are very few studies on the use of technology for proactive policing strategies. Thus, while there has been a significant amount of research that shows hot spots policing is an effective crime-reduction strategy, there needs to be much more research on the effective use of technology for the implementation of hot spots policing as well.

Key Terms

crime analysis: A process involving the use of large amounts of data along with a set of systematic methods and techniques that identify patterns and relationships between crime data and other relevant information to assist police in criminal apprehension, crime and disorder reduction, crime prevention, and evaluation.

criminology of place: a branch of criminology seeking to determine why specific areas have specific crime trends over time.

directed patrol: A patrol tactic involving the use of data to determine areas in which heightened levels of patrol should occur to reduce or stop crime in problem locations.

geographic information systems: A set of computer-based tools that allow the user to modify, visualize, query, and analyze geographic and tabular data.

hot spot: A relatively small geographic area with a disproportionate amount of crime and/or disorder activity.

immediate hot spot: A small area in which a single crime is predicted to occur in an immediate time period.

micro-time hot spot: The emergence of several closely related crimes within a few minutes' travel distance from one another that occurs within a relatively short period of time (several days to weeks). Also known as a crime flare-up.

predictive policing: The use of crime data to anticipate future criminal activity and trends.

risky place: Individual locations, such as one convenience store, one apartment complex, or a specific bus stop, at which there is a concentration of crime or problematic activity.

stratified policing: Systematic ways of deploying resources, tracking responses, and holding people accountable.

Discussion Questions

- What do you think about the influence of technology on policing after reading the chapter?
- Compare the key components of the standard model of policing and hot spots policing.
- The field of crime analysis has not always used technology; discuss why technology has become so integral in how crime analysis is practiced in policing today.
- Compare how technology is used for the different types of hot spots.
- Discuss whether you think it's important to use technology to facilitate resource deployment and accountability for hot spot policing.
- Design a study to test the effectiveness of using technology to support police carrying out hot spots policing. Be specific in your design by selecting one type of technology and one type of hot spot discussed in the chapter.

References

Ariel, B., Sutherland, A., Henstock, D., Young, J., & Sosinski, G. (2018). The deterrence spectrum: Explaining why police body-worn cameras 'work' or 'backfire' in aggressive police-public encounters. *Policing: A Journal of Policy & Practice, 12*(1), 6–26.

Benbouzid, B. (2016, October) Who benefits from the crime? *Books and Ideas.* Retrieved from http://www.booksandideas.net/Who-Benefits-from-the-Crime.html

Bichler, G., & Gaines, L. (2005). An examination of police officers' insights into problem identification and problem solving. *Crime & Delinquency, 51*(1), 53–74.

Boba, R., & Santos, R. G. (2011). *A police organizational model for crime reduction: Institutionalizing problem solving, analysis, and accountability.* Washington DC: Office of Community Oriented Policing Services.

Bond-Graham, D., & Winston, A. (2013, October). All tomorrow's crimes: The future of policing looks a lot like good branding. *SF Weekly.* Retrieved from https://archives.sfweekly.com/sanfrancisco/all-tomorrows-crimes-the-future-of-policing-looks-a-lot-like-good-branding/Content?oid=2827968

Bowers, K. J., & Johnson, S. D. (2005). Domestic burglary repeats and space–time clusters: The dimensions of risk. *European Journal of Criminology, 2*(1), 67–92.

Braga, A. A., Papachristos, A. V., & Hureau, D. M. (2014). The effects of hot spots policing on crime: An updated systematic review and meta-analysis. *Justice Quarterly, 31*(4), 633–663.

Caplan, J. M., & Kennedy, L. W. (2016). *Risk terrain modeling: Crime prediction and risk reduction.* Berkeley, CA: University of California Press.

Chainey, S., & Ratcliffe, J., (2005). *GIS and crime mapping.* Hoboken, NJ: Wiley.

Clarke, R. V., & Eck, J. (2005). *Crime analysis for problem solvers: In 60 small steps.* Washington, DC: Office of Community Oriented Policing Services.

Drawve, G., Belongie, M., & Steinman, H. (2018). The role of crime analyst and researcher partnerships: A training exercise in Green Bay, Wisconsin Policing. *Policing: A Journal of Policy & Practice, 12*(3), 1–11. doi:10.1093/police/pax092

Eck, J., Chainey, S., Cameron, J., Leitner, M., & Wilson, R. (2005). *Mapping crime: Understanding hot spots.* Washington, DC: National Institute of Justice.

Eck, J., Clarke, R. V., & Guerette, R. T. (2007). Risky facilities: Crime concentration in homogeneous sets of establishments and facilities. In G. Farrell, K. J. Bowers, S. D. Johnson,

& M. Townsley (Eds.), *Imagination for crime prevention: Essays in honour of Ken Pease* (pp. 225–264). Portland, OR: Willan.
Galiani, S., & Jaitman, L. (2017). *Predictive policing in a developing country: Experimental evidence from two randomized controlled trials.* Washington DC: Inter-American Development Bank.
Gallager, K., Wartell, J., Gwinn, S., Jones, G., & Stewart, G. (2017). *Exploring crime analysis.* Overland Park, CA: International Association of Crime Analysts.
International Association of Crime Analysts. (2013). *RMS technical requirements of crime analysis* [White Paper 2013-01]. Overland Park, KS: Author.
International Association of Crime Analysts. (2014). *Definition and types of crime analysis* [White Paper 2014-02]. Overland Park, KS: Author.
Irvin-Erickson, Y., La Vigne, N., Levine, N., Tiry, E., & Bieler, S. (2017). What does gunshot detection technology tell us about gun violence? *Applied Geography, 86,* 262–273.
Jackson, D. (2015, April). Motorola Solutions: Rich Payne discusses predictive-policing capabilities. *Urgent Communications.* Retrieved from http://urgentcomm.com/motorola-solutions/motorola-solutions-rich-payne-discusses-predictive-policing-capabilities
Koper, C., Taylor, B., & Woods, D. (2013). A randomized test of initial and residual deterrence from directed patrols and use of license plate readers at crime hot spots. *Journal of Experimental Criminology, 9*(2), 213–244.
McLaughlin, L., Johnson, S. D., Bowers, K. J., Birks, D. J., & Pease, K. (2006). Police perceptions of the long- and short-term spatial distribution of residential burglary. *International Journal of Police Science & Management, 9*(2), 99–111.
Mohler, G. O., Short, M. B., Malinowski, S., Johnson, M., Tita, G. E. Bertozzi, A. L., & Brantingham, P. J (2015). Randomized controlled field trials of predictive policing. *Journal of the American Statistical Association, 110*(512) 1399–1411.
O'Shea, T. C., & Nicholls, K. (2003). Police crime analysis: A survey of U.S. police departments with 100 or more sworn personnel. *Police Practice and Research, 4*(3), 233–250.
Perry, W. L., McInnis, B., Price, C. C., Smith, S. C., & Hollywood, J. S. (2013). *Predictive policing: The role of crime forecasting in law enforcement operations.* Santa Monica, CA; RAND.
PredPol. (2017). *PredPol: The predictive policing company.* Retrieved from http://www.predpol.com
Ratcliffe, J. H., (2006). *Video surveillance of public places.* Washington DC: Office of Community Oriented Policing Services.
Ratcliffe, J. H., & McCullagh, M. (2001). Chasing ghosts? Police perception of high crime areas. *British Journal of Criminology, 41*(2), 330–341.
Ratcliffe, J. H., Taylor, R. B., & Askey, A. P. (2017, September). *The Philadelphia predictive policing experiment: Effectiveness of the prediction models.* Philadelphia, PA: Center for Crime Science, Temple University.
Santos, R. B. (2014). The effectiveness of crime analysis for crime reduction: Cure or diagnosis? *Journal of Contemporary Criminal Justice, 30*(2), 147–168.
Santos, R. B. (2016). *Crime analysis with crime mapping.* Thousand Oaks, CA: SAGE.
Santos, R. B., & Santos, R. G. (2012). The role of leadership in implementing a police organizational model for crime reduction and accountability. *Policing: A Journal of Policy and Practice. 6*(4), 344–353.
Santos R. G., & Santos, R. B. (2015a). Evidence-based policing, "What works" and stratified policing, "How to make it work." *Translational Criminology, 8,* 20–22.
Santos, R. G., & Santos, R. B. (2015b). An ex post facto evaluation of tactical police response in residential theft from vehicle micro-time hot spots. *Journal of Quantitative Criminology, 31*(4), 679–698.
Santos, R. B., & Santos, R. G. (2015c). Examination of police dosage in residential burglary and theft from vehicle micro-time hots spots. *Crime Science, 4*(27), 1–12.

Santos, R. B., & Santos, R. G. (2017). *Crime pattern bulletin study: Results.* Greenwood Village, CO: Adventos.
Santos, R. G. (2017). Police organizational change after implementing crime analysis and evidence-based strategies through stratified policing. *Policing: A Journal of Policy and Practice, 12*(3), 1–15. doi:10.1093/police/pax076
Schuck, A. (2017). Prevalence and predictors of surveillance cameras in law enforcement. *Criminal Justice Policy Review, 28*(1), 41–60.
Sherman, L. W., Gottfredson, D., MacKenzie, D. L., Eck, J., Reuter, P., & Bushway, S. (1997). *Preventing crime: What works, what doesn't, what's promising: A report to the attorney general of the United States.* Washington, DC: U.S. Department of Justice, Office of Justice Programs.
Smith, J., Santos, R. B., & Santos, R. G. (2017). Evidence-based policing and the stratified integration of crime analysis in police agencies: National survey results. *Policing: A Journal of Policy and Practice, 12*(3), 1–13. doi:10.1093/police/pax079
Telep, C. W., Mitchell, R. J., & Weisburd, D. (2014). How much time should the police spend at crime hot spots?: Answers from a police agency directed randomized field trial in Sacramento, California. *Justice Quarterly, 31*(5), 905–933.
Telep, C. W., & Weisburd, D. (2012). What is known about the effectiveness police practices in reducing crime and disorder? *Police Quarterly, 15*(4), 331–357.
Weisburd, D. (2015). The 2014 Sutherland Address: The law of crime concentration and the criminology of place. *Criminology, 53*(2), 133–157.
Weisburd, D., Groff, E., Jones, G., Cave, B., Amendola, K., Yang, S. M, & Emison, R. (2015). The Dallas patrol management experiment: Can AVL technologies be used to harness unallocated patrol time for crime prevention? *Journal of Experimental Criminology, 11*(3), 367–391.
Weisburd, D. L., Groff, E. R., & Yang, S. M. (2012). *The criminology of place: Street segments and our understanding of the crime problem.* New York, NY: Oxford University Press.
Weisburd, D., & Eck, J. (2004). What can police do to reduce crime, disorder, and fear? *The Annals of the American Academy of Political and Social Science, 593,* 42–65.
Weisburd, D. L., & Majimundar, M. K. (2017). *Proactive policing: Effects on crime and communities.* Washington DC: National Academy of Sciences.
Weisburd, D., & McEwen, T. (1997). Crime mapping and crime prevention. In D. Weisburd & T. McEwen (Eds.), *Crime mapping and crime prevention* (pp. 1–26). Monsey, NY: Criminal Justice Press.
White, M., Gaub, J., & Todak, N. (2018). Exploring the potential for body-worn cameras to reduce violence in police-citizen encounters. *Policing: A Journal of Policy & Practice, 12*(1), 66–76.

"Peeking Over the Horizon"

What Does the Future Hold for Policing?

By Kenneth Peak

CHAPTER 16

"The only thing permanent is change."

—Heraclitus

"You cannot fight against the future. Time is on our side."

—W.E. Gladstone

Opening Questions

Answer the following question before reading this chapter:

> What do you know about the issues concerning the future of policing prior to reading this chapter?

Answer the following question while reading the chapter:

> What are some concepts from the chapter that stand out to you? Why do you think they are important?

Introduction

What does the future hold for policing? That vexing question becomes even more perplexing when we consider our present state of affairs, which in many ways are dangerous and volatile. How much easier the police practitioners' lives would be if they had the benefit of a crystal ball! Lacking that, their choice is to either ignore the future until it is upon them or to try to anticipate what the future holds and gear their thoughts and resources to meet and cope with it. This chapter begins with a discussion of an issue that has been vexing the public for several years: Should the police act as guardians or soldiers? That question will loom large in what is expected of the police and, in turn, their mind-set. Then we consider what are termed constitutional policing, procedural justice, and police legitimacy, and how those three elements can help foster community harmony, justice, and changes in police policies. Then the chapter includes brief discussions of several variables that may well affect policing predictions and trends: immigration, technology, the millennial employee, finances, unions, cybercrime, and the changing face of the federal courts.

First Things First: The Constitution as Boss

Guardians or Soldiers?

It may be fairly said that events occurring in Ferguson, Missouri, on August 9, 2014, were an inflection point for the policing to this point and beyond. On that date, a White police officer, Darren Wilson, shot and killed unarmed black teenager, Michael Brown, during an encounter in the street (*New York Times*, 2015). This case sparked intense media coverage and debate over police-citizen race relations and the appropriate use of police force in encounters with unarmed suspects. Although a grand jury determined there was not enough probable cause to conclude that Wilson acted criminally, the killing soon sparked a wave of protests across the country; subsequent uses of police force in other cities (particularly against other unarmed, minority males) kept policing practices and disparate treatment at the forefront of the national consciousness.

For many people, the question of the role occupied by police in their communities has become whether police are acting as *guardians* or as *soldiers*. The 21st Century Task Force on Policing (convened by President Obama in 2015) was compelled to speak on this matter, stating,

> Law enforcement culture should embrace a guardian mindset to build public trust and legitimacy. Toward that end, police and sheriffs' departments should adopt procedural justice as the guiding principle for internal and external policies and practices to guide their interactions with the citizens they serve. (President's Task Force on 21st Century Policing, 2015, p. 1)

In the same vein, former Shoreline, Washington, police chief Susan Rahr asked

> Why are we training police officers like soldiers? Although police officers wear uniforms and carry weapons, the similarity ends there. The missions and rules of engagement are completely different. The soldier's mission is that of a warrior: to conquer. The rules of engagement are decided before the battle. The police officer's mission is that of a guardian: to protect. The rules of engagement evolve as the incident unfolds. Soldiers must follow orders. Police officers must make independent decisions. Soldiers come into communities as an outside, occupying force. Guardians are members of the community, protecting from within. (President's Task Force on 21st Century Policing, 2015, p. 11)

Procedural Justice

Certainly the guardian mind-set that is so strongly hoped for by the public involves the police adopting what is termed procedural justice as the guiding principle for policies and practices; such a mind-set can bring a change in agency culture and contribute to building trust and confidence in the community. At its core, **procedural justice** revolves around four central principles or pillars:

1. Fairness to all: Citizens examine the process by which the officer's decision was made as much as the outcome of a decision—in sum, whether respectful treatment was experienced by the parties involved. If, for example, a person deems he or she was treated fairly when receiving a traffic ticket, he or she will be less likely to lodge a complaint or appeal against the officer.
2. A voice: Citizens want to be heard and believe they have some control over their fate; this encourages a feeling that their opinions matter and that their account of an incident will be given weight.
3. Transparency and openness of process: Here, decisions are made sans secrecy or deception and in the open as much as possible. When officers are as transparent as possible, community members are more likely to accept the outcome, even if unfavorable.
4. Impartiality and unbiased decision making: Decisions are made based on relevant evidence or data rather than on personal opinion, speculation, or guesswork; data or information is used to make decisions (Kunard & Moe, 2015).

Related Concepts: Constitutional Policing and Legitimacy

It is clear that multiple race-related events from 2014 to present have led to a careful review of police practices and calls for reform. At the core of this review are questions concerning police and race relations, which have in turn compelled many police leaders to consider their agency's culture.

Police agencies must first have the trust and support of their communities if they are to form positive and productive relationships. Too often, concerns with constitutional aspects of policing occur only after the fact—when police officials, community members, and the courts look at an officer's actions to determine whether laws, ordinances, or agency policies were violated.

As a result, many police executives are now becoming more involved in what is now termed **constitutional policing**, which can become the cornerstone of their community policing and problem-solving efforts. In sum, constitutional policing means that police policies and practices are intended to protect citizens' rights and afford equal protection under the law. When that occurs, as New Haven (Connecticut) Police Chief Dean Esserman put it, "The Constitution is our boss. We are not warriors, we are guardians. The [police] oath is to the Constitution" (Police Executive Research Forum, 2015, p. 5). Police agencies cannot be part of the community if citizens do not trust the police or have little evidence that the police see their mission as protecting civil rights as well as public safety.

A related concept is police **legitimacy**, or the extent to which the community perceives that police actions are appropriate, proper, and just. If the police have a high level of legitimacy in their community, citizens tend to be more willing to cooperate with the police and accept the outcome of their interactions with them.

Legitimacy, like procedural justice, is reflected in several ways. First, public confidence involves the belief that the police are honest, are trying to do their jobs well, and are striving to protect the community against crime and violence. In addition, legitimacy reflects the willingness of residents to accept police authority. Finally, legitimacy involves the belief that police actions are morally justified and appropriate to the circumstances. Clearly this relationship with the citizenry is what Sir Robert Peel had in mind when he made his oft-quoted statement that "[t]he police are the public, and the public are the police" (quoted in Germann, Day, & Gallati, 1962, p. 63).

Changing Optics

Another point for the police to consider is the so-called *optics* of their responses to mass gatherings. *Considering optics* involves thinking about how police actions, although legal, will appear to the general public. Much controversy was generated in Ferguson concerning the use of the state's National Guard and military equipment and tactics; that concern has since been reflected in other communities. Many citizens have become troubled with the millions of pieces of surplus military equipment that have been given to local police departments across the country. Also of concern is a perceived too-close relationship between police and military in general. What this involves is for police to avoid deploying heavy military equipment to the scene of a demonstration or wearing protective riot gear if there is no indication that a demonstration will be violent. Also, police have learned that interacting with people—such as asking them kindly to move along if necessary—is much more effective (Police Executive Research Forum, 2015).

Generally speaking, then, to advance constitutional policing and legitimacy in the future, a more soft approach is recommended for dealing with demonstrators and mass gatherings, beginning with police communicating with protest leaders before and during events in an attempt to deter any violence and ensure that protests can be conducted peacefully. Put another way, police leaders will likely find it best to use responses that are measured and proportional to what is happening during a demonstration. As Boston Police Commissioner William Evans said, "If we go looking for a fight with demonstrators, that's what we'll get" (quoted in Police Executive Research Forum, 2015, p. 18).

Fomenting Harmony, Justice, and Policy

What approaches might be taken to reestablish peace and harmony in communities that recently witnessed a fatal police shooting and ensuing racial unrest? If someone had an easy answer to that question, he or she could likely realize instant fame (and fortune).

Certainly a future commitment and adoption to the principles and methods described (e.g., constitutional policing, procedural justice) are key elements for this task. First and foremost, the police must understand their communities. In communities such as Ferguson—where 67% of the population but only 5% of police officers are African American—a starting point is to diversify the police department, thereby giving people a greater sense of representation and voice. Other reform ideas (borne out in federal reports and investigations that followed the Ferguson incident) include that police stop blurring the lines with the military, begin wearing body cameras, investigate police shootings to determine whether any civil rights violations occurred, implement training on racial profiling, and create programs to address vestiges of segregation, dehumanization, and stereotyping in our society (President's Task Force on 21st Century Policing, 2015).

In addition, greater emphasis must be placed on police transparency, particularly as it concerns police shootings. Following the shooting death of Michael Brown, legislation was introduced to create a national database tracking such shootings. Indeed, the Death in Custody Reporting Act (Pub. L. No. 113-242) was signed into law in December 2014 mandating that all states report quarterly to the attorney general information regarding the death of any person in the process of arrest or who is otherwise in law enforcement custody, including jails, prisons and juvenile facilities.

Many police agencies also require a change in philosophy and methods. Certain new strategies that are now being tested and employed (e.g., smart policing, intelligence-led policing, predictive policing) indicate that many police chief executives are breaking the bonds of tradition and moving forward. Change and innovation in policing generally has long been felt to be nearly impossible—even being described by Dorothy Guyot in 1979 as akin to "bending granite" (p. 1). Although that is generally an unfair statement in light of the aforementioned changes now occurring in policing, the fact remains that many of today's police chief executives remain stagnant in their thinking and mind-set; or, as one police chief put it, just "trying to survive until Friday night." In sum, agency leaders must take a strategic, 3- to 5-year vision of where the agency needs to be as well as how to get there.

Police organizations, as part of this change, must take into account their culture, which is derived from the agency mission, values, customs, and rituals. Also included is how the agency rewards, recognizes, assigns, and disciplines officers.

Other Factors That Might Influence the Future of Policing

Immigration

The influence of immigration to America and its effect on policing cannot be overstated. However, there is considerable debate among politicians concerning what to do about immigration as a policy matter. Making the issue even more clouded is the fact that U.S. citizens themselves cannot seem to agree on related matters such as whether the police should be aggressive in their enforcement; whether the economy is helped or hurt by the presence of undocumented immigrants; whether those who are living here illegally should be allowed to remain if they have children who were born here or were brought here before age 16; or, if we should spend what appears to be a king's ransom in building a wall along our southern border (Kehaulani Goo, 2015).

Another controversial and related area is so-called **sanctuary cities**, that is, cities known to protect undocumented immigrants from being deported. Today more than 200 state and local jurisdictions have policies that call for not honoring Immigration and Customs Enforcement (ICE) detention requests. Proponents say such policies encourage members of immigrant communities to work with police without fear of deportation to identify and arrest dangerous criminals who might otherwise go undetected. Critics, conversely, say such policies not only allow undocumented immigrants to be here to become victims, but also to become violent criminals as well (Pearson, 2015).

Many state and local police agencies themselves seek to limit immigration enforcement activities. Indeed, a 40-member task force of the National Immigration Forum, composed of law enforcement personnel, argues that immigration enforcement is primarily a federal responsibility and that local enforcement efforts divert limited resources from already financially strapped agencies and limit community policing efforts (National Immigration Forum, 2015).

Still, local police cannot completely avoid dealing with undocumented immigrants. Police come into frequent contact with immigrants and thus should understand the basics of immigration law and policy. Consequently, the federal Office of Community Oriented Policing Services has funded a web-based basic immigration enforcement training program to train officers in such areas as determining immigrant/nonimmigrant status, identifying false identification, and notifying foreign nationals' embassy or consulate (Peak, 2013).

Technology

The Great Recession, beginning in 2008 and lasting about 18 months, forced the police to work smarter and more affordably. One way they opted to do so was to use technology in more efficient ways. It has been argued that information technology (IT) can serve as a **force multiplier** for helping police agencies to combat crime and disorder.

However, future use of new technologies may well present several unresolved issues in terms of legality. First, many IT tools are so new that the courts have not had time to rule on their constitutionality. Furthermore, in some jurisdictions different state and federal courts have handed down conflicting IT rulings. This means that police are often experimenting with little or no guidance from the courts about the constitutionality of their actions.

Another IT issue concerns the matter of legitimacy as they regard privacy issues. A number of legislative issues must be resolved as well; laws governing the use of many police tools were written decades ago and do not reflect current realities. Certainly matters surrounding the use, privacy, and viewing of body camera videos have yet to be resolved; many freedom of information laws were intended to govern the release of written documents, not video footage from body cameras. Another area concerns unmanned aerial vehicles, or drones, which are rapidly being adopted by the public and are beginning to cause a number of problems. Laws covering and restrictions over drones have yet to be fully developed (Jansen, 2015).

The Millennial Employee

As baby boomers continue to retire in tens of thousands over the next 20 years, vacancies in the workforce will be filled by persons born in what is termed generation Y or the millennial generation (those born between 1980 and 2000).

Fairly or not, millennials are viewed by many people as undesirable employees, having been raised in an environment where they received awards simply for showing up. However, this age cohort could benefit and improve law enforcement, especially given their proficiency with technology; they may also be more team oriented—while also likely wanting to find immediate fulfillment and respect at the workplace and expecting educational opportunities and recognition from their careers. Police administrators must adapt to the future workers' views while using their strengths and doing what is necessary to see that they are recruited, trained, and retained. These future administrators must remember, too, that millennials will likely come into the labor force with a very different and casual attitude toward body art, piercings, and the dress code in general (Vaudreuil, 2015; Williams, 2010).

Money, Money, Money

An old criminal justice planning adage holds that if we had unlimited funds, there would be no need for budgeting or planning. Money is the fuel that powers nearly everything the organization does.

The Great Recession impacted police agencies of all sizes and forced police leaders to determine how to do more with less and try to identify where budgets and services could be cut. That mentality has likely carried over to today, creating a new normal. In the future, police administrators must continue to develop expertise in augmenting their operating budgets with different types of grants and in other ways, primarily using the aforementioned IT to collect and analyze data so as to effectively manage and strategically deploy resources and focus on specific problems as they develop. Agencies and policy makers must create proactive, aggressive, and productive problem-solving strategies based on relevant and current data (see, e.g., Office of Community Oriented Policing Services, 2011).

Unions

A topic that is closely related to and will doubtlessly impact the aforementioned topics is that of police unions and collective bargaining. In the mid-2000s, more than one-third of all American workers were members of labor unions. That number has fallen to about 12% overall, with public employee unions left with the only real clout. Nearly 37% of public employees belong to a union (as compared with only about 7.5% in the private sector) (NBC, 2011).

Beginning in 2010, many cities and states started to become alarmed with the affordability of their unions and related benefits, particularly retirement costs. In early 2011, Wisconsin took the bold step of abolishing nearly all collective bargaining rights from the majority of public sector employees. Soon other states (e.g., Iowa, Ohio, Michigan) began examining and amending their collective bargaining laws so as to reduce employees' rights and repeal union pay scales and benefits (Burnett & Horne).

Then, in early 2018, another significant measure was attempted concerning unions, specifically as they concern the mandatory payment of employee dues that cover union bargaining and lobbying efforts. The case *Janus v. AFSCME* involved a state child care specialist who objected to being forced to pay approximately $45 each month in dues to his union; he argued that forcing him and other public workers to pay union dues (as is allowed in 22 states) is a violation of their First Amendment rights. The Trump Administration and about 20 law enforcement groups urged the court not to outlaw the mandatory dues, while the nation's largest police union, the National Fraternal Order of Police, asserted that a ruling for Janus would bring a "death spiral" for law enforcement, as having fewer members would means the union would have to impose higher dues while reducing services. The Supreme Court was expected to decide the case in late 2018 (Weichselbaum, 2018).

Cybercrime

Why would any reasonably intelligent person attempt to rob a bank, thus potentially facing a bevy of security cameras and personnel as well as exploding dye packs, when he or she can obtain funds via **cybercrime**? In fact, bank robberies have declined more than 60% over the past quarter century, due in large part to the increasingly lucrative nature of cybercrime (Jouvenal, 2016). Meanwhile, cybercrime damage is estimated to cost $6 trillion by 2021 (the greatest transfer of economic wealth in history), while cybersecurity will reach about $90 billion per year (Morgan, 2018).

Cybercrime will greatly challenge the police through such activities as data manipulation, software piracy, industrial espionage, bank card counterfeiting, and embezzlement. Hackers of all ages are breaking into computer systems of major corporations and obtaining credit card, telephone, and account information. Other cybercriminals entice children for sexual purposes.

We may not have seen the worst that can happen yet: cyberterrorism. Imagine a world where the information superhighway could be used to remotely access the processing control systems of a cereal manufacturer, changing the levels of iron supplement and thereby sickening and killing children who eat it; to disrupt banks, international financial transactions, and stock exchanges, causing our citizens to lose faith in their economic system; or to attack air traffic control systems and aircraft in-cockpit sensors, causing large civilian aircraft to collide.

Obviously the future of cybercrime will require the development of new investigative techniques, specialized training for police investigators, and employment of individuals with specialized, highly technological backgrounds. If the police are not prepared, these crimes could become the Achilles' heel of our society.

The Impact of the Federal Courts

The federal courts, especially the United States Supreme Court have been a major factor shaping the future of policing for the last century. This is a particularly exciting time for court-watchers. During the first year of his presidency, Donald Trump successfully appointed conservative judge Neil Gorsuch to the Supreme Court as well as 12 lower-court judges. The Trump Administration was thus making good on its campaign promise of swift confirmation of conservative judges (Edmondson, 2018).

These rapid appointments of conservative judges are obviously worrisome for progressives as they represent a major reshaping of the judiciary; for them, a conservative Supreme Court has historically meant advancing a crime control agenda that includes expanded police powers and narrowing civil liberties. It is also said to bring *strict constructionism*—a term whereby justices are said to interpret the U.S. Constitution using "a literal and narrow definition of language in the document without regard to changes that have occurred in American society" since the document was written (Mason, 2017).

Of course, the now more-conservative Supreme Court stands ready to consider cases (and revisit previous decisions) concerning the police such as immigration, gun control, the Fourth Amendment, and technology.

Summary and Conclusion

This chapter has taken a bifurcated view of the future of policing. First it discussed the role of the police, including what has become a primary question of our time: Who are the police and what are they supposed to do? Historically this question was answered simply with "They enforce the law" or "They serve and protect." But policing today is much more complex.

A major obstacle to public understanding of the police role is the crime-fighter image they have long held because of film and media portrayals of nonstop shootouts, car chases, and explosions in the constant pursuit of felons. But, as Jerome Skolnick and David Bayley pointed out, the crimes that terrify Americans the most—robbery, rape, burglary, and homicide—are rarely encountered by police on patrol (Skolnick & Bayley, 1986). Much more common historically, however, have been the welfare tasks that put the police squarely in the role of guardians: checking the welfare of people and communities, being on the lookout, administering death notifications, delivering blood to hospitals, assisting firefighters and animal control units, and so on. Their recent acts resembling a more "soldier" role, including the shootings of unarmed citizens and deployment of military equipment, has caused a chasm with the community that will take much time and effort to close.

Second, we discussed several factors that have traditionally troubled police agencies and will continue to vex and challenge them in the future. Policing always has been and likely always will be a labor-intensive people business, so issues such as immigration, technology, the millennial employee, finances, unions, cybercrime, and the changing face of the federal courts will continue to challenge the police of the future.

Key Terms

constitutional policing: Policing that operates within the parameters set by the U.S. Constitution, state constitutions, the body of court decisions that have interpreted and spelled out in greater detail what the text of the Constitution means in terms of the everyday practices of policing (Police Executive Research Forum, 2015)

cybercrime: Crimes that are either created due to modern reliance on computers or made easier by the presence of computers

force multiplier: A tool that allows an individual or an organization to leverage an effort to gain more output

legitimacy: The rightful use of power. In the case of police legitimacy, it is a concept exploring whether the citizens the police serve see police use of power as appropriate/legitimate or arbitrary/illegitimate

procedural justice: The concept the criminal justice process itself should be fair. It includes not only the concept of due process, but also transparency of the system

sanctuary city: A city known to protect undocumented immigrants from being deported

Discussion Questions

- Name and describe the four main principles of procedural justice.
- How is legitimacy related to procedural justice?
- What do you think would be the best way for police to reestablish peace and harmony in the communities they serve?
- What are your thoughts on sanctuary cities? Are they a smart move by local authorities looking to improve police-community relations or a nuisance to immigration enforcement? Which is more important?
- What are your thoughts about the use of technology in policing?
- How will the national trend in de-unionization affect police?
- What do you think about the future of policing after reading the chapter?

References

Burnett, J., & Horne, J. (2017, July/August). States take on collective bargaining. *The Council of State Governments*. Retrieved from http://www.csg.org/pubs/capitolideas/enews/issue66_2.aspx

Edmondson, C. (2018, December 11). Trump's judicial nominees take heat but largely keep marching through Senate. Retrieved from https://www.nytimes.com/2018/12/11/us/politics/republicans-judges-confirmation-votes.html

Germann, A. C., Day, F. D., & and Gallati, R. R. J. (1962). *Introduction to law enforcement and criminal justice*. Springfield, IL: Charles C. Thomas.

Guyot, D. (1979). Bending granite: Attempts to change the rank structure of American police departments. *Journal of Police Science and Administration, 7*(3), 253–284.

Jansen, B. (2015, February 16). FAA unveils drone rules; Obama orders policy for agencies. *USA Today*. Retrieved from http://www.usatoday.com/story/news/2015/02/15/faa-drone-rule/23440469/

Janus v. American Federation of State, County, and Municipal Employees, Council 31, et al., No. 16-1466 (2018)

Jouvenal, J. (2016, October 6). A quintessentially American crime declines: Robbing banks doesn't pay as it used to. *Washington Post*. Retrieved from https://www.washingtonpost.com/local/public-safety/a-quintessentially-american-crime-on-the-decline--robbing-banks-doesnt-pay-as-it-used-to/2016/09/29/4f54a0a6-e7e9-437c-b484-151a337b0e0a_story.html?utm_term=.e7ed725e4e25

Kehaulani Goo, S. (2015, August 24). What Americans want to do about illegal immigration. *Pew Research Center*. Retrieved from http://www.pewresearch.org/fact-tank/2015/08/24/what-americans-want-to-do-about-illegal-immigration/

Kunard, L., & Moe, C. (2015). *Procedural justice for law enforcement: An overview.* Washington, DC: Office of Community Oriented Policing Services.

Mason, J. (2017, January 26). Trump to nominate "strict constructionist" to Supreme Court: Pence. *Reuters*. Retrieved from https://www.reuters.com/article/us-usa-court-pence/trump-to-nominate-strict-constructionist-to-supreme-court-pence-idUSKBN15A2RR

Morgan, S. (2018, October 10). Top 5 cybersecurity facts, figures and statistics for 2018. *CSO*. Retrieved from https://www.csoonline.com/article/3153707/security/top-5-cybersecurity-facts-figures-and-statistics.html

National Immigration Forum. (2015, July 20). *Chiefs and sheriffs oppose immigration enforcement policies undermining community policing*. Retrieved from https://immigrationforum.org/blog/chiefs-and-sheriffs-oppose-immigration-enforcement-policies-undermining-community-policing/

NBC. (2011, March 11). *Wisconsin governor officially cuts collective bargaining*. Retrieved from http://www.nbcnews.com/id/41996994/ns/politics-more_politics/t/wis-governor-officially-cuts-collective-bargaining/#.Wqv89kxFzcs

New York Times. (2015, August 10). What happened in Ferguson?. Retrieved from https://www.nytimes.com/interactive/2014/08/13/us/ferguson-missouri-town-under-siege-after-police-shooting.html

Office of Community Oriented Policing Services. (2011). *The impact of the economic downturn on American police agencies*. Retrieved from http://www.ncdsv.org/images/COPS_ImpactOfTheEconomicDownturnOnAmericanPoliceAgencies_10-2011.pdf

Peak, K. J. (Ed.). (2013). *Encyclopedia of community policing and problem solving*. Thousand Oaks, CA: Sage Publications.

Pearson, M. (2015, July 8). What's a 'sanctuary city,' and why should you care?. *CNN*. Retrieved from https://www.cnn.com/2015/07/06/us/san-francisco-killing-sanctuary-cities/index.html

Police Executive Research Forum. (2015, April). *Constitutional policing as a cornerstone of community policing*. Washington, DC: Office of Community Oriented Policing Services.

President's Task Force on 21st Century Policing. (2015, May). *Final report of the President's Task Force on 21st Century Policing*. Washington, DC: Office of Community Oriented Policing Services. Retrieved from https://cops.usdoj.gov/pdf/taskforce/taskforce_finalreport.pdf

Skolnick, J. H., & Bayley, D. H. (1986). The new blue line: Police innovation in six American cities. New York, NY: Free Press.

Vaudreuil, S. K. (2015, April 7). Tattoos. Piercings. The workplace. Like it or not, the millennials are the future workforce [Blog post]. *California Public Agency Labor & Employment*. Retrieved from http://www.calpublicagencylaboremploymentblog.com/employment/tattoos-piercings-the-workplace-like-it-or-not-the-millennials-are-the-future-workforce/

Weichselbaum, S. (2018, February 13). A "death spiral" for police unions?. The Marshall Project. Retrieved from https://www.themarshallproject.org/2018/02/23/a-death-spiral-for-police-unions

Williams, C. J. (2010, September 9). Tattoos are free speech protected by Constitution, U.S. appeals court rules. *Los Angeles Times.* Retrieved from http://latimesblogs.latimes.com/lanow/2010/09/tattoos-free-speech.html

ABOUT THE AUTHORS

Dr. Charles J. Kocher is a retired police official, serving first as a police dispatcher and later serving in all civil service ranks up to and including deputy police chief. During his career he was responsible for establishing four community police substations and was founder of the Camden Police Museum. Other assignments included serving as the academic director and resident instructor for the Police Training Academy, Planning and Research Unit and as the administrative assistant to several chiefs of police.

Upon retirement, Kocher served as coordinator for the Criminal Justice program at Cumberland County College, New Jersey, and later served as dean for the Business, Education and Social Sciences division of the college. Currently, he is a full-time, tenured professor at Cumberland County College and is also an adjunct at Fairleigh Dickinson University, Wilmington University, and Saint Joseph's University for both undergraduate and graduate courses.

His formal education includes studies at Villanova University, Rowan University, and Saint Joseph's University. Kocher has earned a Master of Arts from Rowan University and a Master of Science from Saint Joseph's University. His doctorate's studies were conducted at Saint Joseph's University for higher education administration. In addition, he has several certificates from Rutgers University and Harvard University.

Darren K. Stocker, MS, MEd is an associate professor at Cape Cod Community College and is the program coordinator for the Department of Criminal Justice. He is an active member of the American Society of Criminology and the Academy of Criminal Justice Sciences. He has authored or coauthored more than 40 journal articles, book chapters, and criminal justice publications and has spoken at academic conferences, professional meetings, and universities throughout the country and Europe on the topics of criminal justice, policing, terrorism, and other related contemporary topics. Stocker is a graduate of West Chester University and holds graduate degrees from Saint Joseph's University (MS) and the University of Massachusetts (MEd). He is completing his doctoral studies at Northeastern University.

Holly Dershem-Bruce, MA, has been a professor of criminal justice at Dawson Community College in Glendive, Montana for 28 years. She has also taught online courses for Colorado Community Colleges Online for more than 16 years. She teaches a wide variety of courses in the areas of political science, criminal justice, sociology, law enforcement, juvenile delinquency, criminology, and private security. In addition to her instructor duties, Dershem-Bruce is currently the director of DCC's criminal justice law enforcement program. She also serves as the western regional counselor for the community college section of the Academy of Criminal Justice Sciences, a national organization dedicated to the profession of criminal justice. In addition to being a founding member, she has also served as the chair, vice-chair, and immediate past chair for the community college section over the years. Dershem-Bruce also serves on the state of Montana's board of private security, a political board that oversees the private security industry in the state.

Dr. Tiffany Wasserburger graduated with her BA in criminal justice from Chadron State College. She graduated from the University of Nebraska Law School in 2000. After graduation, she returned to western Nebraska to be with her family. During her career she has worked with legal aid and as a prosecutor concentrating on domestic violence, sexual assault, and child abuse cases. Dr. Wasserburger served on the Nebraska Sexual Assault Task Force and in 2010 she received a national award from the Animal Legal Defense Fund for her strong advocacy in animal abuse cases. She now uses her nearly 15 years of experience in the field as the criminal justice program director at Western Nebraska Community College.

Dr. Brian D. Fitch, served for 34 years with the Los Angeles County Sheriff's Department before retiring as a lieutenant. He served as a field training officer, felony investigator, advanced officer training instructor, patrol supervisor, custody supervisor, watch commander, operations lieutenant, and detective bureau commander. He has received a number of Sheriff's Department awards, including the Leadership award, Meritorious Service award, Distinguished Service award, and Exemplary Service award. Dr. Fitch holds adjunct faculty positions in the Psychology Department at California State University, Long Beach and in the Politics and Criminal Justice Department at California State University, Fullerton. Dr. Fitch has held past faculty positions at Woodbury University, Southwestern University School of Law, and Cerritos College. Dr. Fitch is a nationally recognized speaker, teacher, and author in law enforcement communication, leadership, and ethics. He has trained more than 10,000 law enforcement officers throughout the United States, as well as abroad in Oman, Qatar, United Arab Emirates, Saudi Arabia, and Canada. Dr. Fitch holds a master's degrees in communication studies and a doctorate in human development.

Dr. Danny L. McGuire, Jr. is a second-generation law-enforcement professional who spent over 20 years in law enforcement. He began his career as an explorer and community service officer with the Palos Heights Police Department. At the age of 21 Danny earned his first sworn law enforcement position for the Cook County Sheriff's Department and a federally funded narcotics task force called the South Suburban Drug Initiative. From there he was detailed to the NEMEG unit where he was tasked with long-term covert narcotics investigations. After 4 years with the Sheriff's Department, Danny joined the Chicago Police Department where he worked a patrol, special operations, HBT (now known as SWAT), and critical incident response team. Danny was promoted to sergeant and after a short time in patrol was assigned to the SWAT team as weapons of mass destruction safety and support team coordinator and later the chief hostage/crisis negotiator. Dr. McGuire earned a Bachelor of Science in law enforcement management from Calumet College of St. Joseph, a Master of Art in counseling psychology from the Adler School of Professional Psychology, a doctoral degree in education with an emphasis in ethical leadership from Olivet Nazarene University, and a Master of Public Administration from Clemson University. Dr. McGuire is currently the program director for public safety programs and director of the Public Safety Institute at Calumet College of St. Joseph in Whiting, Indiana.

Dr. Mark H. Beaudry, CPP is an assistant professor in criminal justice at Worcester State University. He has been a member of ASIS International since 1982 and a CPP certified protection professional since 1996. He is a frequent researcher and author in security studies, police education and performance, criminology, and the history of the Middle East. In addition to providing book reviews, Dr. Beaudry provides book proposal reviews and a article reviews for varied publishers and journals. Dr. Beaudry is also a retired intelligence chief, area studies analyst, MSG, and a certified anti-terrorism instructor from the USMCR. He holds an AS, BS/MS, and a PhD in human services/criminal justice.

Dr. Marcel F. Beausoleil is an associate professor at Fitchburg State University in Fitchburg, Massachusetts. He is also the academic coordinator for the police program and is the graduate coordinator. He has also taught at Anna Maria College in Paxton, Massachusetts. Prior to entering academia Dr. Beausoleil served with the Woonsocket, Rhode Island, Police Department retiring at the rank of commander. His research focuses on all aspects of policing.

Dr. Paul R. Gormley received his juris doctor degree from New England Law and his doctorate in law and policy from Northeastern University. During undergraduate studies, Dr. Gormley studied and worked in law enforcement before attending law school. His work in law school included drafting an agency opinion involving grand jury secrecy in tax prosecutions, drafting pleadings for the district attorney's office in civil forfeiture in illegal drug distribution cases, and working in a law office focusing on murder and drug distribution defense. He practiced law for 20 years, representing criminal defendants and individuals with mental health issues in state courts and representing convicted sex offenders in sex offender registry classification hearings. Based on his experience in law practice, his research focuses on defense counsel and issues of effective representation of mentally ill criminal defendants. Dr Gormley's numerous presentations include issues of mental illness in criminal proceedings, criminal justice issues, academic assessment, and student writing development. His professional training sessions cover diverse topics including academic assessment by college faculty, criminal justice technology, effective representation of sex offenders in classification hearings, defendant mental health issues, and supervision of cybercrime offenders.

Dr. Jeffrey S. Czarnec served with the Manchester, New Hampshire, Police Department from 1979 to 2002. During his career as a police officer in the largest city north of Boston, he served as a juvenile investigator, SWAT entry-team member, Civil Disturbance Unit member, Undercover Narcotics/Vice detective, and detective in charge of crimes against elder persons.

He embarked on his second career as an assistant professor of criminal justice for Hesser College, where he had served as an adjunct since 1996. He has also served as associate dean with Kaplan University and was chairman of the Department of Criminal Justice at Hesser College located in Manchester, New Hampshire, with five on-ground campuses and an online program, from 2008–2012. He was sought out by the Central Applications Office for the Southern New Hampshire University College of Continuing Education in 2013 to develop the new criminal justice program. From that development, he was hired as an associate dean overseeing the development and delivery of criminal justice, political science, anthropology, sociology, human services and justice studies.

He received his Bachelor of Science in criminal justice from Saint Anselm College, a Master of Science in human services administration from Springfield College, and a doctorate in leadership studies from Franklin Pierce University. His dissertation was a participatory study conducted over a 3-year period with upper-echelon members of the Boston Irish Mafia/Whitey Bulger gang.

In addition, he has successfully completed and distributed a documentary in South Boston with former mayor and ambassador to the Vatican Mr. Raymond Flynn.

He is a member of the Academy of Criminal Justice Sciences, the American Criminological Society, and the New Hampshire Association of Criminal Justice Educators, and he consults regularly with local and regional police and human services leadership.

Christopher James Utecht MS, MA has served as a law enforcement officer in Wisconsin for 15 years, working for the University of Wisconsin-Milwaukee, Washington Island, and Sturgeon Bay police departments as an officer before attaining the rank of chief with the Dover Water Patrol. In addition to the duties incumbent on a chief, during his career Utecht has worked in a variety of police roles, including patrol officer, tactical team member, marine officer, and field-trainer. He began his move into academia by teaching as adjunct faculty at Northeast Wisconsin Technical College in Green Bay, Wisconsin.

Utecht is currently an associate professor in the Criminal Justice Department at the College of Lake County in Grayslake, Illinois. He is a regular presenter at regional and national conferences, including the Academy of Criminal Justice Sciences (ACJS) annual meeting. Chris is also the secretary-treasurer of the ACJS community college section. His writing appears in the journal *Multicultural Perspectives*, and he has co-authored *A Guide to Writing Quality Police Reports* with Ron Connolly. He holds a Master of Science degree in criminal justice from the University of Cincinnati and a Master of Arts in Sociology from the University of Alabama at Birmingham.

Dr. Brandy Benson is a licensed clinical psychologist with a specialized background in forensic and police psychology. Dr. Benson earned her doctorate in clinical psychology from Nova Southeastern University in Fort Lauderdale, Florida. She completed her clinical internship with the Federal Bureau of Prisons. Over the past several years, Dr. Benson has worked closely with various police departments, building a collaborative relationship between law enforcement and mental health. The goal is to not only build resiliency in first responders, but also to assist in their efforts to work in the community and maintain personal safety. She has worked closely with critical response teams implementing hostage negotiation strategies and has completed organized trainings/certifications in critical incident stress management and debriefing. Dr. Benson routinely conducts pre-employment and fitness-for-duty evaluations for public safety personnel and provides post-crisis intervention and general counseling. Dr. Benson is often invited to host first responder trainings on stress management, resiliency, PTSD, suicide and mental health issues in the community. She also has engaged in substantial research with the Crimes Against Children Unit of the FBI, Miami Division, and is well published in the field on commercial sexual exploitation of children. She continues to research and publish in this area. She has taught for South University and Nova Southeastern University in the past; current appointments are Walden University and Southern New Hampshire University.

Dr. Shelly M. Wagers is currently an assistant professor of criminology at the University of South Florida, St. Petersburg (USFSP). Prior to joining the faculty at USFSP, Dr. Wagers worked as a sexual and domestic violence prevention trainer and served as a sworn law enforcement officer. In addition, Dr. Wagers has served as a consultant to the Virginia Batterer Intervention Certification Board regarding evidence-based practices and national trends for batterer intervention programs, and currently she serves on the executive board for the National Partnership to End Interpersonal Violence Across the Lifespan (NPEIV). She has over 20 years of experience developing and delivering educational classes, workshops, and seminars in the area of domestic violence prevention and law enforcement. Dr. Wagers's research on domestic violence has been published in journals such as the *Journal of Interpersonal Violence*, *Violence and Victims*, *Partner Abuse*, and *Police Chief*.

Dr. Patrick J. Solar has been a police officer for nearly 30 years serving as a street officer, detective, sergeant, lieutenant, and small-town chief.

His education includes a bachelor's degree in political science from Northern Illinois University, a master's degree in public administration, specializing in municipal finance and budgeting, and a doctorate in political philosophy, specializing in organizational development, from the Northern Illinois University Graduate School. Solar is also a graduate of the 188th session of the FBI National Academy.

Dr. Solar is currently engaged at the University of Wisconsin–Platteville where he teaches courses on policing and law enforcement at the undergraduate and graduate level. He has written a number of articles related to management and the police function; he is currently working on the development of a new process for police performance assessment reflecting the values of 21st-century policing, and he is the primary author of a new text book titled *Police Community Relations: A Conflict Management Approach*, coming soon from West Academic Publishing.

Dr. Ronald Connolly began his 19-year policing career with the Milwaukee Police Department. After a 5-year break to serve as a chief warrant officer/aviator in the United States Army, he returned to Wisconsin and joined the Appleton Police Department. As a senior sergeant there, he finished his policing career to pursue full-time teaching at Northcentral Technical College, Northeast Wisconsin Technical College, and Marian University, where he is currently an associate professor. Ron has earned a bachelor's degree in criminal justice from Mount Senario College, a Master of Science degree in organizational leadership and quality from Marian University, and an educational doctorate in leadership for the advancement of learning and service from Cardinal Stritch University. Dr. Connolly coordinated the development of the Professional Practice in Public Safety graduate program at Marian University. His presentations include "The Bystander Effect," sponsored by Marian University's Social Justice Committee; "Becoming a 'Superhero' in the Workplace" for Women's Specialty Care Health Clinic; "Building Mindful Relationships" for Bellin Health; "Customer-Focused Leadership" for the Radisson Paper Valley Hotel security staff; and the "Ethics Instructor Update Series" for the Wisconsin Department of Justice. Recently, he co-authored *A Guide to Writing Quality Police Reports* with Christopher Utecht.

Lieutenant Cory Kelly, MA is an 18-year veteran of the Waukegan, Illinois, Police Department (WPD) and serves as the department's only female supervisor out of her 35 male counterparts. She has served in many positions over the years, from a school resource officer, to a detective assigned to the Lake County Children's Advocacy Center, and most recently a patrol shift commander.

Lieutenant Kelly is an instructor within her agency for the following: taser, handcuff, flashlight, pepper spray, baton, and CPR/AED, and she participates in training all officers within the department each year for annual qualifications/certifications. She has received numerous awards over the years, including "Officer of the Year" in 2012 and the Redefine Leadership award in 2018, and was given a lifetime achievement award for her time as liaison with the Waukegan Citizen's Police Academy. She also sits on the Lake County United Way Women's Leadership Counsel, representing the WPD.

Lieutenant Kelly graduated from Western Illinois University (WIU) with both her bachelor's and master's degrees. Lieutenant Kelly uses her academic achievements to teach the next generation of law enforcement officers. She has taught for the University of Phoenix and is currently an adjunct faculty member at the College of Lake County (Illinois), where she currently teaches Traffic Enforcement and Community Policing.

Dr. Mark A. Tallman is an adjunct professor at Colorado State University's Center for the Study of Homeland Security (CSHS) and is a private security and emergency planning consultant. Dr. Tallman is the author of *Ghost Guns: Hobbyists, Hackers, and the Homemade Weapons Revolution*, for release by Praeger in 2019. Tallman's professional experience includes risk and threat assessment, security technology research, weapons policy research, counterterrorism policy research, organizational continuity, emergency planning, security management planning, energy security, cultural and historic resource protection (CHR), and exercise planning. Dr. Tallman was a project manager for the Program on Terrorism and Insurgency Research at the Sie Center for International Security and Diplomacy, and he currently teaches homeland, international, and cyber security at Colorado State University, Pueblo's Center for the Study of Homeland Security (CSHS) and Center for Cyber Security Education and Research

(CCSER). Mark has a PhD in international studies with a security concentration from the University of Denver's Josef Korbel School of International Studies, an MA in global politics from Illinois State University, and a BA in international relations from Northern Illinois University. He is a certified associate business continuity planner (ABCP), range safety officer (RSO), and wilderness first responder (WFR).

Dr. Rachel B. Santos is currently a professor of criminal justice and director of the Center for Police Practice, Policy, and Research at Radford University, in Radford, Virginia. Her interests include conducting practice-based research, which is implementing and evaluating evidence-based practices in the "real world" of criminal justice. In particular, she seeks to improve crime prevention and proactive crime-reduction efforts by police in areas such as crime analysis, problem solving, accountability, as well as leadership and organizational change. She and Dr. Roberto Santos co-created stratified policing, which is an organizational model for systemizing proactive crime-reduction strategies in police departments. Other areas of research include police/researcher partnerships, police/community collaboration, hot spot and problem-oriented policing, predictive policing, environmental criminology, crime and place, police/crime data and technology, experimental research methodology, and program evaluation.

Dr. Roberto G. Santos is currently a tenure-track assistant professor of criminal justice as well as associate director of the Center for Police Practice, Policy and Research at Radford University in Radford, Virginia. He is a retired police commander from a large police agency in Florida where, for 22 years, he either worked in, supervised, or commanded every division within the agency. He assists police agencies nationally and internationally and conducts evidence-based and practice-based research to "translate" research to practice and vice versa. He and Dr. Rachel Santos co-created stratified policing, which is an organizational model for systemizing proactive crime-reduction strategies in police departments. Dr. Santos focuses on areas of proactive crime reduction approaches and strategies, crime and place, environmental criminology, police use of force, police training, criminal investigations, organizational change and leadership, police and community partnerships, crime analysis, and experimental research methodology.

Dr. Kenneth Peak is emeritus professor and former chairman of the Department of Criminal Justice, University of Nevada, Reno, where he was named "Teacher of the Year" by the university's honor society. He has authored or coauthored 38 textbooks (on introductory criminal justice, general policing, community policing, justice administration, police supervision and management, and women in law enforcement), two historical books (on Kansas bootlegging and temperance), and more than 60 journal articles. Following 4 years as a municipal police officer in Kansas, he subsequently held positions as a nine-county criminal justice planner for southeast Kansas; director of a four-state technical assistance institute for the Law Enforcement Assistance Administration (based at Washburn University in Topeka); director of university police at Pittsburg State University (Kansas); acting director of public safety at University of Nevada, Reno; and assistant professor of criminal justice at Wichita State University. He received two gubernatorial appointments to statewide criminal justice committees while residing in Kansas, served as chairman of the Police Section, Academy of Criminal Justice Sciences, and is past president of the Western Association of Criminal Justice.

Index

D

Q

R

Z

CPSIA information can be obtained
at www.ICGtesting.com
Printed in the USA
LVHW060013090419
613404LV00004B/6/P

9 781516 595976